The

LITTLE BOOK

Of

CYBERSECURITY

HARRY KATZAN JR.

THE LITTLE BOOK OF CYBERSECURITY

iUniverse books may be ordered through booksellers or by contacting:

iUniverse
1663 Liberty Drive
Bloomington, IN 47403
www.iuniverse.com
844-349-9409

Because of the dynamic nature of the Internet, any web addresses or links contained in this book may have changed since publication and may no longer be valid. The views expressed in this work are solely those of the author and do not necessarily reflect the views of the publisher, and the publisher hereby disclaims any responsibility for them.

Any people depicted in stock imagery provided by Getty Images are models, and such images are being used for illustrative purposes only. Certain stock imagery © Getty Images.

ISBN: 978-1-6632-3776-7 (sc)
ISBN: 978-1-6632-3777-4 (hc)
ISBN: 978-1-6632-3778-1 (e)

Library of Congress Control Number: 2022915493

Print information available on the last page.

iUniverse rev. date: 03/23/2022

To Margaret, as always

PREFACE

This is little book is a collection of chapters written by the author on the subject of Cybersecurity. They represent papers that have been peer reviewed and prepared for a variety of conferences and other academic events. Some chapters have been written to suit a general audience, and others have been prepared for a select class of readers. There are some formatting differences due to the basic requirements of the varying circumstances.

The essays are intended to be read separately resulting in a minimal amount of definitional material being repeated throughout the book. The reader is able to comfortably read the entries on a topic of interest and disregard the remainder. The chapters are related, but each has a unique focus.

The subject matter can be viewed as two separate collections. The first is the relation of cybersecurity to the newly dispatched subject of service science. The second is the application of modern technology to everyday affairs. The objective of the chapters is to provide insight into what is new to the areas of business and management. The scope of the subject matter is introductory, foundational, and applicative. The introductory chapters are straightforward and give a gentle introduction to what the disciplines are all about. The foundational chapters provide a basis for the study of the concepts and methods of the two disciplines. The applicative essays are general in nature, so as to provide insight to what does and can go on in the world of service and technology.

The table of contents is unique in that the entries give an introduction to the respective chapters. This is an aid to selection and gives a summary of the subject matter that is covered. The chapters were assembled to support a recent look into the various subjects.

Service and cybersecurity are new fields of study and learning. Unfortunately, insufficient time has elapsed for the development of a set of case studies suitable for that form of study. It is hoped that this collection will partially fill that void.

Harry Katzan, Jr.
April 2022

CONTENTS

Section One - Introduction to Cybersecurity

1   Essentials of Cybersecurity **1**

The effectiveness and efficiency of modern networked computer systems is a function of five basic attributes: availability, accuracy, authenticity, confidentiality, and integrity. The concepts apply to information, computers, networks, and other elements of coordination, cooperation, and control, and they apply to government, business, education, and private individuals. The concerns normally involve the Internet as a communication facility – hence the name *Cybersecurity*. Some of the concerns that immediately come to mind are identity, personal privacy, intellectual property, secure maintenance of the critical infrastructure, and organizational sustainability. The purpose of this chapter is to give a composite picture of what cybersecurity is all about, identify the important literature on the subject, and describe how it differs from everyday information security affecting individuals and computer activities. This paper requires knowledge of basic information systems, computer, and network security technology for an understanding of the implications of many of the topics.

2   Cybersecurity Service Model **11**

The efficacy of modern computer systems is normally regarded as a function of five basic attributes of computer and information security: availability, accuracy, authenticity, confidentiality, and integrity. The concepts generally apply to government, business, education, and the ordinary lives of private individuals. The considerations normally involve extended applications of the Internet – hence the name *Cybersecurity*. Achieving and maintaining a secure cyberspace is a complicated process, and some of the concerns involve personal identity, privacy and intellectual property, secure maintenance of the critical infrastructure, and the sustainability of organizations. The threats to a secure operating infrastructure are serious and profound: cyber terrorism, cyber war, cyber espionage, and cyber crime, to which the technical community has responded with a plethora of ad hoc safeguards and procedures, usually supplied by the competitive private sector. This chapter proposes a fresh view of the cyber domain based on service science with the ultimate objective of developing a cybersecurity service model.

3   Fundamentals of Applied Cybersecurity for
     Business and Management.. 27

It is well established that cybersecurity is a complicated and complex subject encompassing computer security, information assurance, comprehensive infrastructure protection, commercial integrity, and ubiquitous personal interactions. The concepts apply to information, computers, networks, and other elements of coordination, cooperation, and control, and they apply to government, business, education, and the ordinary lives of private individuals. The concerns normally involve the Internet as a communication facility – hence the name *Cybersecurity*. Achieving and maintaining cybersecurity is a never-ending process, much like national security, bank security, and so forth, so it is important to know the essential foundations of how to manage the risks of using technical interactions in order to obtain the inherent benefits. Some of the concerns that immediately come to mind are identity, personal privacy, intellectual property, secure maintenance of critical infrastructure, and the continued operation of necessary organizations. There is a plethora of printed and online literature on various aspects of cybersecurity – including computer security, information assurance, infrastructure security, personal security, and associated government policy information. The purpose of this chapter is to give a composite picture of what cybersecurity is all about, identify the important literature on the subject, and describe how it differs from everyday information security affecting individuals and computer activities. This chapter requires knowledge of basic information systems, computer, and network security technology for an understanding of the implications of many of the topics.

4   Advances in Cybersecurity for Business and
     Management 37

The value of modern computer systems and applications is generally conceived as being a function of five characteristics normally associated with cybersecurity: availability, accuracy, authenticity, confidentiality, and integrity. The concepts generally apply to government, business, education, and the ordinary lives of private individuals, and take place in an environment associated with the Internet. Maintaining a secure cyberspace is a multidimensional process involving personal identity, privacy, intellectual property, the critical infrastructure, and the sustainability of organizations. The threats inherent in a secure operating infrastructure are profound:

cyber terrorism, cyber war, cyber espionage, and cyber crime, to which the technical community has responded with safeguards and procedures. This chapter provides a contemporary view of security in the cyber domain with the ultimate objective of developing a science of cybersecurity. Two recent advances are covered: automated intrusion detection and application containers. Individuals and organizations involved with computer and information security should be aware of major developments in this important area.

5   Contemporary Issues in Cybersecurity Research
for Business and Management **49**
The effectiveness of modern computer applications is normally regarded as a function of five basic attributes of secure computer and information systems: availability, accuracy, authenticity, confidentiality, and integrity. The concepts generally apply to government, business, education, and the ordinary lives of private individuals. The considerations normally involve extended Internet applications – hence the name *Cybersecurity*. Achieving and maintaining a secure cyberspace is a complicated process, and some of the concerns involve personal identity, privacy, intellectual property, the critical infrastructure, and the sustainability of organizations. The threats to a secure operating infrastructure are serious and profound: cyber terrorism, cyber war, cyber espionage, and cyber crime, to which the technical community has responded with safeguards and procedures, usually supplied by the private sector. This chapter provides a comprehensive view of security in the cyber domain with the ultimate objective of developing a science of cybersecurity.

Section Two - Cybersecurity and Service

6   Service Concepts **63**
This chapter gives a conspectus of Service for academicians and practitioners with the express purpose of defining the scope of the discipline. The subject of services is the up and coming discipline for the 22nd century, and it encompasses technology, entrepreneurship, business growth, and innovation – four subjects that are generally of interest to most managers and scientists, alike. Services are important to people in business, government, education, health care and management, religion, military, scientific research, engineering, and other endeavors that are too numerous to mention,

because most service providers – be they individuals, businesses, governments, and so forth – are also consumers of services. This is the first of three introductory chapters on the subject. The second chapter, entitled "Service Management," covers the operational environment for services, and the last chapter, entitled "Service Technology " covers the technical and architectural basis for the Service discipline.

7   Service Management **103**

In the multifaceted domain of services, management and business are intertwined. An enterprise, taken in this paper to be a business, government entity, or educational organization, simultaneously manages its own services and services provided to clients by adopting the role of service provider or service client. In short, an enterprise is likely to be a provider and a user of services. In fact, many internal services are managed as a business and in some instances evolve into external service providers – all with the same or similar functional deployments. So the fine line of separation between management and business is nonexistent, and that phenomenon is clearly evident in the chapters on service.

8   Service Technology **135**

This chapter concludes the conspectus of Service for academicians and practitioners. It follows the two previous chapters, entitled *Service Concepts* and *Service Management* with the express purpose of defining the scope of the discipline. An eclectic background in service technology and service architecture is required to fully explore the potential of a science as an academic discipline. This chapter reviews the technical concepts needed to apply the concepts that have previously been introduced.

9   Identity as a Service **183**

Identity service is an important subject in information systems in general and cloud computing in particular. Normally associated with digital security and privacy, the scope of identity is much greater and affects most aspects of everyday life. Related subjects are behavioral tracking, personal-identifiable information (PII), privacy data relevance, data repurposing, and identity theft. Cloud computing is currently portrayed as a model for providing on-demand access to computing service via the Internet and also serves as a focus for modern security and privacy concerns. Adoption of cloud computing practically eliminates the upfront costs of acquiring computational resources and the time delay of building and deploying software applications. The technology is not without a downside, which, in this case, is the privacy of business and personal information for which identity is a major consideration. **Identity service** is an admixture of the major issues in the privacy and security of individual rights in a complex informational environment. This is a working paper on this important subject.

10   Principles of Service Systems: An Ontological Approach.. **199**
This paper delineates the principles of service systems, based on an ontological foundation of the subject matter developed independently of a particular endeavor, that are required to enable communication among researchers and assist in the ongoing theoretical development of the constituent topics. The chapter begins with the presentation of service elements and progresses through the various topics until the requisite concepts, relations, and vocabulary are formulated. The subjects are presented in a developmental manner to promote clarity and readability by a broad service science audience and to support research in the discipline.

Section Three - Advanced Subjects

11   Toward a Unified Ontology of Trusted Identity in Cyberspace... **229**
The nation's digital infrastructure is in jeopardy because of inadequate provisions for privacy, identity, and security. Recent Internet activity has resulted in an onslaught of identity theft, fraud, digital crime, and an increasing burden to responsible citizens. The computer security and Internet communities have been generally responsive but apparently ineffective, so it is time for a third party to step in, take charge, and provide an infrastructure to assist in protecting individuals and non-person entities. This chapter is a contribution to the domain of ontological commitment as it applies to a description of subjects, objects, actions, and relationships as they pertain to the National Strategy of Trusted Identity in Cyberspace initiative.

12 Essentials of Ransomware for Business and Management **255**

Ransomware is one of the most vicious and troublesome forms of cyber terrorism to surface in recent years, and the reported incidents of it are increasing rapidly. In this form of cyber crime, a malicious program takes over a victim's computer making use of the computer and access to files unavailable unless a victim pays a ransom. The problem affects individuals and organizations, including in one instance, a health-care facility. Typically, the victim does not know how to respond when a ransomware attack takes place, since payment of the amount of the requested ransom does not necessarily resolve the situation. This chapter describes the various forms of ransomware and gives insight on effective countermeasures. It is a short chapter on a new subject in cybersecurity.

13 Watchlist Concepts for Business and Management – Getting Started **263**

A *watchlist* is generally regarded as a database the government uses to track terrorists. While that is partially true, there is clearly more to it. Otherwise, all of the terrorists would be easily rounded up and the world would be free of the immense security problems that we now face. It follows that if the methodology were genuinely effective, then the inherent techniques could perhaps be used for marketing and other business and societal concerns. Although the methods developed thus far by government agencies are indeed impressive, they necessarily have to be updated as the underlying problems mature. Many subjects need to be analyzed and solutions implemented. The problem domain must be precisely defined and related considerations delineated. To start, a few basic questions need to be answered concerning where society is essentially going with the notion of watch listing and whether or not the concepts of listing are applicable to other areas of business, government, and education. This essay gives an introduction to this very important topic.

14 Cyberspace Policy Review And The National Strategy For Trusted Identity In Cyberspace **273**

This chapter gives a brief but substantial review of two documents promulgated by the U.S. Office of the President: the *Cyberspace Policy Review* and the *National Strategy for Trusted Identity in Cyberspace*. An identity ecosystem, consisting of participants and infrastructure, is proposed and an operational framework is envisioned. The underlying concepts are comprehensive, and the overall implications should be of interest to the academic, business, and government communities.

15 Introduction to Terrorism for Managers 285

Most persons are well aware of the nature and danger of terrorism, although they haven't had the least inclination to define the term and related concepts. Throughout history, there have been many examples of terrorism as a threat to individual freedom and national security, and those threats have taken the form of a wide variety of actions resulting in large-scale losses of life, destruction of public, private, and personal property, widespread illness and injury, displacement of large numbers of people, and devastating economic loss. There are several dimensions to terrorism, including its very nature, cause, perpetration, targets, methods, and defense against it, and numerous papers, reports, and books have been published on the subject. However, a civilian awareness of methods for self-defense has yet to be stimulated and most businesses, institutions, and other agencies have little preparation or knowledge of a response to a terrorist attack. Business and institutional management has a responsibility to stakeholders, employees, customers, and the general public for an effective response in the event of a terrorist attack. An introduction to the essential methods for establishing an appropriate response to terrorism is the subject of the chapter.

1

ESSENTIALS OF CYBERSECURITY

INTRODUCTION

It is well established that cybersecurity is a complicated and complex subject encompassing computer security, information assurance, comprehensive infrastructure protection, commercial integrity, and ubiquitous personal interactions. Most people look at the subject from a personal perspective. Is my computer and information secure from outside interference? Is the operation of my online business vulnerable to outside threats? Will I get the item I ordered? Are my utilities safe from international intrusion? Have I done enough to protect my personal privacy? Are my bank accounts and credit cards safe? How do we protect our websites and online information systems from hackers? The list of everyday concerns that people have over the modern system of communication could go on and on. Clearly, concerned citizens and organizations look to someone or something else, such as their Internet service provider or their company or the government, to solve the problem and just tell them what to do.

So far, it hasn't been that simple and probably never will be. The digital infrastructure based on the Internet that we call cyberspace is something that we depend on every day for a prosperous economy, a strong military, and an enlightened lifestyle. Cyberspace, as a concept, is a virtual world synthesized from computer hardware and software, desktops and laptops, tablets and cell phones, and broadband and wireless signals that power our schools, businesses, hospitals, government, utilities, and personal lives through a sophisticated set of communication systems, available worldwide. However, the power to build also provides the power to disrupt and destroy. Many persons associate cybersecurity with cyber crime, since it costs persons, commercial organizations, and governments more than a $1 trillion per year. However, there is considerably more to cybersecurity than cyber crime, so it is necessary to start off with concepts and definitions.

CONCEPTS AND DEFINITIONS

Cyberspace has been defined as the interdependent network of information technology infrastructure, and includes the Internet, telecommunications networks, computer systems, and embedded processors and controllers in critical industries. Alternately, cyberspace is often regarded as any process, program, or protocol relating to the use of the Internet for data processing transmission or use in telecommunication. As such, cyberspace is instrumental in sustaining the everyday activities of millions of people and thousands of organizations worldwide.

The strategic plan for the U.S. Department of Homeland Security lists five main missions for the period 2012-2016, listed as follows:

> Mission 1: Preventing Terrorism and Enhancing Security
>
> Mission 2: Securing and Managing Our Borders
>
> Mission 3: Enforcing and Administering Our Immigration Laws
>
> Mission 4: Safeguarding and Securing Cyberspace

Mission 5: Ensuring Resilience to Disaster

Clearly, the placement of cybersecurity as one of the five major strategic missions of the Department of Homeland Security (DHS) is a sure-fire indication that an underlying problem exists with the global dependence on the Internet that is summarized in the following introductory quote from the DHS report:

> Cyberspace is highly dynamic and the risks posed by malicious cyber activity often transcend sector and international boundaries. Today's threats to cybersecurity require the engagement of the entire society – from government and law enforcement to the private sector and most importantly, members of the public – to mitigate malicious activities while bolstering defensive capabilities.

Ensuing policy goals and objectives to achieve cybersecurity could therefore include:

Goal 4.1: Create a Safe, Secure, and Resilient Cyber Environment

Objective 4.1.1: Understand and prioritize cyber threats

Objective 4.1.2: Manage risks to cyberspace

Objective 4.1.3: Prevent cyber crime and other malicious uses of cyberspace

Objective 4.1.4: Develop a robust public-private cyber incident response capability

Goal 4.2: Promote Cybersecurity Knowledge and Innovation

Objective 4.2.1: Enhance public awareness

Objective 4.2.2: Foster a dynamic workforce

Objective 4.2.3: Invest in innovative technologies, techniques, and procedures

While the line between policy and operations may be a blurred line in some instances, a necessary requirement of cybersecurity is to have security operations be part of a stated set of objectives.

CYBER ATTACKS

Cyber attacks can be divided into four distinct groups: cyber terrorism, cyber war, cybercrime, and cyber espionage. It would seem that cybercrime and cyber espionage are the most pressing issues, but the others are just offstage. Here are some definitions:

> *Cyber crime* is the use of computers or related systems to steal or compromise confidential information for criminal purposes, most often for financial gain.

> *Cyber espionage* is the use of computers or related systems to collect intelligence or enable certain operations, whether in cyberspace or the real world.

> *Cyber terrorism* is the use of computers or related systems to create fear or panic in a society and may not result in physical destruction by cyber agitation.

> *Cyber war* consists of military operations conducted within cyberspace to deny an adversary, whether a state or non-state actor, the effective use of

information systems and weapons, or systems controlled by information technology, in order to achieve a political end.

As such, cybersecurity has been identified as one of the most serious economic and national security challenges facing the nation.

THE COMPREHENSIVE NATIONAL CYBERSECURITY INITIATIVE

In order to achieve cybersecurity, from individual, national, organizational, or global perspectives, a proposed set of major goals has been developed:

To establish a front line of defense against today's immediate threats
To defend against the full spectrum of threats
To strengthen the future cybersecurity environment

Starting from the top, the President has directed the release of a summary description of the Comprehensive National Cybersecurity Initiatives, summarized as follows:

Initiative #1. Manage the Federal Enterprise Network as a single network enterprise with Trusted Internet Connections.

Initiative #2. Deploy an intrusion detection system of sensors across the Federal enterprise.

Initiative #3. Pursue deployment of intrusion prevention systems across the Federal enterprise.

Initiative #4. Coordinate and redirect research and development (R&D) efforts.

Initiative #5. Connect current cyber ops centers to enhance situational awareness.

Initiative #6. Develop and implement a government-wide cyber counterintelligence (CI) plan.

Initiative #7. Increase the security of our classified networks.

Initiative #8. Expand cyber education.

Initiative #9. Define and develop enduring "leap-ahead" technology, strategies, and programs.

Initiative #10. Define and develop enduring deterrence strategies and programs.

Initiative #11. Develop a multi-pronged approach for global supply chain risk management.

Initiative #12. Define the Federal role for extending cybersecurity into critical infrastructure domains.

The basic idea of the twelve initiatives is to address current and future cybersecurity issues by combining the resources of the Federal government, local and state governments, and the private sector to provide a strong response to future cyber incidents and by strengthening public/private relationships.

CRITICAL INFRASTRUCTURE AND KEY RESOURCES

The present concern over cybersecurity is the result of a variety of cyber attacks, intrusions, and countermeasures that have occurred globally in recent years. The threat scenarios are multidimensional and attribution is cumbersome to ascertain. Moreover, exposure to cyber threats can be direct or indirect, resulting from a dependence on one or more elements of critical infrastructure. The scope of inherent infrastructure has grown from ten in the year 2003 to eighteen in the year 2012. The underlying philosophy is that once the critical areas are identified, a public/private dialog can be established to achieve a measurable amount of cybersecurity. Each of the six critical areas are classed as major and are assigned a Sector Specific Agency (SSA) by the Department of Homeland Security as part of the National Infrastructure Protection Plan (NIPP), intended to set national priorities, goals, and requirements for effective allocation of resources. The major areas are:

Chemical
Commercial Facilities
Critical Manufacturing
Dams
Emergency Services
Nuclear Reactors, Materials, and Waste

The manner in which the public/private coordination and collaboration is executed is a matter of public debate. The key point is that a cyber intrusion in a major area can indirectly endanger a large number of people, governmental organizations, and commercial facilities.

The remaining twelve critical areas are assigned to existing governmental offices, as reflected in the following list:

Agriculture and food – Department of Agriculture and the Food and Drug Administration

Banking and Finance – Department of the Treasury

Communications – Department of Homeland Security

Defense Industrial Base – Department of Defense

Energy – Department of Energy

Governmental Facilities – Department of Homeland Security

Information Technology – Department of Homeland Security

National Monuments and Icons – Department of the Interior

Postal and Shipping – Transportation Security Administration

Healthcare and Public Health – Department of Health and Human Services

Transportation Systems – Transportation Security Administration and the U.S. Coast Guard

Water – Environmental Protection Agency

National and global protection necessarily involves the establishment of a framework to provide the following:

The exchange of ideas, approachs, and best practices
The facilitation of security planning and resource allocation
The establishment of structure for effective coordination among partners
The enhancement of coordination with the international community
The building of public awareness

The identification of the areas of critical infrastructure is significant because of the wide diversity of cyber threats, vulnerabilities, risk, and problem domains. Moreover, critical elements possess a wide variety of technological attributes that require a range of solutions.

SUMMARY

The paper gives an overview of the emerging discipline of cybersecurity that adds a policy level to the longstanding subjects of information security, computer security, and network security. Concepts and some basic definitions are covered. Cyber attacks are divided into cyber crime, cyber espionage, cyber terrorism, and cyber war. A comprehensive overview of the subject matter is given through the National Cybersecurity Initiative, and the notion of the critical infrastructure is explored in some detail.

REFERENCES

Remarks by the U.S. President on Securing Our Nation's Cyber Infrastructure, East Room, May 29, 2009.

National Security Presidential Directive 54/Homeland Security Presidential Directive 23 (NSPD-54/HSPD-23).

Shackelford, Scott L., In Search of Cyber Peace: A Response to the Cybersecurity Act of 2012, *Stanford Law Review,* March 8, 2012, (http://www.stanfordlawreview.org).

Lord, K.M. and T. Sharp (editors), *America's Cyber Future: Security and Prosperity in the Information Age* (Volume I), Center for New American Security (June 2011), (http://www.cnas.org).

National Security Council, *The Comprehensive National Cybersecurity Initiative,* The White House, (http://www.whitehouse.gov/cybersecurity/comprehensive-national-cybersecurity-initiative).

The White House, *The National Strategy to Secure Cyberspace,* February, 2003.

Homeland Security, *More About the Office of Infrastructure Protection*, (http:// www.dhs.gov/xabout/structure/gc_1189775491423.shtm).

The Department of Homeland Security, *National Infrastructure Protection Plan: Partnering to enhance protection and resiliency*, 2009.

***** End of Chapter 1 *****

2

CYBERSECURITY
SERVICE MODEL

INTRODUCTION

The Internet is the newest form of communication between organizations and people in modern society. Everyday commerce depends on it, and individuals use it for social interactions, as well as for reference and learning. To some, the Internet is a convenience for shopping, information retrieval, and entertainment. To others, such as large organizations, the Internet makes expansion cost effective and allows disparate groups to profitably work together through reduced communication costs. It gives government entities facilities for providing convenient service to constituents. The Internet is also efficient, because it usually can provide total service on a large variety of subjects in a few seconds, as compared to a much longer time for the same results that would have been required in earlier times. [11]

From a security perspective, the use of the term "cyber" generally means more than just the Internet, and usually refers to the use of electronics to communicate between entities. The subject of cyber includes the Internet as the major data transportation element, but can also include wireless, fixed hard wires, and electromagnetic transference via satellites and other devices. Cyber elements incorporate networks, electrical and mechanical devices, individual computers, and a variety of smart devices, such as phones, tablets, pads, and electronic game and entertainment systems. A reasonable definition would be that cyber is the seamless fabric of the modern information technology infrastructure that enables organizations and private citizens to sustain most aspects of modern everyday life.

Cyber supports the commercial, educational, governmental, and critical national infrastructure. Cyber facilities are pervasive and extend beyond national borders. As such, individuals, organizations, and nation-states can use cyber for productive and also destructive purposes. A single individual or a small group can use cyber for commercial gain or surreptitious invasion of assets. Activities in the latter category are usually classed as penetration and include attempts designed to compromise systems that contain vital information. In a similar vein, intrusion can also effect the operation of critical resources, such as private utility companies.

Interconnectivity between elements is desirable and usually cost effective, so that a wide variety of dependencies have evolved, and cyber intrusions have emerged. Thus, a small group of individuals can compromise a large organization or facility, which is commonly known as an *asymmetric* threat against which methodological protection is necessary. In many cases, a single computer with software obtained over the Internet can do untold damage to a business, utility, governmental structure, or personal information. Willful invasion of the property of other entities is illegal, regardless of the purpose or intent. However, the openness of the Internet often makes it difficult to identify and apprehend cyber criminals.

CYBERSECURITY OPERATIONS

It is well established that cybersecurity is a complicated and complex subject encompassing computer security, information assurance, comprehensive infrastructure protection, commercial integrity, and ubiquitous personal interactions. Most people look at the subject from a personal perspective. Is my computer and information secure from outside interference? Is the operation of my online business vulnerable to outside threats? Will I get the item I ordered? Are my utilities safe from international intrusion? Have I done enough to protect my personal privacy? Are my bank accounts and credit cards safe? How do we protect our websites and online information systems from hackers? Can my identity be stolen? The list of everyday concerns that people have over the modern system of communication could go on and on. Clearly, concerned citizens and organizations look to someone or something else, such as their Internet service provider or their company or the government, to solve the problem and just tell them what to do.

So far, it hasn't been that simple and probably never will be. The digital infrastructure based on the Internet that we call cyberspace is something that we depend on every day for a prosperous economy, a strong military, and an enlightened lifestyle. Cyberspace, as a concept, is a virtual world synthesized from computer hardware and software, desktops and laptops, tablets and cell phones, and broadband and wireless signals that power our schools, businesses, hospitals, government, utilities, and personal lives through a sophisticated set of communication systems, available worldwide. However, the power to build also provides the power to disrupt and destroy. Many persons associate cybersecurity with cyber crime, since it costs persons, commercial organizations, and governments more than a $1 trillion per year.[1] However, there is considerably more to cybersecurity than cyber crime, so it is necessary to start off with a few concepts and definitions.

Cyberspace has been defined as the interdependent network of information technology infrastructure, and includes the Internet, telecommunication networks, computer systems, and embedded processors and controllers in critical industries. Alternately, cyberspace is often regarded as any process, program, or protocol relating to the use of the Internet for data processing transmission or use in telecommunication.

---

[1] Remarks by the U.S. President on Securing Our Nation's Cyber Infrastructure, East Room, May 29, 2009. [1]

As such, cyberspace is instrumental in sustaining the everyday activities of millions of people and thousands of organizations worldwide.

Cyber Attacks

Cyber attacks can be divided into four distinct groups: cyber terrorism, cyber war, cyber crime, and cyber espionage. It would seem that cyber crime and cyber espionage are the most pressing issues, but the others are just offstage. Here are some definitions:

> *Cyber crime* is the use of computers or related systems to steal or compromise confidential information for criminal purposes, most often for financial gain.

> *Cyber espionage* is the use of computers or related systems to collect intelligence or enable certain operations, whether in cyberspace or the real world.

> *Cyber terrorism* is the use of computers or related systems to create fear or panic in a society and may result in physical destruction by cyber agitation.

> *Cyber war* consists of military operations conducted within cyberspace to deny an adversary, whether a state or non-state actor, the effective use of information systems and weapons, or systems controlled by information technology, in order to achieve a political end.

As such, cybersecurity has been identified as one of the most serious economic and national security challenges facing the nation.[2] There is

---

[2] National Security Council, The Comprehensive National Cybersecurity Initiative, The White House, (http://www.whitehouse.gov/cybersecurity/comprehensive-national-cybersecurity-initiative). [2]

also a personal component to cybersecurity. The necessity of having to protect one's identity and private information from outside intrusion is a nuisance resulting in the use of costly and inconvenient safeguards.

Cyberspace Domain, its Elements and Actors

Cyberspace is a unique domain that is operationally distinct from the other domains of land, sea, air, and space. It provides, through the Internet, the capability to create, transmit, manipulate, and use digital information.[3] The digital information includes data, voice, video, and graphics transmitted over wired and wireless facilities between a wide range of devices that include computers, tablets, smart phones, and control systems. The Internet serves as the transport mechanism for cyberspace. The extensive variety of content is attractive to hackers, criminal elements, and nation states with the objective of disrupting commercial, military, and social activities. Table 1 gives a list of areas at risk in the cyberspace domain.[4] Many cyber events, classified as cyber attacks, are not deliberate and result from everyday mistakes and poor training. Others result from disgruntled employees. Unfortunately, security metrics include non-serious as well as serious intrusions, so that the cybersecurity threat appears to be overstated in some instances. This phenomenon requires that we concentrate on deliberate software attacks and how they are in fact related, since the object is to develop a conceptual model of the relationship between security countermeasures and vulnerabilities.

Many of the software threats can be perpetrated by individuals or small groups against major organizations and nation-states – referred to as *asymmetric attacks*. The threats are reasonably well known and

---

[3] McConnell, M., *Cyber Insecurities: The 21st Century Threatscape*, Chapter II in Lord, K.M. and T. Sharp (editors), America's Cyber Future: Security and Prosperity in the Information Age (Volume II), Center for New American Security (June 2011), (http://www.cnas.org). [18]

[4] Stewart, J., *CompTIA Security+ Review Guide*, Indianapolis: Wiley Publishing, Inc., 2009. [21]

are summarized in Table 2. It's clear that effective countermeasures are both technical and procedural, in some instances, and must be linked to hardware and software resources on the defensive side. The security risks that involve computers and auxiliary equipment target low-end firmware or embedded software, such as BIOS, USB devices, cell phones and tablets, and removable and network storage. Operating system risks encompass service packs, hotfixes, patches, and various configuration elements. Established counter measures, include intrusion detection and handling systems, hardware and software firewalls, and antivirus and anti-spam software.

Here is a list of service threats: privilege escalation, virus, worm, trojan horse, spyware, spam, hoax, adware, rootkit, botnet, and logic bomb.

The cybersecurity network infrastructure involves unique security threats and countermeasures. Most of the threats relate to the use of out-of-date network protocols, specific hacker techniques, such as packet sniffing, spoofing, phishing and spear phishing, man-in-the-middle attacks, denial-of-service procedures, and exploiting vulnerabilities related to domain name systems. Countermeasures include hardware, software, and protective procedures of various kinds. Hardware, software, and organizational resources customarily execute the security measures. There is much more to security threats and countermeasures, and the information presented here gives only a flavor to the subject.

There is an additional category of threats and countermeasures that primarily involves end-users and what they are permitted to do. In order for a threat agent to infiltrate a system, three elements are required: network presence, access control, and authorization. This subject is normally covered as the major features of information assurance and refers to the process of "getting on the system," such as the Internet or a local-area network. A threat agent cannot address a system if the computer is not turned on or a network presence is not possible. Once an end user is connected to the computer system or network, then access control and authorization take over. It has been estimated that 80% of security violations originate at the end-user level.[5] *Access control* concerns the identification of the entity requesting accessibility and whether that entity is permitted to use the system. *Authorization* refers to precisely what that entity is permitted to do, once permitted access. There is a high-degree of specificity to access-control and authorization procedures. For example, access control can be based on something the requestor knows or what it is. Similarly, authorization can be based on role, group membership, level in the organization, and so forth. Clearly, this category reflects considerations which the organizations has control over, and as such, constitutes security measures that are self-postulated.

The above information constitutes a synopsis of cybersecurity necessary for this paper. Cybersecurity, as an academic discipline, is considerably more extensive.

Naïve Service Science

It is well established that a *service* is a provider/client interaction that creates and captures value. Both parties participate in the transaction, and in the process, both benefit from it. In a sense, the provider and client co-produce the service event, because one can't do without the other. [15] Another view of service is that it is the deployment of service assets by a set of service participants for the benefit of another set of service participants, defined here as economic entities including individuals, businesses, educational institutions, and government agencies and are generally classed as providers and clients when a service event is instantiated. In fact, some economists have classed most products as service providers, since they provide tangible or intangible benefit to a service entity. [12, 19, 22]

Informational systems that are used by people, such as computer systems and the Internet, are also classed as services. In fact, the phenomena of users interacting with computer-based service systems that rely on other computers, as in web services, are also classed as

---

[5] Stewart, *op cit.*

services. In general, the role of service provider and a service client are *complementary*, since one cannot do without the other, and this concept is known as *service duality*. [14] When two entities work together to achieve a common purpose, on the other hand, their form of behavior is regarded as *supplementary*. [13]

Normally, systems that provide services exhibit a lifecycle consisting of the following layers of activity: commitment, production, availability, delivery, analysis, and termination. Many societal systems reflect a lifecycle, and that group includes facilities for cybersecurity and information assurance. [13]

Service Collectivism

Most services operate in a well-defined area of endeavor, such as a university, newspaper, or a medical group. In an operational domain of this sort, there exists a set of providers, a set of clients, and a set of available services. In a colloquial sense, an element of the provider set interacts with an element of the client set instantiating a service from the service set; the interaction creates a service event. [14] The connection between the provider and client sets is viewed as a mapping between the sets in the same sense that a function is a mapping between the domain and co-domain in mathematics. A common means of representing this mapping can be denoted by:

$$S: P \rightarrow C$$

where the service (S) assigns to each provider p in P an element c in C. Clearly, P refers to the set of providers and C refers to the client set. The concept is slightly more complicated. Take a university as an example. The set of services provided to students is commonly partitioned as administrative services, academic services, and student services, where the last group addresses the wide variety of personal concerns normally related to students. The service providers in each category commonly coordinate amongst themselves as well as between categories. Some students require multiple services while others need few, if any. An analogous case is a newspaper where readers chose between sections of interest.

Two considerations are of particular interest. The first, and perhaps most important, is the salient fact that service providers in the categories of P collaborate between themselves and with service providers in other sections. Thus, the set P is a *service collective*. Later, we are going to reflect on the possibility of elements in P performing service on elements of themselves.

The second consideration serves to initiate the notion of *service duality*. In the mapping of an element of P with an element of C, mathematical function theory serves as a useful model. Three forms are identified: surjection, injection, and bijection. With surjection, every element in C is a service interaction for at least one provider in P. Thus, every element of C is covered. With injection, every element in C is a service interaction for most one provider in P. The relationship is a bijection if it is a surjection and an injection for all elements in P and C. Thus, the phenomena that a provider gives service to multiple clients, i.e., injection, is true only if a temporal form is established.

The key point concerning service duality is that if there is no need for a particular form of service within a given domain, then the necessity of related activity is diminished. If a service provider doesn't have any clients, is it really a service provider or does it exist in some intermediate form. Economic considerations would certainly apply to this situation, so then the question is "To what types of service does this form of analysis apply?"

Collaboration Service

A *collaboration service* exists when a total provider set P supplies a totality of services for a specific domain to a complete client set C. Not every provider p_i performs the same service but the members of P can collectively supply all of the service needed for that domain. If a product-as-a-service is incorporated in that domain, then it is incorporated in that collaboration group. If a form of service included procedures that must be performed by the client to achieve a service, then that process is additionally included in the collaboration group. Similarly, if certain conditions, or state of the system, must exist within the client area in order for a particular service event to be accomplished, then those *a priori* conditions should be part of the collaboration group. Thus, a collection of potential provider services, products, processes, and conditions is regarded as a *collaboration group* that provides service to clients in a complex operational domain.

Cybersecurity Collaboration Group

The controls that constitute a cyber security domain form a collaboration group. Diverse elements of hardware and software are used for network and operating system security. Processes are necessary for gaining network presence, access control, and authentication. Intrusion detection and prevention systems (IPDS) are implemented to perform continuous monitoring and cyber protection. Access roles and operational rules are developed to facilitate use of cyber security procedures and elements. Clearly, cybersecurity is a service, albeit a special kind of service in which the distinction between providers and clients is more often blurred rather than being strictly defined.

When a client adopts cybersecurity principles for network presence, access control, and authentication, for example, it applies the inherent methods for and by itself, thereby assuming the dual role of provider and client. Similarly, when an organization installs a hardware or software firewall for network protection, it is effectively applying a product for its own security.

In a service system, service entities exchange information and behavior in order to achieve mutually beneficial results. As service systems become more complex, the service entities adapt to optimize their behavior – a process often referred to as *evolution*. [17] Differing forms of organization emerge such that the system exhibits intelligent behavior based on information interchange and the following nine properties: emergence, co-evolution, sub-optimal, requisite variety, connectivity, simple rules, self organization, edge of chaos, and nestability. Systems of this type are usually known as *complex adaptive systems*. [12] Complex adaptive systems are often known as "smart systems," and cybersecurity researchers are looking at the operation of such systems as a model for the design of cybersecurity systems that can prevent attacks through the exchange of information between security elements.

Distributed Security

The major characteristic of a cybersecurity system designed to prevent and mediate a cyber attack is that the totality of security elements in a particular domain are organized into a smart service system. This characteristic refers to the facility of cyber elements to communicate on a real-time basis in response to cyber threats. Currently, threat determination is largely manual and human-oriented. An intrusion detection system recognizes an intrusion and informs a security manager. That manager then contacts other managers via email, personal contact, or telephone to warn of the cyber threat. In a smart cybersecurity system, the intrusion detection software would isolate the cyber threat and automatically contact other elements in the domain to defend their system. Thus, the security service would handle intruders in a manner similar to the way biological systems handle analogous invasions: recognize the threat; attempt to neutralize it; and alert other similar elements.

In a definitive white paper on distributed security, McConnell [18] recognizes the need for cyber devices to work together in near real-time to minimize cyber attacks and defend against them. This is a form of continuous monitoring and referred to as a *cyber ecosystem* in which relevant participants interact to provide security and maintain a persistent state of security. Clearly, a cyber ecosystem would establish a basis for cybersecurity through individually designed hierarchies of security elements, referred to as security devices. Ostensibly, security devices would be programmed to communicate in the event of a cyber attack. The conceptual building blocks of an ecosystem are automation, interoperability, and authentication. *Automation* refers to the notion of security devices being able to detect intrusion detection and respond to other security devices without human intervention. Thus, the security ecosystem could behave as a security service and provide speed and in the activation of automated prevention systems. *Interoperability* refers to the ability of the cyber ecosystem to incorporate differing assessments, hardware facilities, and organizations with strategically distinct policy structures. *Authentication* refers to the capability to extend the ecosystem across differing network technologies, devices, organizations, and participants.

Thus, the cyber ecosystem responds as a service system in requests for security service to participants that are members of the ecosystem, namely private firms, non-profit organizations, governments, individuals, processes, cyber devices comprised of computers, software, and communications equipment.

Monroe Doctrine for Cybersecurity

Internet governance refers to an attempt at the global level to legislate operations in cyberspace taking into consideration the economic, cultural, developmental, legal, political, and cultural interests of its stakeholders. [9] A more specific definition would be the development and application by governments and the private sector of shared principles, norms, rules, decision-making, and programs that determine the evolution and use of the Internet. [9] Internet governance is a difficult process because it encompasses, web sites, Internet service providers, and hackers and activists and involves differing forms of content and operational intent ranging from pornography to terrorist information to intrusion and malicious content. Cybersecurity is a complex form of service that purports to protect against intrusion, invasion, and other forms of cyber terrorism, crime, espionage, and war. But, attacks can be carried out by anyone with an Internet connection and a little bit of knowledge of hacking techniques. NATO has addressed the subject of cyber defense with articles that state the members will consult together in the event of cyber attacks but are not duty bound to render aid. [8] It would seem that deterrence, where one party is able to suggest to an adversary that it is capable and willing to use appropriate offensive measures, is perhaps a useful adjunct to cybersecurity service. However, successful attribution of cyber attacks is not a fail proof endeavor so that offensive behavior is not a total solution.

Cybersecurity is a pervasive problem that deserves different approaches. Davidson [10] has noted an interesting possibility, based on the volume of recent cyber attacks. The context is that we are in a cyber war and a war is not won on defense. A "Monroe Doctrine in Cyberspace" is proposed, similar to the Monroe Doctrine of 1823 that "here is our turf; stay out or face the consequences."

SUMMARY

The Internet is a seamless means of communication between organizations and people in modern society; it supports an infrastructure that permits cost effective commerce, social interaction, reference, and learning. The use of the term "cyber" means more than just the Internet and refers to the use of electronics in a wide variety of forms between entities. Cyber facilities are pervasive and extend beyond national borders and can be used by individuals, organizations, and nation states for productive and destructive purposes. A single individual or small group can use cyber technology for surreptitious invasion of assets to obtain vital information or to cause the disruption of critical resources.

Cybersecurity is conceptualized as a unique kind of service in which providers and clients collaborate to supply service through shared responsibility, referred to as *collaborative service*. Cybersecurity is achieved through distributed security implemented as a smart service system with three important attributes: automation, interoperability, and authentication. A Monroe Doctrine for Cybersecurity is proposed.

REFERENCES

1   Remarks by the U.S. President on Securing Our Nation's Cyber Infrastructure, East Room, May 29, 2009.

2   National Security Presidential Directive 54/Homeland Security Presidential Directive 23 (NSPD-54/HSPD-23).

3   National Security Council, *The Comprehensive National Cybersecurity Initiative*, The White House, (http://www.whitehouse.gov/cybersecurity/comprehensive-national-cybersecurity-initiative).

4   The White House, *The National Strategy to Secure Cyberspace*, February 2003.

5   The Department of Homeland Security, *More About the Office of Infrastructure Protection*, (http://www.dhs.gov/xabout/structure/gc_1189775491423.shtm).

6   The Department of Homeland Security, *National Infrastructure Protection Plan: Partnering to enhance protection and resiliency*, 2009.

7   Working Group on Internet Governance, Report Document WSIS-II/PC-3/DOC/5-E, August 2005.

8   Cavelty, M., Cyber-Allies: Strengths and Weaknesses of NATO's Cyberdefense Posture, *IP – Global Edition*, ETH Zurich, 3/2011.

9   Conway, M., Terrorism and Internet Governance: Core Issues, Dublin: *Disarmament Forum 3*, 2007.

10 Davidson, M., *The Monroe Doctrine in Cyberspace*, Testimony given to the Homeland Security Subcommittee on Emerging Threats, Cybersecurity, and Technology, March 10, 2009.

11 Katzan, H., *Foundations of Service Science: A Pragmatic Approach*, New York: iUniverse, Inc., 2008.

12 Katzan, H., *Service Science: Concepts, Technology, Management*, New York: iUniverse, Inc., 2008.

13 Lord, K.M. and T. Sharp (editors), *America's Cyber Future: Security and Prosperity in the Information Age* (Volume I), Center for New American Security (June 2011), (http://www.cnas.org).

14 Mainzer, K., *Thinking in Complexity: The Complex Dynamics of Matter, Mind, and Mankind*, New York: Springer, 1997.

15 McConnell, B. (co-author) and The Department of Homeland Security, *Enabling Distributed Security in Cyberspace: Building a Healthy and Resilient Cyber Ecosystem with Automated Collective Action*, http://www.dhs.gov/ xlibrary/assets/nppd-cyber-ecosystem-white-paper-03-23-2011.pdf, 23 March 2011.

16 Norman, D., *Living with Complexity*, Cambridge: The MIT Press, 2011. Shackelford, Scott L., In Search of Cyber Peace: A Response to the Cybersecurity Act of 2012, *Stanford Law Review*, March 8, 2012, (http:// www.stanfordlawreview.org).

***** End of Chapter 2 *****

3

FUNDAMENTALS OF APPLIED CYBERSECURITY FOR BUSINESS AND MANAGEMENT

INTRODUCTION

It is well established that cybersecurity is a complicated and complex subject encompassing computer security, information assurance, comprehensive infrastructure protection, commercial integrity, and ubiquitous personal interactions. Most people look at the subject from a personal perspective. Is my computer and information secure from outside interference? Is the operation of my online business vulnerable to outside threats? Will I get the item I ordered? Are my utilities safe from international intrusion? Have I done enough to protect my personal privacy? Are my bank accounts and credit cards safe? How do we protect our websites and online information systems from hackers? The list of everyday concerns that people have over the modern system of communication could go on and on. Clearly, concerned citizens and organizations look to someone or something else, such as their Internet service provider or their company or the government, to solve the problem and just tell them what to do.

So far, it hasn't been that simple and probably never will be. The digital infrastructure based on the Internet that we call cyberspace is something that we depend on every day for a prosperous economy, a strong military, and an enlightened lifestyle. Cyberspace, as a concept, is a virtual world synthesized from computer hardware and software, desktops and laptops, tablets and cell phones, and broadband and wireless signals that power our schools, businesses, hospitals, government, utilities, and personal lives through a sophisticated set of communication systems, available worldwide. However, the power to build also provides the power to disrupt and destroy. Many persons associate cybersecurity with cyber crime, since it costs persons, commercial organizations, and governments more than a $1 trillion per year. However, there is considerably more to cybersecurity than cyber crime, so it is necessary to start off with concepts and definitions.

CONCEPTS AND DEFINITIONS

Cyberspace has been defined as the interdependent network of information technology infrastructure, and includes the Internet, telecommunications networks, computer systems, and embedded processors and controllers in critical industries. Alternately, cyberspace is often regarded as any process, program, or protocol relating to the use of the Internet for data processing transmission or use in telecommunication. As such, cyberspace is instrumental in sustaining the everyday activities of millions of people and thousands of organizations worldwide.

The strategic plan for the U.S. Department of Homeland Security lists five main missions for the period 2012-2016, listed as follows:

Mission 1: Preventing Terrorism and Enhancing Security

Mission 2: Securing and Managing Our Borders

Mission 3: Enforcing and Administering Our Immigration Laws

Mission 4: Safeguarding and Securing Cyberspace

Mission 5: Ensuring Resilience to Disaster

Clearly, the placement of cybersecurity as one of the five major strategic missions of the Department of Homeland Security (DHS) is a sure-fire indication that an underlying problem exists with the global dependence on the Internet that is summarized in the following introductory quote from the DHS report

> Cyberspace is highly dynamic and the risks posed by malicious cyber activity often transcend sector and international boundaries. Today's threats to cybersecurity require the engagement of the entire society – from government and law enforcement to the private sector and most importantly, members of the public – to mitigate malicious activities while bolstering defensive capabilities.

Ensuing policy goals and objectives to achieve cybersecurity could therefore include:

Goal 4.1: Create a Safe, Secure, and Resilient Cyber Environment

Objective 4.1.1: Understand and prioritize cyber threats

Objective 4.1.2: Manage risks to cyberspace

Objective 4.1.3: Prevent cyber crime and other malicious uses of cyberspace

Objective 4.1.4: Develop a robust public-private cyber incident response capability

Goal 4.2: Promote Cybersecurity Knowledge and Innovation

Objective 4.2.1: Enhance public awareness

Objective 4.2.2: Foster a dynamic workforce

Objective 4.2.3: Invest in innovative technologies, techniques, and procedures

While the line between policy and operations may be a blurred line in some instances, a necessary requirement of cybersecurity is to have security operations be part of a stated set of objectives.

CYBER ATTACKS

Cyber attacks can be divided into four distinct groups: cyber terrorism, cyber war, cybercrime, and cyber espionage. It would seem that cybercrime and cyber espionage are the most pressing issues, but the others are just offstage. Here are some definitions:

Cyber crime is the use of computers or related systems to steal or compromise confidential information for criminal purposes, most often for financial gain.

Cyber espionage is the use of computers or related systems to collect intelligence or enable certain operations, whether in cyberspace or the real world.

Cyber terrorism is the use of computers or related systems to create fear or panic in a society and may not result in physical destruction by cyber agitation.

Cyber war consists of military operations conducted within cyberspace to deny an adversary, whether a state or non-state actor, the effective use of information systems and weapons, or systems controlled by information technology, in order to achieve a political end.

As such, cybersecurity has been identified as one of the most serious economic and national security challenges facing the nation.

THE COMPREHENSIVE NATIONAL CYBERSECURITY INITIATIVE

In order to achieve cybersecurity, from individual, national, organizational, or global perspectives, a proposed set of major goals has been developed:

To establish a front line of defense against today's immediate threats

To defend against the full spectrum of threats

To strengthen the future cybersecurity environment

Starting from the top, the President has directed the release of a summary description of the Comprehensive National Cybersecurity Initiatives, summarized as follows:

Initiative #1. Manage the Federal Enterprise Network as a single network enterprise with Trusted Internet Connections.

Initiative #2. Deploy an intrusion detection system of sensors across the Federal enterprise.

Initiative #3. Pursue deployment of intrusion prevention systems across the Federal enterprise.

Initiative #4. Coordinate and redirect research and development (R&D) efforts.

Initiative #5. Connect current cyber ops centers to enhance situational awareness.

Initiative #6. Develop and implement a government-wide cyber counterintelligence (CI) plan.

Initiative #7. Increase the security of our classified networks.

Initiative #8. Expand cyber education.

Initiative #9. Define and develop enduring "leap-ahead" technology, strategies, and programs.

Initiative #10. Define and develop enduring deterrence strategies and programs.

Initiative #11. Develop a multi-pronged approach for global supply chain risk management.

Initiative #12. Define the Federal role for extending cybersecurity into critical infrastructure domains.

The basic idea of the twelve initiatives is to address current and future cybersecurity issues by combining the resources of the Federal government, local and state governments, and the private sector to provide a strong response to future cyber incidents and by strengthening public/private relationships.

CRITICAL INFRASTRUCTURE AND KEY RESOURCES

The present concern over cybersecurity is the result of a variety of cyber attacks, intrusions, and countermeasures that have occurred globally in recent years. The threat scenarios are multidimensional and attribution is cumbersome to ascertain. Moreover, exposure to cyber threats can be direct or indirect, resulting from a dependence on one or more elements of critical infrastructure. The scope of inherent infrastructure has grown from ten in the year 2003 to eighteen in the year 2012. The underlying philosophy is that once the critical areas are identified, a public/private dialog can be established to achieve a measurable amount of cybersecurity. Each of the six critical areas are classed as major and are assigned a Sector Specific Agency (SSA) by the Department of Homeland Security as part of the National Infrastructure Protection Plan (NIPP), intended to set national priorities, goals, and requirements for effective allocation of resources. The major areas are:

Chemical
Commercial Facilities
Critical Manufacturing
Dams
Emergency Services
Nuclear Reactors, Materials, and Waste

The manner in which the public/private coordination and collaboration is executed is a matter of public debate. The key point is that a cyber intrusion in a major area can indirectly endanger a large number of people, governmental organizations, and commercial facilities.

The remaining twelve critical areas are assigned to existing governmental offices, as reflected in the following list:

Agriculture and food – Department of Agriculture and the Food and Drug Administration

Banking and Finance – Department of the Treasury

Communications – Department of Homeland Security

Defense Industrial Base – Department of Defense

Energy – Department of Energy

Governmental Facilities – Department of Homeland Security

Information Technology – Department of Homeland Security

National Monuments and Icons – Department of the Interior

Postal and Shipping – Transportation Security Administration

Healthcare and Public Health – Department of Health and Human Services

Transportation Systems – Transportation Security Administration and the U.S. Coast Guard

Water – Environmental Protection Agency

National and global protection necessarily involves the establishment of a framework to provide the following:

The exchange of ideas, approaches, and best practices

The facilitation of security planning and resource allocation

The establishment of structure for effective coordination among partners

The enhancement of coordination with the international community

The building of public awareness

The identification of the areas of critical infrastructure is significant because of the wide diversity of cyber threats, vulnerabilities, risk, and problem domains. Moreover, critical elements possess a wide variety of technological attributes that require a range of solutions.

SUMMARY

The paper gives an overview of the emerging discipline of cybersecurity that adds a policy level to the longstanding subjects of information security, computer security, and network security. Concepts and some basic definitions are covered. Cyber attacks are divided into cyber crime, cyber espionage, cyber terrorism, and cyber war. A comprehensive overview of the subject matter is given through the National Cybersecurity Initiative, and the notion of the critical infrastructure is explored in some detail.

REFERENCE

Remarks by the U.S. President on Securing Our Nation's Cyber Infrastructure, East Room, May 29, 2009.

National Security Presidential Directive 54/Homeland Security Presidential Directive 23 (NSPD-54/HSPD-23).

Shackelford, Scott L. (2012). In Search of Cyber Peace: A Response to the Cybersecurity Act of 2012, *Stanford Law Review*, March 8, 2012, (http://www.stanfordlawreview.org).

Lord, K.M. and T. Sharp (editors) (2011). *America's Cyber Future: Security and Prosperity in the Information Age* (Volume I), Center for New American Security (June 2011), (http://www.cnas.org).

National Security Council, *The Comprehensive National Cybersecurity Initiative*, The White House, (http://www.whitehouse.gov/cybersecurity/comprehensive-national-cybersecurity-initiative).

The White House, *The National Strategy to Secure Cyberspace*, February, 2003.

Homeland Security, *More About the Office of Infrastructure Protection*, (http://www.dhs.gov/xabout/structure/gc_1189775491423.shtm).

The Department of Homeland Security, *National Infrastructure Protection Plan: Partnering to enhance protection and resiliency*, 2009.

****** End of Chapter 3 *****

4

ADVANCES IN CYBERSECURITY FOR BUSINESS AND MANAGEMENT

(Some commonality with Chapter 3)

Introduction

The Internet is the newest form of communication between organizations and people in modern society. Everyday commerce depends on it, and individuals use it for social interactions, as well as for reference and learning. To some, the Internet is a convenience for shopping, information retrieval, and entertainment. To others, such as large organizations, the Internet makes national and global expansion cost effective and allows disparate groups to profitably work together through reduced storage and communication costs. It gives government entities facilities for providing convenient service to constituents. The Internet is also efficient, because it usually can provide total service on a large variety of subjects in a few seconds, as compared to a much longer time for the same results that would have been required in earlier times (Katzan, 2012).

From a security perspective, the use of the term "cyber" generally means more than just the Internet, and usually refers to the use of electronics to communicate between entities. The subject of cybersecurity includes the Internet as the major data transportation element, but can also include wireless, fixed hard wires, and electromagnetic transference via satellites and other devices. Cyber elements incorporate networks, electrical and mechanical devices, individual computers, and a variety of smart devices, such as phones, tablets, pads, and electronic game and entertainment systems. The near future portends road vehicles that communicate and driverless automobiles. A reasonable view would be that cyber is the seamless fabric of the modern information technology infrastructure that enables organizations and private citizens to sustain most aspects of modern everyday life.

It is important to place cybersecurity in its proper operational domain. Cybersecurity resides in a domain named *cyberspace* that is distinct from the other established domains of land, sea, air, and space. Cyberspace uses the Internet as the transport mechanism that supports computers, tablets, smart phones, and control systems, and sustains communication of digital information including data, voice, video, and graphics. The variety of content and its extensive distribution is attractive to hackers, criminal elements, and nation with the objective is disrupting commercial, military, and social activities. Some of areas at risk in the cyberspace domain are commercial, industry, trade, finance, security, intellectual property technology, culture, policy, and diplomacy. The subject of cybersecurity in complicated because many cyber events, often classified as cyber attacks, are not deliberate and result from everyday mistakes, poor training, and disgruntled employees. Cybersecurity metrics usually include non-serious and well as serious intrusions, so that the cybersecurity threat is commonly overstated.

Cyber supports the commercial, educational, governmental, and critical national infrastructure. Cyber facilities are pervasive and extend beyond national borders. As such, individuals, organizations, and nation-states can use cyber for productive and also destructive purposes. A single individual or a small group can use cyber for commercial gain or surreptitious invasion of assets. Activities in the latter category are usually classed as penetration and include attempts designed to compromise systems that contain vital information. In a similar vein, intrusion can also effect the day-to-day operation of critical resources, such as private utility companies.

Interconnectivity between elements is desirable and usually cost effective, so that a wide variety of dependencies have evolved in normal circumstances, and cyber intrusions have emerged. Thus, a small group of individuals can compromise a large organization or facility, which is commonly known as an *asymmetric* threat against which methodological protection is necessary. In many cases, a single computer with software obtained over the Internet can do untold damage to a business, utility, governmental structure, or personal information. Willful invasion of the property of other entities is illegal, regardless of the purpose or intent. However, the openness of the Internet often makes it difficult to identify and apprehend cyber criminals – especially when the subject's illegal activities span international borders.

Cybersecurity Operations

Cybersecurity is a complicated and complex subject encompassing computer security, information assurance, comprehensive infrastructure protection, commercial integrity, and ubiquitous personal interactions. Most people look at the subject from a personal perspective. Is my computer and information secure from outside interference? Is the operation of my online business vulnerable to outside threats? Will I get the item I ordered? Are my utilities safe from international intrusion? Have I done enough to protect my personal privacy? Are my bank accounts and credit cards safe? How do we protect our websites and online information systems from hackers? Can my identity be stolen? The list of everyday concerns that people have over the modern system of communication could go on and on. Clearly, concerned citizens and organizations look to someone or something else, such as their Internet service provider or their company or the government, to solve the problem and just tell them what to do.

Cybersecurity hasn't been a simple problem and probably never will be. Cyberspace is a virtual world synthesized from computer hardware and software, desktops and laptops, tablets and cell phones, and broadband and wireless signals that power our schools, businesses, hospitals, government, utilities, and personal lives through a sophisticated set of communication systems, available worldwide. However, the power to build also provides the power to disrupt and destroy. Many persons associate cybersecurity with cyber crime, since it costs persons, commercial organizations, and governments more than a $1 trillion per year. However, there is considerably more to cybersecurity than cyber crime, so it is necessary to start off with a few concepts and definitions.

The term *cybersecurity* refers to two things: the state of possessing a secure operational environment and also the process of achieving a secure operational environment.

Cyber Attacks

Cyber attacks can be divided into four distinct groups: cyber terrorism, cyber war, cyber crime, and cyber espionage. It would seem that cyber crime and cyber espionage are the most pressing issues, but the others are just offstage. Here are some definitions:

> *Cyber crime* is the use of computers or related systems to steal or compromise confidential information for criminal purposes, most often for financial gain.
>
> *Cyber espionage* is the use of computers or related systems to collect intelligence or enable certain operations, whether in cyberspace or the real world.

Cyber terrorism is the use of computers or related systems to create fear or panic in a society and may result in physical destruction by cyber agitation.

Cyber war consists of military operations conducted within cyberspace to deny an adversary, whether a state or non-state actor, the effective use of information systems and weapons, or systems controlled by information technology, in order to achieve a political end.

As such, cybersecurity has been identified as one of the most serious economic and national security challenges facing the nation. There is also a personal component to cybersecurity. The necessity of having to protect one's identity and private information from outside intrusion is a nuisance resulting in the use of costly and inconvenient safeguards.

Cyber terrorism is and has been of particular to analysts in developed countries. In fact, cyber terrorism has engendered in an entire industry of consultants and other relevant services. The basic idea is that a terrorist event perpetrated via the Internet could disrupt one or more of the critical resources such as power, water, and transportation. Why a critical resource should be capable of being controlled through the Internet is an interesting question that cannot be easily answered. But, nevertheless, after years of warnings and discussion, to this date, it hasn't been done. (Weimann, 2006)

The Cyberspace Domain, its Elements and Actors

Cyberspace provides, through the Internet, the capability to create, transmit, manipulate, and use digital information. The digital information includes data, voice, video, and graphics transmitted over wired and wireless facilities between a wide range of devices that include computers, tablets, smart phones, and control systems.

The Internet serves as the transport mechanism for cyberspace. The extensive variety of content is attractive to hackers, criminal elements, and nation states with the objective of disrupting commercial, military, and social activities. Many cyber events, classified as cyber attacks, are not deliberate and result from everyday mistakes and poor training. Others result from disgruntled employees. Unfortunately, security metrics include non-serious as well as serious intrusions, so that the cybersecurity threat appears to be overstated in some instances. This phenomenon requires that we concentrate on deliberate software attacks and how they are in fact related, since the object is to develop a conceptual model of the relationship between security countermeasures and vulnerabilities.

Many of the software threats can be perpetrated by individuals or small groups against major organizations and nation-states – referred to as *asymmetric attacks,* as mentioned previously. The threats are reasonably well known and are summarized in the following list: privilege escalation, virus, worm, Trojan horse, spyware, spam, hoax, adware, rootkit, botnet, and logic bomb. It's clear that effective countermeasures are both technical and procedural, in some instances, and must be linked to hardware and software resources on the defensive side. The security risks that involve computers and auxiliary equipment target low-end firmware or embedded software, USB devices, cell phones and tablets, and removable and network storage. Operating system risks encompass service packs, hotfixes, patches, and various configuration elements. Established counter measures, include intrusion detection and handling systems, hardware and software firewalls, and antivirus and anti-spam software.

The cybersecurity network infrastructure involves unique security threats and countermeasures. Most of the threats relate to the use of out-of-date network protocols, specific hacker techniques, such as packet sniffing, spoofing, phishing and spear phishing, man-in-the-middle attacks, denial-of-service procedures, and exploiting vulnerabilities related to domain name systems. Countermeasures include hardware, software, and protective procedures of various kinds. Hardware, software, and organizational resources customarily execute the security measures. There is much more to security threats and countermeasures, and the information presented here gives only a flavor to the subject.

There is an additional category of threats and countermeasures that primarily involves end-users and what they are permitted to do. In order for a threat agent to infiltrate a system, three elements are required: network presence, access control, and authorization. This subject is normally covered as the major features of information assurance and refers to the process of "getting on the system," such as the Internet or a local-area network. A threat agent cannot address a system if the computer is not turned on or a network presence is not possible. Once an end user is connected to the computer system or network, then access control and authorization take over. It has been estimated that 80% of security violations originate at the end-user level. *Access control* concerns the identification of the entity requesting accessibility and whether that entity is permitted to use the system. *Authorization* refers to precisely what that entity is permitted to do, once permitted access. There is a high-degree of specificity to access-control and authorization procedures. For example, access control can be based on something the requestor knows, a physical artifact, or a biometric attribute. Similarly, authorization can be based on role, group membership, level in the organization, and so forth. Clearly, this category reflects considerations which the organizations has control over, and as such, constitutes security measures that are self-postulated.

Automated Intrusion Detection

Intrusion detection is the process of monitoring the events occurring in a computer system or network and analyzing them for signs of possible security [sec] incidents. Intrusion prevention is the process of performing intrusion detection and attempting to stop detected possible incidents. Intrusion detection and prevention systems (IDPS) are primarily focused on identifying possible incidents, logging information about them, attempting to stop them, and reporting them to security administrators. An intrusion detection system (IDS) is software that automates the intrusion detection process. (Scarfone and Mell, 2007, p. ES-1) This is definitely the way of the future in this regard, but for proprietary reasons, it is not possible to delineate detailed specifics.

Application Containers

An application container is an operating system in which each application can only see itself, thereby limiting intrusion by unwanted programs. The technology that underlies the use of application containers is based on the notion of an hypervisor, initially developed for large mainframe computer systems. (Katzan, 1986) An application-container is a minimalist operating system designed to run only containers with all other functionality disabled. The configuration is standard for a prescribed class of applications and the file-system is read only. Essentially, an application container is analogous to the operating system on a smartphone. The parent operating system, that is the hypervisor, is designed to run a set of distinct application containers. Thus, a set of application containers is a portable, reusable, and automatable way to package and run applications. (Souppaya, Morello, and Scarfone, 2017)

Distributed Security

The major characteristic of a cybersecurity system designed to prevent and mediate a cyber attack is that the totality of security elements in a particular domain are organized into a smart service system. This characteristic refers to the facility of cyber elements to communicate on a real-time basis in response to cyber threats. Currently, threat determination is largely manual and human-oriented. An intrusion detection system recognizes an intrusion and informs a security manager. That manager then contacts other managers via email, personal contact, or telephone to warn of the cyber threat. In a smart cybersecurity system, the intrusion detection software would isolate the cyber threat and automatically contact other elements in the domain to defend their system. Thus, the security service would handle intruders in a manner similar to the way biological systems handle analogous invasions: recognize the threat; attempt to neutralize it; and alert other similar elements.

In a definitive white paper on distributed security, McConnell (2011) recognizes the need for cyber devices to work together in near real-time to minimize cyber attacks and defend against them. This is a form of continuous monitoring and referred to as a *cyber ecosystem* in which relevant participants interact to provide security and maintain a persistent state of security. Clearly, a cyber ecosystem would establish a basis for cybersecurity through individually designed hierarchies of security elements, referred to as security devices. Ostensibly, security devices would be programmed to communicate in the event of a cyber attack. The conceptual building blocks of an ecosystem are automation, interoperability, and authentication. *Automation* refers to the notion of security devices being able to detect intrusion detection and respond to other security devices without human intervention. Thus, the security ecosystem could behave as a security service and provide speed and in the activation of automated prevention systems. *Interoperability* refers to the ability of the cyber ecosystem to incorporate differing assessments, hardware facilities, and organizations with strategically distinct policy structures. *Authentication* refers to the capability to extend the ecosystem across differing network technologies, devices, organizations, and participants.

Thus, the cyber ecosystem responds as a service system in requests for security service to participants that are members of the ecosystem, namely private firms, non-profit organizations, governments, individuals, processes, cyber devices comprised of computers, software, and communications equipment.

Monroe Doctrine for Cybersecurity

Internet governance refers to an attempt at the global level to legislate operations in cyberspace taking into consideration the economic, cultural, developmental, legal, political, and cultural interests of its stakeholders (Conway, 2007). A more specific definition would be the development and application by governments and the private sector of shared principles, norms, rules, decision-making, and programs that determine the evolution and use of the Internet (Conway, <u>op cit.</u>). Internet governance is a difficult process because it encompasses, web sites, Internet service providers, hackers, and activists, involving differing forms of content and operational intent ranging from pornography and terrorist information to intrusion and malicious content. Cybersecurity is a complex form of service that purports to protect against intrusion, invasion, and other forms of cyber terrorism, crime, espionage, and war. But, attacks can be carried out by anyone with an Internet connection and a little bit of knowledge of hacking techniques. NATO has addressed the subject of cyber defense with articles that state the members will consult together in the event of cyber attacks but are not duty bound to render aid (Cavelty, 2011). It would seem that deterrence, where one party is able to suggest to an adversary that it is capable and willing to use appropriate offensive measures, is perhaps a useful adjunct to cybersecurity service. However, successful attribution of cyber attacks is not a fail proof endeavor so that offensive behavior is not a total solution to the problem of deterrence.

Cybersecurity is a pervasive problem that deserves different approaches. Davidson (2009) has noted an interesting possibility, based on the volume of recent cyber attacks. The context is that we are in a cyber war and a war is not won on strictly defensive behavior. A "Monroe Doctrine in Cyberspace" is proposed, similar to the Monroe Doctrine of 1823 that states "here is our turf; stay out or face the consequences."

Summary

The Internet is a seamless means of communication between organizations and people in modern society; it supports an infrastructure that permits cost effective commerce, social interaction, reference, and learning. The use of the term "cyber" means more than just the Internet and refers to the use of electronics in a wide variety of forms between disparate entities. Cyber facilities are pervasive and extend beyond national borders and can be used by individuals, organizations, and nation states for productive and destructive purposes. A single individual or small group can use cyber technology for surreptitious invasion of assets to obtain vital information or to cause the disruption of critical resources.

Cybersecurity is conceptualized as a unique kind of service in which providers and clients collaborate to supply service through shared responsibility, known as *collaborative security*. Cybersecurity is achieved through distributed security implemented as a smart system with three important attributes: automation, interoperability, and authentication. A Monroe Doctrine for Cybersecurity is proposed.

Two reasonably new classes of cybersecurity technology are automated intrusion detection and application containers.

References and Selected Bibliographic Material

Remarks by the U.S. President on Securing Our Nation's Cyber Infrastructure (2009). East Room, May 29, 2009.

National Security Presidential Directive 54/Homeland Security Presidential Directive 23 (NSPD-54/HSPD-23).

The White House. National Security Council, *The Comprehensive National Cybersecurity Initiative*, (http://www.whitehouse.gov/cybersecurity/comprehensive-national-cybersecurity-initiative).

The White House (2003). *The National Strategy to Secure Cyberspace*, February 2003.

The Department of Homeland Security. *More About the Office of Infrastructure Protection*, (http://www.dhs.gov/xabout/structure/gc_1189775491423.shtm).

The Department of Homeland Security (2009). *National Infrastructure Protection Plan: Partnering to enhance protection and resiliency.*

Working Group on Internet Governance (2005). Report Document WSIS-II/PC-3/DOC/5-E, August 2005.

Cavelty, M., (2011).Cyber-Allies: Strengths and Weaknesses of NATO's Cyberdefense Posture, IP-Global Edition, ETH Zurich, 3/2011.

Conway, M. (2007). Terrorism and Internet Governance: Core Issues, Dublin: *Disarmament Forum 3*, 2007.

Davidson, M. (2009). *The Monroe Doctrine in Cyberspace,* Testimony given to the Homeland Security Subcommittee on Emerging Threats, Cybersecurity, and Technology, March 10, 2009.

Katzan, H. (2012). Cybersecurity Service Model, *Journal of Service Science,* 5(2): 71-78.

Katzan, H. (1986). *Operating Systems: A Pragmatic Approach,* New York: Van Nostrand Reinhold.

Lord, K.M. & T. Sharp (editors, 2011). *America's Cyber Future: Security and Prosperity in the Information Age* (Volume I), Center for New American Security (June 2011), (http://www.cnas.org).

McConnell, B. & The Department of Homeland Security (2011). *Enabling Distributed Security in Cyberspace: Building a Healthy and Resilient Cyber Ecosystem with Automated Collective Action,* http://www.dhs.gov/xlibrary/assets/nppd-cyber-ecosystem-white-paper-03-23-2011.pdf, 23 March 2011.

Scarfone, K. and P. Mell (2007). *Guide to Intrusion and Prevention Systems (IDPS),* Computer Security Division, Information Technology Laboratory, National Institute of Standards and Technology, Gaithersburg, MD, NIST Special Publication 800-94.

Shackelford, S.L. (2012). In Search of Cyber Peace: A Response to the Cybersecurity Act of 2012, *Stanford Law Review,* March 8, 2012, (http://www.stanfordlawreview.org).

Souppaya, M., Morello, J, and K. Scarfone, (2017). *Application Container Security Guide* Computer Security Division, Information Technology Laboratory, National Institute of Standards and Technology, Gaithersburg, MD, NIST Special Publication 800-190.

Weimann, G. (2006), *Cyber Terrorism: How Real is the Threat?* United States Institute of Peace, (www.usip.org).

****** End of Chapter 4 *****

5

CONTEMPORARY ISSUES IN CYBERSECURITY RESEARCH FOR BUSINESS AND MANAGEMENT

INTRODUCTION

The Internet is the newest form of communication between organizations and people in modern society. Everyday commerce depends on it, and individuals use it for social interactions, as well as for reference and learning. To some, the Internet is a convenience for shopping, information retrieval, and entertainment. To others, such as large organizations, the Internet makes national and global expansion cost effective and allows disparate groups to profitably work together through reduced storage and communication costs. It gives government entities facilities for providing convenient service to constituents. The Internet is also efficient, because it usually can provide total service on a large variety of subjects in a few seconds, as compared to a much longer time for the same results that would have been required in earlier times (Katzan, 2012).

From a security perspective, the use of the term "cyber" generally means more than just the Internet, and usually refers to the use of electronics to communicate between entities. The subject of cyber includes the Internet as the major data transportation element, but can also include wireless, fixed hard wires, and electromagnetic transference via satellites and other devices. Cyber elements incorporate networks, electrical and mechanical devices, individual computers, and a variety of smart devices, such as phones, tablets, pads, and electronic game and entertainment systems. The near future portends road vehicles that communicate and driverless automobiles. A reasonable view would be that cyber is the seamless fabric of the modern information technology infrastructure that enables organizations and private citizens to sustain most aspects of modern everyday life.

Cyber supports the commercial, educational, governmental, and critical national infrastructure. Cyber facilities are pervasive and extend beyond national borders. As such, individuals, organizations, and nation-states can use cyber for productive and also destructive purposes. A single individual or a small group can use cyber for commercial gain or surreptitious invasion of assets. Activities in the latter category are usually classed as penetration and include attempts designed to compromise systems that contain vital information. In a similar vein, intrusion can also effect the day-to-day operation of critical resources, such as private utility companies.

Interconnectivity between elements is desirable and usually cost effective, so that a wide variety of dependencies have evolved in normal circumstances, and cyber intrusions have emerged. Thus, a small group of individuals can compromise a large organization or facility, which is commonly known as an *asymmetric* threat against which methodological protection is necessary. In many cases, a single computer with software obtained over the Internet can do untold damage to a business, utility, governmental structure, or personal information. Willful invasion of the property of other entities is illegal, regardless of the purpose or intent. However, the openness of the Internet often makes it difficult to identify and apprehend cyber criminals – especially when the subject's illegal activities span international borders.

CYBERSECURITY OPERATIONS

It is well established that cybersecurity is a complicated and complex subject encompassing computer security, information assurance, comprehensive infrastructure protection, commercial integrity, and ubiquitous personal interactions. Most people look at the subject from a personal perspective. Is my computer and information secure from outside interference? Is the operation of my online business vulnerable to outside threats? Will I get the item I ordered? Are my utilities safe from international intrusion? Have I done enough to protect my personal privacy? Are my bank accounts and credit cards safe? How do we protect our websites and online information systems from hackers? Can my identity be stolen? The list of everyday concerns that people have over the modern system of communication could go on and on. Clearly, concerned citizens and organizations look to someone or something else, such as their Internet service provider or their company or the government, to solve the problem and just tell them what to do.

So far, it hasn't been that simple and probably never will be. The digital infrastructure based on the Internet that we call cyberspace is something that we depend on every day for a prosperous economy, a strong military, and an enlightened lifestyle. Cyberspace, as a concept, is a virtual world synthesized from computer hardware and software, desktops and laptops, tablets and cell phones, and broadband and wireless signals that power our schools, businesses, hospitals, government, utilities, and personal lives through a sophisticated set of communication systems, available worldwide. However, the power to build also provides the power to disrupt and destroy. Many persons associate cybersecurity with cyber crime, since it costs persons, commercial organizations, and governments more than a $1 trillion per year. However, there is considerably more to cybersecurity than cyber crime, so it is necessary to start off with a few concepts and definitions.

Cyberspace has been defined as the interdependent network of information technology infrastructure, and includes the Internet, telecommunication networks, computer systems, and embedded processors and controllers in critical industries. Alternately, cyberspace is often regarded as any process, program, or protocol relating to the use of the Internet for data processing transmission or use in telecommunication. As such, cyberspace is instrumental in sustaining the everyday activities of millions of people and thousands of organizations worldwide. The key terminology is that in a security event, a *subject* executes the crime against an *object* and that both entities incorporate computer and networking facilities.

CYBER ATTACKS

Cyber attacks can be divided into four distinct groups: cyber terrorism, cyber war, cyber crime, and cyber espionage. It would seem that cyber crime and cyber espionage are the most pressing issues, but the others are just offstage. Here are some definitions:

> *Cyber crime* is the use of computers or related systems to steal or compromise confidential information for criminal purposes, most often for financial gain.

> *Cyber espionage* is the use of computers or related systems to collect intelligence or enable certain operations, whether in cyberspace or the real world.

> *Cyber terrorism* is the use of computers or related systems to create fear or panic in a society and may result in physical destruction by cyber agitation.

> *Cyber war* consists of military operations conducted within cyberspace to deny an adversary, whether

a state or non-state actor, the effective use of information systems and weapons, or systems controlled by information technology, in order to achieve a political end.

As such, cybersecurity has been identified as one of the most serious economic and national security challenges facing the nation. There is also a personal component to cybersecurity. The necessity of having to protect one's identity and private information from outside intrusion is a nuisance resulting in the use of costly and inconvenient safeguards.

Cyberspace Domain, its Elements and Actors

Cyberspace is a unique domain that is operationally distinct from the other operational domains of land, sea, air, and space. It provides, through the Internet, the capability to create, transmit, manipulate, and use digital information. The digital information includes data, voice, video, and graphics transmitted over wired and wireless facilities between a wide range of devices that include computers, tablets, smart phones, and control systems. The Internet serves as the transport mechanism for cyberspace. The extensive variety of content is attractive to hackers, criminal elements, and nation states with the objective of disrupting commercial, military, and social activities. Table 1 gives a list of areas at risk in the cyberspace domain. Many cyber events, classified as cyber attacks, are not deliberate and result from everyday mistakes and poor training. Others result from disgruntled employees. Unfortunately, security metrics include non-serious as well as serious intrusions, so that the cybersecurity threat appears to be overstated in some instances. This phenomenon requires that we concentrate on deliberate software attacks and how they are in fact related, since the object is to develop a conceptual model of the relationship between security countermeasures and vulnerabilities.

Table 1. Areas at Risk in the Cyberspace Domain

Commerce
Industry
Trade
Finance
Security
Intellectual property
Technology
Culture
Policy
Diplomacy

Many of the software threats can be perpetrated by individuals or small groups against major organizations and nation-states – referred to as *asymmetric attacks,* as mentioned previously. The threats are reasonably well known and are summarized in Table 2. It's clear that effective countermeasures are both technical and procedural, in some instances, and must be linked to hardware and software resources on the defensive side. The security risks that involve computers and auxiliary equipment target low-end firmware or embedded software, such as BIOS, USB devices, cell phones and tablets, and removable and network storage. Operating system risks encompass service packs, hotfixes, patches, and various configuration elements. Established counter measures, include intrusion detection and handling systems, hardware and software firewalls, and antivirus and anti-spam software.

Table 2. Security Threats

Privilege escalation
Virus
Worm
Trojan horse

Spyware

Spam

Hoax

Adware

Rootkit

Botnet

Logic bomb

The cybersecurity network infrastructure involves unique security threats and countermeasures. Most of the threats relate to the use of out-of-date network protocols, specific hacker techniques, such as packet sniffing, spoofing, phishing and spear phishing, man-in-the-middle attacks, denial-of-service procedures, and exploiting vulnerabilities related to domain name systems. Countermeasures include hardware, software, and protective procedures of various kinds. Hardware, software, and organizational resources customarily execute the security measures. There is much more to security threats and countermeasures, and the information presented here gives only a flavor to the subject.

There is an additional category of threats and countermeasures that primarily involves end-users and what they are permitted to do. In order for a threat agent to infiltrate a system, three elements are required: network presence, access control, and authorization. This subject is normally covered as the major features of information assurance and refers to the process of "getting on the system," such as the Internet or a local-area network. A threat agent cannot address a system if the computer is not turned on or a network presence is not possible. Once an end user is connected to the computer system or network, then access control and authorization take over. It has been estimated that 80% of security violations originate at the end-user level. *Access control* concerns the identification of the entity requesting accessibility and whether that entity is permitted to use the system. *Authorization* refers to precisely what that entity is permitted to do, once permitted access. There is a high-degree of specificity to access-control and authorization procedures. For example, access control can be based on something the requestor knows, a physical artifact, or a biometric attribute. Similarly, authorization can be based on role, group membership, level in the organization, and so forth. Clearly, this category reflects considerations which the organizations has control over, and as such, constitutes security measures that are self-postulated.

CYBERSECURITY COLLABORATION

A *collaboration group* exists when a set of service providers **P** supplies a totality of services for a specific operational domain to a set of clients **C**. Not every provider p_i performs the same service but the members of **P** can collectively supply all of the service needed for that domain. The client set **C** constitutes the functions in the operational system that require protection.

The controls that constitute a cyber security domain form a collaboration group. Diverse elements of hardware and software are used for network and operating system security. Clearly, processes are necessary for gaining network presence, access control to a given resource, and user authentication. Intrusion detection and prevention systems (IPDS) are implemented to perform continuous monitoring and cyber protection. Access roles and operational rules are developed to facilitate use of cyber security procedures and elements.

When a client adopts cybersecurity principles for network presence, access control, and authentication, for example, it applies the inherent methods for and by itself, thereby assuming the dual role of provider and client. Similarly, when an organization installs a hardware or software firewall for network protection, it is effectively applying a product for its own security.

In a security system, security controls exchange information and behavior in order to achieve mutually beneficial results. As security systems become more complex, the security entities adapt to optimize their behavior – a process often referred to as *evolution* (Mainzer, 1997). Differing forms of organization emerge such that the system exhibits intelligent behavior based on information interchange and the following nine properties: emergence, co-evolution, sub-optimal, requisite variety, connectivity, simple rules, self organization, edge of chaos, and nestability. Systems of this type are usually known as *complex adaptive systems* (Katzan 2012). Complex adaptive systems are often known as "smart systems," and cybersecurity researchers are looking at the operation of such systems as a model for the design of cybersecurity systems that can prevent attacks through the exchange of information between security elements.

DISTRIBUTED SECURITY

The major characteristic of a cybersecurity system designed to prevent and mediate a cyber attack is that the totality of security elements in a particular domain are organized into a smart service system. This characteristic refers to the facility of cyber elements to communicate on a real-time basis in response to cyber threats. Currently, threat determination is largely manual and human-oriented. An intrusion detection system recognizes an intrusion and informs a security manager. That manager then contacts other managers via email, personal contact, or telephone to warn of the cyber threat. In a smart cybersecurity system, the intrusion detection software would isolate the cyber threat and automatically contact other elements in the domain to defend their system. Thus, the security service would handle intruders in a manner similar to the way biological systems handle analogous invasions: recognize the threat; attempt to neutralize it; and alert other similar elements.

In a definitive white paper on distributed security, McConnell (2011) recognizes the need for cyber devices to work together in near real-time to minimize cyber attacks and defend against them. This is a form of continuous monitoring and referred to as a *cyber ecosystem* in which relevant participants interact to provide security and maintain a persistent state of security. Clearly, a cyber ecosystem would establish a basis for cybersecurity through individually designed hierarchies of security elements, referred to as security devices. Ostensibly, security devices would be programmed to communicate in the event of a cyber attack. The conceptual building blocks of an ecosystem are automation, interoperability, and authentication. *Automation* refers to the notion of security devices being able to detect intrusion detection and respond to other security devices without human intervention. Thus, the security ecosystem could behave as a security service and provide speed and in the activation of automated prevention systems. *Interoperability* refers to the ability of the cyber ecosystem to incorporate differing assessments, hardware facilities, and organizations with strategically distinct policy structures. *Authentication* refers to the capability to extend the ecosystem across differing network technologies, devices, organizations, and participants.

Thus, the cyber ecosystem responds as a service system in requests for security service to participants that are members of the ecosystem, namely private firms, non-profit organizations, governments, individuals, processes, cyber devices comprised of computers, software, and communications equipment.

Monroe Doctrine for Cybersecurity

Internet governance refers to an attempt at the global level to legislate operations in cyberspace taking into consideration the economic, cultural, developmental, legal, political, and cultural interests of its stakeholders (Conway, 2007). A more specific definition would be the development and application by governments and the private sector of shared principles, norms, rules, decision-making, and programs that determine the evolution and use of the Internet (Conway, op cit.). Internet governance is a difficult process because it encompasses, web sites, Internet service providers, hackers, and activists, involving differing forms of content and operational intent ranging from pornography and terrorist information to intrusion and malicious content. Cybersecurity is a complex form of service that purports to protect against intrusion, invasion, and other forms of cyber terrorism, crime, espionage, and war. But, attacks can be carried out by anyone with an Internet connection and a little bit of knowledge of hacking techniques. NATO has addressed the subject of cyber defense with articles that state the members will consult together in the event of cyber attacks but are not duty bound to render aid (Cavelty, 2011). It would seem that deterrence, where one party is able to suggest to an adversary that it is capable and willing to use appropriate offensive measures, is perhaps a useful adjunct to cybersecurity service. However, successful attribution of cyber attacks is not a fail proof endeavor so that offensive behavior is not a total solution to the problem of deterrence.

Cybersecurity is a pervasive problem that deserves different approaches. Davidson (2009) has noted an interesting possibility, based on the volume of recent cyber attacks. The context is that we are in a cyber war and a war is not won on strictly defensive behavior. A "Monroe Doctrine in Cyberspace" is proposed, similar to the Monroe Doctrine of 1823 that states "here is our turf; stay out or face the consequences."

SUMMARY

The Internet is a seamless means of communication between organizations and people in modern society; it supports an infrastructure that permits cost effective commerce, social interaction, reference, and learning. The use of the term "cyber" means more than just the Internet and refers to the use of electronics in a wide variety of forms between disparate entities. Cyber facilities are pervasive and extend beyond national borders and can be used by individuals, organizations, and nation states for productive and destructive purposes. A single individual or small group can use cyber technology for surreptitious invasion of assets to obtain vital information or to cause the disruption of critical resources.

Cybersecurity is conceptualized as a unique kind of service in which providers and clients collaborate to supply service through shared responsibility, referred to as *collaborative security*. Cybersecurity is achieved through distributed security implemented as a smart system with three important attributes: automation, interoperability, and authentication. A Monroe Doctrine for Cybersecurity is proposed.

REFERENCES AND SELECTED BIBLIOGRAPHIC MATERIAL

Remarks by the U.S. President on Securing Our Nation's Cyber Infrastructure (2009). East Room, May 29, 2009.

National Security Presidential Directive 54/Homeland Security Presidential Directive 23 (NSPD-54/HSPD-23).

The White House. National Security Council, *The Comprehensive National Cybersecurity Initiative*, (http://www.whitehouse.gov/cybersecurity/comprehensive-national-cybersecurity-initiative).

The White House (2003). *The National Strategy to Secure Cyberspace,* February 2003.

The Department of Homeland Security. *More About the Office of Infrastructure Protection*, (http://www.dhs.gov/xabout/structure/gc_1189775491423.shtm).

The Department of Homeland Security (2009). *National Infrastructure Protection Plan: Partnering to enhance protection and resiliency.*

Working Group on Internet Governance (2005). Report Document WSIS-II/PC-3/DOC/5-E, August 2005.

Cavelty, M. (2011). Cyber-Allies: Strengths and Weaknesses of NATO's Cyberdefense Posture, *IP – Global Edition,* ETH Zurich, 3/2011.

Conway, M. (2007). Terrorism and Internet Governance: Core Issues, Dublin: *Disarmament Forum 3,* 2007.

Davidson, M. (2009). *The Monroe Doctrine in Cyberspace,* Testimony given to the Homeland Security Subcommittee on Emerging Threats, Cybersecurity, and Technology, March 10, 2009.

Katzan, H. (2012). Essentials of Cybersecurity, *Southeastern INFORMS Conference*, Myrtle Beach, SC, October 4-5, 2012.

Katzan, H. (2008). *Foundations of Service Science: A Pragmatic Approach*, New York: iUniverse, Inc.

Katzan, H. (2010). Service Analysis and Design, *International Applied Business Research Conference*, Orlando, FL, January 4-6, 2010.

Katzan, H. (2010). Service Collectivism, Collaboration, and Duality Theory, *International Applied Business Research Conference*, Orlando, FL, January 4-6, 2010.

Katzan, H. (2008). *Service Science: Concepts, Technology, Management*, New York: iUniverse, Inc.

Lord, K.M. & T. Sharp (editors, 2011). *America's Cyber Future: Security and Prosperity in the Information Age* (Volume I), Center for New American Security (June 2011), (http://www.cnas.org).

Mainzer, K. (1997). *Thinking in Complexity: The Complex Dynamics of Matter, Mind, and Mankind*, New York: Springer.

McConnell, B. & The Department of Homeland Security (2011). *Enabling Distributed Security in Cyberspace: Building a Healthy and Resilient Cyber Ecosystem with Automated Collective Action*, http://www.dhs.gov/xlibrary/assets/nppd-cyber-ecosystem-white-paper-03-23-2011.pdf, 23 March 2011.

Norman, D. (2011). *Living with Complexity*, Cambridge: The MIT Press.

Shackelford, S.L. (2012). In Search of Cyber Peace: A Response to the Cybersecurity Act of 2012, *Stanford Law Review*, March 8, 2012, (http://www.stanfordlawreview.org).

Stewart, J. (2009). *CompTIA Security + Review Guide*, Indianapolis: Wiley Publishing, Inc.

Vargo, S. & Akaka, M. (2009). Service-Dominant Logic as a Foundation for Service Science: Clarification, *Service Science*, 1, 32-41.

***** End of Chapter 5 *****

6

SERVICE CONCEPTS

HISTORICAL OVERVIEW

Service Science has the potential to change the way we think about and subsequently view the new world order and may eventually change the predominant economic focus from products to services. Since services are the cornerstone of most modern businesses, there is a high level of interest in the subject by persons from business, government, and education. Major corporations have supported intellectual activity on the subject by giving introductory presentations at many conferences and by providing liberal access to relevant information on corporate Web sites.

Service

A *service* is generally regarded as work performed by one person or group that benefits another person or group. It is an activity and not an element of property. Another definition is that it is a type of business that provides assistance and expertise rather than a tangible product. Still another definition is that it is after-purchase support offered by a product manufacturer or retailer. In employment, it is work done for business as an occupation. We are going to refer to it as a provider/ client interaction in which both parities participate and both parties obtain some benefit from the relationship. The provider and the client exchange information and adopt differing roles in the process. A service is a form of activity, consumed at the point of production.

Normally, an element of service is a *process* – or a diverse collection of activities – applicable in principle to business, education, government, and personal endeavors.

System

A *service system* is a socially constructed collection of service events in which participants exchange beneficial actions through a knowledge-based strategy that captures value from a provider-client relationship. The definition is based on the notion of a system, which is a group of interdependent components that form a coherent whole and operate together to achieve a purpose.

The inherent service strategy is a dynamic process that orchestrates (or coordinates) infrastructure, employees, partners, and clients in the co-production of value. Based on a theoretical framework for creating economies of coordination, research on service systems incorporates a detailed analysis of various and diverse service events, so as to develop a view of the service scape.

Characteristics

The concept of service has its roots in economic activities that are classified as extractive, secondary, and services. *Extractive* refers to agriculture, mining, forestry, fishing, and so forth. *Secondary* refers to manufacturing and processing. *Services* refer to everything else, usually subdivided into domestic, trade and commerce, information services, and personal. This is a very general definition intended for the reporting by the government of economic conditions. In order to get a handle on services, we need better definitions.

A *service* is a provider/client interaction that creates and captures value. A unique characteristic of services, unlike agriculture and manufacturing, is that both parties participate in the transaction, and in the process, both capture value. In a sense, the provider and the client co-produce the service event, because one can't do without the other. It stands to reason that the roles of the client and the provider are different. In a doctor/patient service event, for example, the physician brings knowledge, time, and the necessary infrastructure. The patient brings him or herself, a medical history, and a perceived situation that requires attention. During the service process, the participants exchange information in various forms, resulting in a change to the people involved. The doctor's experience level and assets change, as do the patient's information level and physical or mental condition. There is more to it, of course, but this is the basic idea.

Organizations

For organizations, the case is slightly different. Some companies, such as professional firms, are totally service oriented. Other service companies, such as airlines and restaurants, have more complicated arrangements. An airline company, for example, could contract out its telephone reservation service to another company. This process is called *outsourcing*.

Continuing with the airline example, let's assume that an agreement is made with a company in another country to run a call center whereby passengers can make reservations and obtain information. The airline is the client and the call center company is the provider. How does the client (that is the airline company, in this case), who is a stakeholder with something to gain or lose, effectively control the situation? They collectively draw up a *service level agreement* that governs the quality of service, the number of calls to be handled in a specified period of time, the duration of the agreement, and the costs involved. Why don't the patient and the doctor have a service level agreement? They do, but it is implicit in the social setting in which medical services are performed. In many areas of service management, the key element is the service-level agreement.

Business Service

Some firms further complicate the picture by essentially being in two related service businesses at the same time. Consider an information technology (IT) company that provides services in two forms: consulting and outsourcing. With consulting, the firm tells a client how to do something, and with outsourcing, the firm does it for the client. As an example, the IT firm could advise on what information systems the client needs and then develop those systems. Similarly, it could provide information on how to set up an IT operation and then run that shop after it is set up.

Related to IT services is a general class of activities known as *business services*. With business services, like IT services, there are two options: consulting and outsourcing. With business service consulting, organizations are advised about business function, such as customer relationship management (CRM) and enterprise resource planning (ERP). With outsourcing, the business services firm does it for you – perhaps in the areas of finance and accounting.

What we have at this point are multiple organizations, collections of people and technology connected by value propositions and shared information, operating as a service system. More specifically, a *service system* can be viewed as a configuration of people and technology connected to another system of people and technology in order to co-create value for both organizations.

Products and Service

It is useful to consider the differences between products and services. Products are tangible and services are intangible An automobile, a garment, a table, and even a fast-food hamburger are examples of products. A doctor's visit, swimming pool cleaning, and package delivery are examples of services. On the surface, one could conclude that products are produced through some relevant sequence of operations, but that is not a defining characteristic, since most services also go through a sequence of steps. The answer is that a product is an artifact – something you can see or touch. Clearly, a service results in something worthwhile – otherwise, why engage in it – but the result is a change in a person or possession, not in the creation of something.

Products are storable; services are non-storable. You can store any of the examples of products, given above. If you have your car cleaned or your lawn mowed, you can't exactly save that service. When a service is finished, it is done forever. Perhaps, a record of the service is archived, explicitly or implicitly, but once the stop button is pushed, that service machine is off. If a service has to be repeated, then it is another service event.

Another related difference is that services are generally regarded as perishable. The implication here is that if a seat on an airline flight is not used, then the value of that opportunity is lost. There are many parallels between services and events in everyday life. If you buy a fresh banana and don't eat it within a reasonable time period, its value is lost. You can buy another, but again, that is a different thing. Product and services are two different things.

With products, consumption follows production. In fact, the build-store-sell and the sell-build-ship business models apply here. With services, consumption and production occur at the same time. This characteristic is related to the difference between product quality and service quality. With products, a quality assessment can be made before the customer enters the scene. With services, the client's view of quality is determined during the service process. As product classes mature, they become standardized and competition shifts to price. Services are almost always customized. In general, product development is capital intensive, and the delivery of services is labor intensive. It is important to recognize, however, that the creation of products may include services in the production process, and that services may also accompany production in the form of follow-on activity.

Classification

Given that services are pervasive in modern economies, there would appear to be so much diversity between them that it would be impossible to make any sense of the subject. On the other hand, there has to be a set of common denominators that we could use to classify services so that we could draw some conclusions about organization, performance, and quality.

Services are generally classified by at least five criteria: service process, service nature, service delivery, service availability, and service demand. The major factor is a qualitative concept, known as "service nature" that consists of service object and service result. We will focus on the service object, because it reflects whether a service is performed on a person, a possession, or information. In a previous section, we covered the subject of distinguishing services from goods. The service object is useful for distinguishing services from services, and it preserves the roles of the provider and the client. In a generic sense, the question of who or what gets the service is the determining factor in exactly how much of the other four criteria are applied to a particular service event.

People Processing

In people processing services, the provider performs corporeal actions to the client. The client is part of the service production process and remains in the domain of the provider during service delivery. There is simultaneity of production with consumption in a people processing service event, and the provider and client, are regarded as co-producing the service. Various forms of transportation service, for example, are placed in this category.

Possession Processing

In possession processing services, the provider changes the state of one or more tangible objects under the jurisdiction of the client. Many possession processing services are straightforward, as in car washing and other maintenance activities. These services relate to the condition of an object and are regarded as physical services.

Clearly, there are other attributes of service objects and one of the most common is ownership that puts retailing into the domain of service processing. In fact, some manufacturing operations consist of a sequence of services applied to a physical object or system. Another physical attribute is location, and an operation that provides components to a just-in-time production process is a form of service. Package delivery, for example, is a form of possession processing.

Information Processing

Information processing services deal with the collection, manipulation, interpretation, and transmission of data to create value for the client. Accounting, banking, consulting, education, insurance, legal, and news are commonly experienced examples of information processing services. There are important issues with information processing services, such as representation (as with lawyers and accountants), infrastructure (as with computers, databases, and the Internet), and self service (as with online facilities, ATM machines, and other administrative functions).

Characteristics

In business, services are commonly referred to as the non-material equivalent of a good. Services can be sold, purchased, and scheduled. To many people, a service represents something they cannot do themselves or do not want to do, or perhaps more importantly, something that can be done more efficiently or in a less costly manner by a specialized business entity. Here are some characteristics of services:

> *A service is a process.* This notion is paramount to recognizing the far-reaching importance of service science as an academic discipline. A service takes input and produces output. In between the input and the output, there exist one or more steps that constitute the service process.

A service is heterogeneous. This characteristic reflects the fact that each client/provider interaction in the form of a service event is unique.

A service captures value. A service event creates a benefit to both the client and the provider, in the form of a change of state that is reflected in their physical condition or location, a change in their possessions, or in their assets.

A service cannot be inventoried. The notion of opportunity loss is fundamental to service science. An empty seat on an airline flight cannot be resold. The value lost to a service provider due to a missed appointment cannot be regained. This characteristic gives a time dimension to services. Thus, a service capacity is said to be *perishable,* referring to the fact that it is "perished" when unused.

A service is intangible. A service event does not produce a physical product as a result; however, a service can produce a noticeable result.

A service is consumed at the point of production. This characteristic adds specificity to the recognition that a service is a process, even though it may be summarized for descriptive purposes as a service event. When a service terminates, it is finished. After the final step in a service process, the event is archived along with the consequent change of states of the client and provider.

A service cannot be resold or given away. It is not possible to pass a service on to another economic entity. The result of a service event is unique to that event, although information gained during the service process could theoretically be used by another entity. However, information resulting from a service event is not the same as the service event, because of the consumption characteristic.

A service is co-produced. This characteristic emphasizes the fact that because of the simultaneity of client and provider participation and the fact that a service event does not result in the production of a good, but rather in the state of something, it is commonly referred to as the co-production of value in the sense that if either of the participants were not present for the service event, it could not be interpreted as being a service.

Service characteristics are useful for distinguishing one service event from another and for defining classes of services.

SERVICE SYSTEM

A *service system* is a collection of resources and economic entities, capable of engaging in or supporting one or more service events. The resources are the infrastructure and other facilities necessary to support the service process. The economic entities are the service provider and service client that co-produce the service event. In the case of possession processing services, the service environment would also consist of one or more tangible objects that serve as the service object of the service process. In most cases, a service system is required to sustain a service event. A service system consisting of a provider, a client, and a service target is conceptualized. In this instance, the service target could be the client, a possession of the client, or an individual or an organizational entity over which the client has responsibility.

Service Facilities

If a service provider and client can co-produce a service event, there must be some degree of geographical locality to the situation, in the sense that the client travels to the provider or the provider travels to the client or the client and provider execute the service event in a third-party location or they communicate via some form of interactive device and its corresponding media. In other words, they have to get together.

> **The Service Factory.** Let's first consider the case where the customer travels to facilities associated with the provider, such as an airline terminal, hospital, restaurant, retail establishment, or hotel – to name only a few examples. We will refer to the provider facilities, in this case, as the *service factory*. The basic idea is that the customer remains at the service factory during service delivery. The situation quickly gets complicated because it depends on whether or not the service is associated with a tangible object, an intangible object, or a production supply chain. A *pure service* is a service not associated with tangible objects, such as in medical treatment, hair coloring, and personal transportation. The service event is scheduled, initiated, terminated, and archived – all in the service factory. Many service processes are comprised of several steps called the *service chain*. Other services, not just pure services, consist of a service chain, but this characteristic is normally associated with pure services. When a service process consists of a service chain, it is

said to be "scripted." Clearly, a service script may be implicit in the service, such as a doctor's visit, or it may be explicitly prescribed as part of a formal service agreement. Depending upon the complexity of the situation, services can also be a part of a goods production process or a conventional supply chain. A related consideration is whether the service is classified as being discrete or continuous. A *discrete service* takes place in s short time interval – such as hours. A *continuous* service takes place over a longer period of time – such as days or longer. Moreover, a continuous service may be comprised of several service events, as in insurance or banking. Hospital service is continuous consisting of a series of service events. Moreover, the service events may be dynamic in the sense that they are not necessarily planned beforehand. A doctor's visit, on the other hand, ordinarily consists of a service chain of planned events, wherein the services might include check in, get weighed, interact with the physician, and so forth. Some continuous services, such as insurance and banking, incorporate a service factory that is closely associated with the provider but not the client. Clearly, services of this type have a service initiation, service steps, and eventually a termination; but in-between service events are dynamic in the sense that they may occur on an unscheduled and unplanned basis. Still other services in this category may utilize more than one service facility, such as a check-in terminal and a transportation vehicle. However, the classification applies since the client occupies provider facilities for the duration of the service. Branch banking is a form of continuous service with more than one service facility.

The Service Shop. Some services involve leaving a possession of the client at a service shop for later pick-up, as in the cases of dry cleaning and auto repair. Clearly, the service shop is associated with the service provider, and the service object, owned by the client, occupies physical space in the service facility for the duration of the service process. Child day care, for example, would be placed in this category.

The Service Portal. Other services engage a virtual service facility for the duration of the service event. All of this sounds like the Internet, and that's the idea. However, the category also includes telecommuting and a variety of online and telephone services. In fact, any activity, generally classed as e-Commerce, falls under the umbrella of a service portal. Included in the category of service portals are a variety of information services and "do it yourself" activities.

Mobile Service Facilities. In the previous categories, the emphasis has been on provider resources that occupy a fixed space, incorporating personnel, buildings, equipment, machines, vehicles, and supplies. The scenario has been that the client travels to the service facility or accesses it via some modern convenience. In other cases, the client moves as in navigation services and various forms of satellite communication, such as radio, information providing, and related services – such as car unlocking.

Client Facilities. The subject of service provisioning would not be complete without the mention of client facilities, as in the case where the service provider travels to the client to perform a service. In most instances in this group, the service is performed on a possession of the client – even though that is not a necessary condition.

Implementation of Services

All organizations and all persons do not have the same service requirements and accordingly, the same problems. Moreover, it is impossible to look at services from solely an industry perspective or even a personal point of view. Clearly, services differ between industries and between persons. On the other hand, the diverse set of activities, universally called *services,* wouldn't be called *services* if there weren't some degree of commonality among them. Accordingly, we are going to take a look at steps in the service process, not necessarily service interactions, per se, that are commonly incorporated into the service chain. Service *initiation* refers to the steps necessary to schedule a service and establish a provider/client interaction. Appointments with professional service providers are normally scheduled, whereas arrangements with nonprofessionals are commonly scheduled on an informal basis. Some service providers use appointments to manage demand as a means of achieving service efficiency. Entry service *administration* initiates customer input, such as filling out forms, and establishes a service agreement encompassing fees and expectations. Legal documents may be involved with this step, and client requirements are delineated. Service *interactions* are the steps in the service process. For discrete service processes, service interactions are statically planned with expected variations, since most services are customized by the provider for each client. For continuous service processes, service interactions are dynamically engaged – as in the case of banking, insurance, and hospital care. Service *termination* represents the end of a set of service interactions, regardless if they are statically or dynamically executed. Follow-on services or referrals are established during this step. Exit service *administration* initiates the record-keeping process and deals with the economic aspects of the service process. Service *archiving* handles information storage and legal requirements.

Collectively, the six generic functions are normally present, explicitly or implicitly, in practically all service processes, and are referred to as the *service platform*. The intended meaning of the terminology is that the service platform supports the service process.

Business Services

The basis of business service systems is the evolution from collaboration to automation. The first phase, entitled *Collaboration*, utilizes human engineering principles and is characterized as "assistance by doing some of the work." The next phase, entitled *Augmentation*, utilizes technology to increase productivity by using tools to supplement human activity. The third phase, entitled *Delegation*, is the outsourcing to service providers of non-core business processes that do not provide competitive advantage. The final phase, entitled *Automation*, employs technology to provide self-service systems. Employing the four elements of business service systems, namely organization, technology, management, and information systems, service businesses can move among the phases by considering the following elements: business value (*Should we?*), technology (*Can we?*), governance (*May we?*), and business priorities (*Will we?*).

Globalization

A business service system is a complex socio-techno-economic system that combines people, technology, value, and clients along four dimensions: information sharing, work sharing, risk sharing, and goods sharing. There is some evidence that some elements of all four dimensions are present in all business service systems. Before globalization, services were performed between provider and client with some degree of locality. After Globalization Three, business value creation through services is created by sharing. Information and communications technology (ICT) is the key business driver in value creation and is the form of technology most closely aligned with business service systems.

Outsourcing

Outsourcing is the transfer of the ownership of a business process to a supplier, which includes management and day-to-day execution of that function. The most commonly outsourced business processes are information technology, human resources, accounting, customer support, and call center operations. The key characteristics of outsourcing are "transfer" and ownership; it is different from the process in which the buyer retains control and tells the supplier how to do the work. The objective of outsourcing can be and often is one of the following: reducing costs, focusing the capability of a particular business on more profitable activities, and to obtain special capabilities that the provider firm may possess. Core business competencies are usually not outsourced. For example, airlines commonly outsource telephone reservation and information systems to foreign companies in order to reduce costs and focus on flight operations. Another example, more close to home, is the outsourcing of business cleaning services to benefit from economies of scale for that type of service.

With outsourcing, the client and the provider enter into a business relationship, established with a substantial business agreement, and then the service provider takes over the business process. Outsourcing is usually – actually, almost always – associated with offshoring, but that need not necessarily be the case.

Offshoring

Offshoring is a general term that describes the relocation of a business process from one country to another. Although the present context is services, the practice also applies to manufacturing and production. If a country can provide services in a less expensive manner than other countries, it gives them a comparative advantage to freely trade those services. In the modern world of ICT for the appropriate services, therefore, offshoring can be achieved by establishing the necessary business ecosystem.

To be more specific, offshoring is the practice of transferring an internal business process of a company in one country to another country, to be executed by the same or a different company. Service offshoring is particularly appealing to modern business since many services can be digitized thereby facilitating inter-country relocation.

Offshoring may involve the transfer of intellectual property and training to the receiving country and is related to the availability of educated and trained labor as factors in production – the others being land and capital. Accordingly, many design and development services are being redirected offshore.

Outsourcing and Offshoring

It follows from the above discussion that a company that engages in the transfer of an entire business function to another company in another country is both outsourcing and offshoring. As mentioned previously, common examples of outsourcing are call centers, accounting, customer support, human relations, and information technology (IT). It is now appropriate to add medical diagnosis, design services, and engineering services to the list and recognize that both outsourcing and offshoring are involved.

Public opinion on combined outsourcing and offshoring (O&O) is negative, because it is generally felt that the process adversely affects individuals and the total labor market. Even in cases in which O&O is associated with lower jobless rates, it is felt that O&O tends to shift displaced workers into lower paying jobs.

Sharing

The major tenet of services is that the provider and the client co-produce a service event and the composite interaction creates value for both of the participants. To a greater or lesser degree, a service is enacted by sharing, as covered previously. Information sharing is more closely aligned with services in which persons interact, such as medical provisioning and consulting. Work sharing is characterized by outsourcing. Risk sharing (although not covered so far) is associated with continuous form of service, such as insurance, and is related to transformational outsourcing. Goods sharing is involved with certain formal tangible people-oriented services, such as hotel and auto rental.

Service Process Organization

Practically everyone has heard of or experienced service providers that traditionally have clients backed up with very long waiting times. A common example is the "not so fast" fast-food restaurant. In the world of services, organization is everything. While it is literally impossible to solve all service problems in a few pages, it is feasible to deliver an organizational design that is relevant to most service systems. A definition of a service system is:

> A *service system* is a system of people and technology
> that adapts to the changing value of information in
> the system. It is important to emphasize that the
> "changing value of information" also refers to the
> service process itself. So it should be expected that
> a particular service organization would adjust to
> changing conditions in the workplace.

In the production of goods, a measure of organization is the level of inventory, even though the management of inventory can be a subject in its own right. With services, capacity is a key element, and long waiting lines are evidence of insufficient service capacity, ineffective demand management, or inadequate organization. In this section, a working model of service organization is presented that should serve as a starting point for looking at organizational issues.

Retailing and Services

The importance of service organization is inherent in retailing. Retailing is a service, as covered previously, and the sales service event changes the ownership attribute of a product. A significant aspect of retailing exists, however, that is associated with service organization.

There is a component in retailing that is directly related to the level of expected service as a function of the price of the product. Most customers possess a nominal price for a given product. If the sales price is lower than nominal value, then less service is expected. If the sales price is higher than the nominal price, then more service is expected or the product is deemed overpriced. Buyer behavior, therefore, is governed by a combination of price and retail service, so that buyer behavior is influenced to some degree by service organization.

INFORMATION SERVICES

Through information and communications technology, modern society has made enormous advances in how we live and work. How far we have progressed is summarized by Microsoft chairman Bill Gates in a recent email message. "The ability to access and share information instantly and communicate in ways that transcend the boundaries of time and distance has given rise to an era of unprecedented productivity and innovation that has created new economic opportunities for hundreds of millions of people around the world and paved the way for global growth that is unparalleled in human history."

An *information service* is a resource capable of supporting a service event or instantiating a service event based on information. In other words, an information service can assist in the execution of a service, such as in retailing, or it can actually be the service as when buying a pair of shoes on the Internet – actually, the World Wide Web, but that distinction is not required at this point. The resource is a service provider that can take the form of a person or a computer.

The execution of an information service event requires a service client that can also take the form of a person or computer, and the provider and client must interact in order to co-produce the service. The execution of a service event changes the state of the provider and the client, but a tangible object is not produced. An information service is commonly associated with computer technology, but that is not a necessary condition. The most definitive characteristic of an information service is that the information travels, which gives rise to new models of information management and communications technology.

A Personal Dimension

Most of the information that is communicated between people is about something. Clearly, there is some form of informational interchange that accompanies practically all services. Information service is more than the incidental exchange of information.

With information services, the client specifically requests information and the provider supplies it using some form of communications channel. The service request may be implicit in some other form of activity or it may be "ordered" on a demand basis, but it is nevertheless requested.

Data and Information

Each provider/client interaction in an information service requires a context, and here is why. Pure unadulterated facts are known as *data*. *Information* is data in a particular context so it has a specific meaning. When you request some information about a subject from an Internet web site, for example, the context is supplied in some manner, such as from the site itself, the nature of the query, or even information in a previously requested web page. The context effectively gives meaning to data and turns it into information. The bits that flow through wires or through the air as electromagnetic radiation are nothing more than data, at best. Accordingly, it would be proper to say that it is an *information service* that turns a bunch of bits into something useful, such as a news story or downloaded music.

Ordinary Mail

Not all information services necessarily require a computer. The United States Postal Service is a case in point, as is its international equivalent, known as the PTT (Post, Telephone, and Telegraph), which do not require a computer in their basic form. Electronic mail (email as we generally know it) is also an information service, and it does require a computer. Each element has a sender and an intended recipient. Who is the service provider? It is certainly not the sender or recipient. Clearly, it is the mail service itself. The mail serves as the communications channel between the sender and the recipient. In most other information services, the communications channel is only a channel for communication and nothing more. With mail service, pickup, transportation, and delivery would appear to be the service, and the informational content of the message is not brought into the analysis.

Is Software a Service?

Yes. Software would appear to be a service, such as in document preparation and as suggested by the example of ordinary mail. Information is moved from one place to another and perhaps it is transformed a bit in the process. In document preparation, or word processing, as it is usually called, information is moved from an origin, such as a person's brain, through the nervous system, the person's fingers, and the keyboard to the computer and software and then to a document file. Nevertheless, it is transferred from one place to another. If electronic mail is considered to be a service, then it would seem that word processing is also. Consider another example. If you go to a tax preparation agency to have your return prepared, you consider it to be a service. If you buy a program for a small fee that does the same work as the tax agency, does it perform a service?

Most people would agree that tax software is a service. In the same vein, presentation, spreadsheet, and database software would also be regarded as services.

There is another aspect to all of this, as exemplified by the word processing and email examples. The provider and client participate in the exchange of information, even though they may not be, and probably won't be, in close proximity. Thus, the distance metric is not necessarily significant in word processing, and in the case of email, even the time metric is also not significant.

Is *all* software a service? Perhaps, that should have been the original question. It is an open item. It is easy to conceptualize that office software for document preparation, presentation, graphics, data management, and data analysis could be regarded as services, since that software facilitates the transfer of information from one place to another. In the area of information systems, DSS (Decision Support System) software, for example, provides timely information to managers to aid in decision making. DSS software is definitely a service. What about AI (Artificial Intelligence) software, such as software that monitors gauges in a nuclear reactor? Then, if something goes wrong, the computer program shuts the reactor down before a meltdown occurs. Again, most people, especially those that work in nuclear power plants, would agree that it is a service. The debate could go on. For this paper, at least, software is a service.

Enterprise Information Services

Information is the cornerstone of modern business, and government as well, and is the major ingredient in everyday commerce. In the study of information services, the distinction between information and the system to handle the information is often blurred. In this section, we will establish the difference between information and services.

A lot of information is about things: about a product or service, about travel arrangements, about how to do something, about an event, about a person or group, about something that has happened in the past, and so forth. We are going to refer to this type of information as *operand information*, and we are additionally going to refer to information that is involved with the service process itself as *operant information*. When the focus of an information service is the result, then as Vargo and Lusch might put it, we are using goods-dominant logic and the result is referred to as the operand. When the focus of an information service is on the process, then we are employing service-dominant logic and the operant resources are the information and the other steps in the service process.

Business Information

Business information services are usually divided into two categories: operational services and management services. Operational services are employed to run the enterprise and management services are used to manage the enterprise. Some of the same basic concepts are used in both categories, but the time and distance characteristics are different. For example, a database management system and a database are normally used to store persistent data for the enterprise. With operational services, the database is dynamic and is updated for each transaction. With management services, static data is needed to make effective decisions. Accordingly, a static database would ordinarily be created from the dynamic database so that timely management reports could be generated. Of course, this is a bit of a simplification, but the basic idea is there.

The management of information is an enterprise service in its own right. Clearly, the transfer of information from operational databases to a data warehouse is a concrete example of an enterprise information service.

Transaction Services

When you make an airline reservation or check a flight schedule using the Internet, you are using a transaction processing system. Most information services that support operational systems in today's world use transaction processing. At the most general level, you interact with the server using the communications channel. You are the client, the server is the provider, and the service is the transaction. The entire process is mediated by hardware and software and the only thing that moves is the information.

Client and Provider Input to an Information Service

An information service requires client and provider input, just as in any other kind of service. Usually, the client – whether it is a person or a computer – enters a small amount of information into the service process. The provider – usually a computer information system – has access to a larger store of information, so that we can say the provider provisionally supplies a larger amount of information. The informational output of an information service is a function of the inputs and the nature of the service.

The client may have help supplying input to an information service through hardware and software facilities known as "interaction services." The provider may have assistance from database services and auxiliary services via a service bus.

Interaction Services

An interaction service is normally a socially-constructed collection of structural elements and behavioral patterns, such as action buttons, list boxes, and pull-down menus. Interaction services are dependent upon what the client expects to do with the information service. Here are some examples:

- Information exploration (e.g., find out about service science)
- Accomplish something (e.g., reserve a seat)
- Find a "good enough" answer to a question (e.g., how do we get to New York)
- Change the direction of a search operation (e.g., what about service systems)

- Establish a point of reference (e.g., mark my place to come back to at a later time)

Designing effective interaction services is not so easy, but one approach is to think about the elements with which you have to work. A common set of such elements is composed of objects (such as icons), actions (such as a file menu), subject (such as the information that you have to work with), and tools (such as calendars and appointments).

Interaction services are a small part of service science, but nevertheless an important part.

Service Bus

A *service bus* is a high-speed data link between two computing platforms that operate in a request/response mode. The client requests an item of information (such as the price of IBM stock on Monday at 11:00 on a given date) and the provider, which operates in a server mode, supplies it in an expeditious manner. A service bus requires software that is called *middleware*.

An example of the need for a service bus is inherent in the following example. A stock broker is on a line to a client who requests the price of IBM stock. The brokerage firm has a computer (the server) that gets an up-to-the-second feed from the stock exchange. There is a high speed link between the stock brokers and the server, and each broker has a specialized thick client interface. The broker enters the stock symbol for IBM into a text box and clicks a send button. The server responds in a fraction of a second with the requested price.

Collaboration

Collaboration operates at the intellectual level and often benefits from decentralization and varying degrees of academic and personal diversity. Collaboration is a unique form of service. The service provider in the information service modality is established through information and communications technology, and is an instance of where the "service is the service provider," because it allows the clients in a collaboration service to exchange meaningful information.

Collaboration requires at least two clients interacting in what is referred to as a *multi-client service*. A multi-client service is frequently leaderless and is known as a *virtual organization structure*. Traditional workflow where a document is passed between team members is a common form of collaboration.

Pull versus Push

It is perhaps a bit of an oversimplification, but "the manner in which you approach an information service determines what you get." The characteristics of the *pull model* are succinctly summarized in the following sentence. "Rather than 'push,' this new approach focuses on 'pull' – creating platforms that help people to mobilize appropriate resources when the need arises."

Push models are essentially scripted and thrive in stable environments with little uncertainty. Forecasting, as in demand forecasting, is key in push environments and allows high levels of efficiency to be developed in business processes. Most of modern business and governmental activity uses the push modality. A business pushes a product into the marketplace and people buy it. Push programs are top-down processes with the following steps: design, deploy, execute, monitor, and refine.

Pull models increase value creation for both clients and providers. For clients, "pull" activity expands the scope of available resources. For providers, pull systems expand the market for services. Pull platforms are associated with the following attributes: uncertain demand, emergent design, decentralized environment, loosely coupled modular construction of facilities, and on-demand service provisioning. Pull models are more amenable to uncertain business conditions.

From both the client's and the provider's perspectives, pull services focus on the following activities: find, select, purchase, deliver, and service. If all of this sounds familiar, it should be. It represents how you buy shoes on the Internet.

Enterprise Services

The seven constituents of an enterprise information service are providers, clients, messages, communications, information processing, persistent storage, and the user interface that collectively take into consideration the requisite technology including database facilities, email archives, protocols, business rules, operational procedures, and a variety of service interactions needed for enterprise applications. Since information, and not people, move in information services, this category of service is based on information and communications technology. It is important that when we discuss information services at the enterprise level, we are primarily concerned with functionality and not necessarily with computing platforms.

Information Services

Information service systems typically operate in a client/server mode, which means that the end user is the service client, the enterprise application running on a computing platform is the service provider, and the means of client and provider interaction is some form of communications channel. Typically, the client enters information into the system through a well-defined interface and the provider does something in return. Exactly what the provider does is of primary importance to the information service system.

There are at least three distinct possibilities:

- The provider accesses some form of persistent storage and returns selected information to the client.
- The provider performs some element of information processing and returns an indicator to the client that it was done.

- The client and the provider enter into an interactive dialog concerning specific informational elements and a supply chain operation is initiated to accomplish the corresponding enterprise operation.

As such, information service systems are instrumental in supporting daily activities. Typical enterprise applications are order processing, purchasing, accounting, inventory control, human resources, marketing and sales support, manufacturing, and various forms of service support including data collection and information management.

SElectronic Information Services

It is possible to be more definitive about electronic information services. Three main constituents are identified: business, government, and the consumer. How the information services are related is important. B2C indicates business-to-consumer. B2B indicates business-to-business. G2B indicates government-to-business. C2C indicates consumer-to-consumer. G2G indicates government-to-government. G2C indicates government-to-consumer. In the symbols, the leftmost letter reflects the provider and the rightmost letter represents the client.

Electronic Commerce

Electronic commerce is an enterprise information service application supported by the Internet and the World Wide Web, and can be viewed as an opportunistic means of doing business with minimal cost. In short, the information services of the Internet and the Web are used to conduct business.

Electronic commerce is usually known as e-commerce or B2C for short. Conventional business establishments are referred to as "brick and mortar" facilities characterized by a shopping area in which customers can view products, and business personnel can conduct commerce. The equivalent in the digital world is an e-commerce web site where a consumer can conduct analogous functions. The service provider is the e-commerce web site and the customer is the client connected to the web site via the Internet. In this instance, the Internet is the communications channel. The service process is the set of interactions between the customer and one or more web sites that go through the following steps: find, select, purchase, deliver, and service.

Find is an Internet service process, which is usually a set of service interactions, to navigate to the desired Internet retailer. After the electronic retailer is chosen, the *select* and *purchase* services represent the online equivalent of the traditional processes of making a purchase. Purchasing involves payment that invokes a secure service designed for that specific purpose. *Deliver* is another service process initiated by the retailer for physically delivering the product to the consumer. *Service* is the Web enabled service process of providing customer support. Each of the steps in the B2C service process (i.e., find, select, purchase, deliver, and service) involves at least one service, so the entire process can be properly regarded as a *multiservice*, driven by a series of constituent information services.

B2C transactions are characterized by increased convenience, enhanced efficiency, additional buying choice, and lower prices, from the consumer's perspective, and by an increased return on retailing investment for the electronic retailer. An electronic retailer need not have a related "brick and mortar" facility, but that is often the case.

Electronic Business

Electronic business is the use of the Internet and the World Wide Web to conduct business operations, including intra-business and inter-business transactions. This is a broad category and ranges from relatively simple information services to obtain tacit business information from within a single organization to complex Web Services and REST web services.

Electronic business is usually known as e-business or B2B for short and has its roots in electronic data interchange (EDI) commonly used to exchange information on business operations within an organization, and between business partners, suppliers, and wholesalers. The use of the Internet for communications services reduces operational costs for computer networks and increases the value obtained from costs that are incurred.

The major advantage of B2B operations is that companies can utilize an information service known as the "B2B Electronic Marketplace," wherein they can buy and sell products and exchange information through a *virtual marketplace*. Not only can companies create supply chains, but they can create business partnerships in which one company can take advantage of information services of another company. The process, known as the *componentization of information services*, facilitates the creation of web services that allow the company to be a more responsive (to market and economic conditions) enterprise.

B2B is similar to B2C in one respect. Modern company operations require the purchase of certain *indirect materials*, typically referred to as MRO materials, where MRO stands for "maintenance, repair, and operations," and include such items as ball pens, repair parts, and office equipment. Through the B2B electronic marketplace, various companies can collectively achieve lower cost through *demand aggregation*. *Direct materials* are items used in production or retail operations as part of a company's core business. B2B operations can also be sustained through web services.

Electronic Marketplace

Information services, such as the electronic marketplace, permit companies to engage in B2B market operations in horizontal and vertical electronic marketplaces. In a *horizontal marketplace*, buyers and sellers can interact across many industries. Travel and financial services are common examples, because they are applicable to almost any type of business, such as the process industries (oil and gas) and conventional and electronic retailing.

In a *vertical marketplace*, buyers and sellers are in the same industry and primarily engage in information services that relate to direct material.

Electronic Government

Information services are a means of transforming the management and operations of government to be more responsive, efficient, and reliable in delivering services to the electorate – at all governmental levels, including federal, state, and local communities. The objective is to enhance informational facilities that already exist so they may properly be regarded as click and mortar," with the options of obtaining information and services via the Internet and World Wide Web while continuing to have a physical presence. Three flavors have been identified: Government to Business (G2B), Government to Consumer (G2C), and Government to Government (G2G). In the latter case, there are two possibilities: inter-government and intra-government. Inter-government refers to the vertical alignment of information services between governmental levels on the same initiative, such as the coordination of federal, state, and local agencies on air pollution. Intra-government refers to the horizontal alignment of services between agencies at the same level of government, such as disaster response coordination between police, fire, and emergency medical departments.

Government to business operations reflect information services that cover purchasing of MRO materials, and the provisioning of information facilities for procedures, regulations, reporting, and compliance. In the latter case, governmental reporting facilities (by business to government) are commonly available to submit requisite documentation through Internet and World Wide Web services.

Most citizens are familiar with Government to consumer information services for taxes and various forms of registration. For taxpayers, the ability to download forms and directions, and the ability to submit completed tax forms is paramount. For those of us fortunate enough to receive a tax refund, the increased efficiency is money in the bank. Vehicle and voter registration are other information services that are efficient from both client and provider perspectives.

Overall, however, the availability of information on dates, procedures, directions, and so forth, at the click of a mouse via the Internet and the World Wide Web – pure information services – is the greatest advantage of G2C services.

PERSONAL SERVICES

Personal information services are an ever expanding collection of Internet and World Wide Web applications. The prevalence of the applications, however, brings up a fundamental question about exactly what constitutes the clients, providers, and the services in the various forms of information service. The resources appear to be different among the applications, so the presentation of the subject matter will be instructive for determining the scope of personal information services. Accordingly, we will cover the following services: chat rooms, instant messaging, Internet telephone, web auctions, user-generated media, social networking, and newsgroups. This is only a sample of relevant applications but is indicative of how information services are used to support those applications.

Chat Rooms

One of the most popular means of communicating on the Internet is through a chat room, the best known of which is IRC (Internet Relay Chat). IRC operates in the client/server mode and requires an IRC server; clients require special IRC software, usually downloaded from the Internet.

When using chat, the user selects a channel, which establishes the conversation in which the user will participate. Characteristically, other users, throughout the world, will have chosen the same channel.

The idea being that they will exchange information on a certain subject.

During operation, users type messages on their local client computer and the information is relayed via the Internet to the server. The message is then forwarded to other users signed on to the same channel and is displayed on their screens. A user may just listen, figuratively speaking, or may participate in the conversation. Ostensibly, users respond to other user's transmissions, so that an identifying name (sometimes called a *handle*) accompanies each submission. Since chat rooms are a global phenomenon, a network of IRC servers is required to service all of the users in a specific domain. A recent development is "voice chat," which is an audio equivalent to the traditional text-based chat.

At the end-user level, a chat room can be viewed as a collection of clients whose interpersonal communications is being managed by the chat server system operating as a service provider. The chat server system consists of the hardware, software, and Internet facilities, necessary to do the task. The service process consists of a set of dynamically determined client/server interactions, where the end-user is the client and the chat server is the service provider.

Instant Messaging

Instant messaging is the private real-time communication of textual messages between two users logged on to an instant messaging (IM) server over the Internet. Messages are forwarded through an IM server that uses the "sender" client's buddy list to determine the destination for forwarded messages. Many Internet specialists consider instant messaging to be a form of chat room operations, since it has similar information service characteristics.

Front and Back Stages

Internet chat and instant messaging, among other information services, incorporate a value chain of component services, divided between front and back stages. Essentially, the front stage is what the end-user conceptualizes and the back stage is what is going on under the covers, so to speak.

The noteworthy aspect of the division is that human clients are only part of the process, if they are involved at all, and the front stage represents the client's experience supplemented by the back stage that represents the information service support structure based on ICT facilities. The participants (Human or ICT) may possess different but complementary views of the service process.

Internet Telephone

Using the Internet for making telephone calls is appealing to many people because of the cost, which may be free in some cases, over and above the cost of the Internet connection. Several methods and associated software facilities are available. They generally fall into two broad categories.

In the first case, you use special hardware and software to communicate through your personal computer (PC) using a microphone and speakers. If you are calling someone who is also using the same method, the call is totally free, as it is with web browsing and email, and it is also applicable to users anywhere in the world.

In the second case, you use your ordinary "land line" telephone handset, and the call is routed over the Internet using a service process generally known as Voice over IP (VoIP). With VoIP, your voice is digitized and routed through the Internet as information packets, similar to other information services such as web pages and email. At the receiving end, the voice packets are converted to normal telephone signals.

With Internet telephone, the conceptualized front and back stages coincide. The clients are the telephone users and the service provider is the value chain of Internet activities.

Web Auctions

A *web auction* is an Internet and World Wide Web service that connects buyers and sellers in a consumer-to-consumer (C2C) mode to conduct an online version of traditional auction. A well-known web site that manages the web auction process is *eBay*, but there are notably other sites that perform the same service.

In this instance, the information service is the posting and delivery of information concerning products for sale and associated bids. The clients are the buyers and sellers and the information service consists of the information processing facilities to sustain the auction. In this instance, the Internet and the World Wide Web serve only as a communication channel.

User Generated Media

There are three major forms of information dissemination normally originating from individuals that use the Internet and World Wide Web services: web logs, podcasts, and RSS feeds. The services are related and are covered together in this section.

A *web log* (called a *blog*) is a medium for presenting information without restrictions or review over the Internet and accessible through the World Wide Web. People who participate in the service of creating information content in this category are known as *bloggers,* and the process itself is known as *blogging*. The following three information services are normally associated with this form of activity: (1) Obtaining information on how to set up and access a blog web site; (2) Providing services that assist in actually setting up a blog web site; and (3) Using services that assist in making entries in a web log. Each blog site has a uniform resource locator (URL) and a theme, subsequently used for search and discovery.

A *podcast* is an audio blog, serviced by the Internet that serves the same purpose as a personal radio station. Using your PC and a microphone, you can record a document and store it on an appropriate blog site. Other users can then download the audio blog to their PC for listening or for transfer to a music player. Podcasts are used to listen to broadcast media and educational material. In the latter category, a podcast is an effective means of delivering course material to students.

An *RSS feed* is a means of generating a wider audience for blogs and podcasts, through an Internet technique known as Really Simple Syndication. RSS feeds utilize special web formatted material and deliver automatically generated downloads to registered end users using push technology.

User-generated media operations are generally considered to be a front stage process. All communications are *asynchronous*, which means they are created (or uploaded) as a process at one time and accessed (or downloaded) by another process at another time, using push technology.

Social Networking

Social networking is usually regarded as the process of keeping up with friends and family, and it is no surprise that the process has migrated to the World Wide Web. The inherent information service is social networking is known as "shared space."

A *shared space* is an online virtual public space in which a person – commonly a young person – can display information about themselves, including text, audio, and video. Special web sites, such as MySpace and Facebook, are designed to handle social networking. Actually, the video is predominantly photographs taken with a digital camera and uploaded to an appropriate web site set up for social networking. A person's virtual space is subsequently accessible by friends. The conceptual model for a shared space is that of a private room to which one can invite friends to look around, thus giving the owner a private virtual space not otherwise available in everyday life. As with information services that support media, social networking services are asynchronous and use pull technology.

Newsgroups

A *newsgroup* is a collection of people that participate in a discussion on a particular subject using Internet facilities. The usual form of communication is email, and the mode of communication is question and answer. The largest and most widely known online news group is *usenet*. A participant subscribes to a particular topic. When that participant logs on to the newsgroup server, the entries on the selected topic are automatically sent to that participant. Special client software is required to participate in a newsgroup. User interactions are organized by thread, so that a given user effectively engages in a conversation, as required, with participants in the same interest group. If a thread is *moderated*, questions are sent to a human moderator who screens the questions for appropriateness. Otherwise, questions are simply listed by topic. Most threads are archived by date.

Newsgroup software employs the same information service modality as email, and in fact, is dependent upon email for its operational infrastructure. Newsgroup facilities are also available through most information service portals, such as America Online and Google.

QUICK SUMMARY

1. The subject of services is important to most people because they are employed in services and are also consumers of services. In the year 2000, U.S. service employment comprised 80% of the workforce. Surprisingly, very little attention is given to the service sector, in spite of the fact that most of us work in it.

2. A *service* is a provider/client interaction that creates and captures value. A unique characteristic of services, unlike agriculture and manufacturing, is that both parties participate in the transaction, and in the process, both capture value. In a sense, the provider and the client co-produce the service event, because one can't do without the other.

3. There are several definitive characteristics of services. They are summarized as follows. A service is a process. A service is heterogeneous. A service captures value. A service cannot be

inventoried. A service is intangible. A service is consumed at the point of production. A service cannot be resold or given away. And finally, a service is co-produced.

4. A service system is a system of people and technology that adapts to the changing value of knowledge in the system. The participants in a service system are the provider and client and the relationship between them is the service process. Systems of this type require an environment in which to operate that can take the form of a service factory in which the client resides for the duration of the service process and the service shop in which a possession of the client resides for the duration of the service event.

5. Service systems are facilitated by information and communications technology and enhanced by globalization. Service provisioning is inherent in outsourcing and offshoring. Innovation in supplying services is required because services are usually customized and labor intensive.

6. Core business processes are not customarily outsourced, and outsourcing predominantly does not provide differentiation in the marketplace.

7. An *information service* is a resource capable of supporting a service event or instantiating in a service event based on information. In other words, an information service can assist in the execution of a service, such as in retailing, or it can actually be the service as when buying a pair of shoes on the Internet.

8. Most of the information that is communicated between people is about something. With information services, the client requests information and the provider supplies it using some form of communications channel.

9. Software would appear to be a service, such as in document preparation and as suggested by the example of ordinary mail. Information is moved from one placed to another and perhaps it is transformed a bit in the process.

10. Information is the cornerstone of modern business, and government as well, and is the major ingredient in everyday commerce. Business information services are usually divided into two categories: operational services and management services.

11. Operational services are employed to run the enterprise and management services are used to manage the enterprise.

12. Teams are the accepted norm in the modern enterprise, and collaboration is the process by which they progress toward a common goal. With information services, collaboration between groups and individuals can be effected from geographically dispersed locations.

13. Major enterprise information service applications are electronic commerce, electronic business, and electronic government. Major personal information service applications are chat rooms, instant messaging, Internet telephone, web auctions, web logs, podcasts, RSS feeds, social networking, and newsgroups.

REFERENCES

1   Friedman, T.L. (2006), *The World is Flat: A Brief History of the Twenty-First Century*, New York: Farrar, Straus and Giraux.

2   Gralla, P. (2004), *How the Internet Works*, Indianapolis, IN: Que Publishing.

3   Hagel, J. and J. Brown (2007), *From Push to Pull: Emerging Models for Mobilizing Resources*, www.edgeperspectives.com.

4   IBM Almaden Services Research (2006), *Service Science, Management, and Engineering (SSME): Challenges, Frameworks, and Call for Participation*, http://almaden.ibm.com/ssme, p. 13.

5   IBM Almaden Services Research (2006), *SSME: What are services?* http://almaden.ibm.com/ssme.

6   Katzan, H. (2008), "Foundations of Service Science: Concepts and Facilities," *Journal of Service Science*, 1(1), 1-22.

7   Katzan, H. (2008), *Service Science: Concepts, Technology, Management*, New York: iUniverse, Inc.

8   Maglio, P. (2007), *Service Science, Management, and* Engineering (SSME): *An Interdisciplinary Approach to Service Innovation*, IBM Almaden Research Center, http://almaden.ibm.com/ssme, p. 14.

9   Maglio, P. and J. Spohrer (2007), *Fundamentals of Service Science*, IBM Almaden Research Center.

10   *Offshoring* (2007), http://en.wikipedia.org/wiki/Offshoring.

11   *Ontology* (2007), http://en.wikipedia.org/wiki/Ontology.

12   *Outsourcing* (2007), http://en.wikipedia.org/wiki/Outsourcing.

13   Richardson, L. and S. Ruby (2007), *RESTful Web Services*, Sebastopol, DA; O'Reilly Media, Inc.

14   Spohrer, J. Maglio, P., Bailey, J. and D. Gruhl (2007), *Steps Toward a Science of Service Systems*, IBM Almaden Research Center, San Jose, CA, www.almaden.ibm.com/asr, 2007.

15   Spohrer, J., Vargo, S.C., Caswell, N., and P.P. Maglio (2007), *The Service System is the Basic Abstraction of Service Science*, IBM Research, Almaden Research Center, San Jose, CA, www.almaden.ibm.com/asr.

16   Stair, R.M. and G.W. Reynolds (2008), *Principles of Information Systems: A Managerial Approach*, Boston: Thomson Course Technology.

17   Tabas, L. (2007), *Designing for Service Systems*, UCB iSchool Report 2007-008, February, 2007.

18   Tapscott, D. and A.D. Williams (2006), *Wikinomics: How Mass Collaboration Changes Everything*, New York: Penguin Group, Inc.

19   Tidwell, J. (2006), *Designing Interfaces*, Sebastopol, CA: O'Reilly Media, Inc.

20   Vargo, S. and B. Lusch (2004), "Evolving to a New Dominant Logic for Marketing," *Journal of Marketing*, 69 (January, 2004), 1-17.

21   Vargo, S. and B. Lusch (2007), *Service-Dominant Logic Basics*, www.sdlogic.net.

***** End of Chapter 6 *****

7

SERVICE MANAGEMENT

ENTERPRISE SERVICE CONCEPTS

In the domain of services, management and business are intertwined. An enterprise, taken in this essay to be a business, government entity, or educational organization, simultaneously manages its own services and services provided to clients by adopting the role of service provider or service client. In short, an enterprise is likely to be a provider and a user of services. In fact, many internal services are managed as a business and in some instances evolve into external service providers – all with the same or similar functional deployments. So the fine line of separation between management and business is nonexistent, and that phenomenon is clearly evident in the following sections.

MANAGEMENT

Historically, the focus of service management has been on the application of traditional management concepts to enterprise processes that primarily involve services. Typical business examples are banking and health care that have greatly benefited from the application of scientific principles to everyday operations. Two common applications are the use of waiting-line methods for the front office and process scheduling techniques for the back office. Through the application of information and communications technology (ICT), many organizations have adjusted everyday operations enabling them to go through a transformational process to achieve revenue growth by being able to respond more quickly to changing market conditions and by being more effective and efficient in the application of services. This section describes modern services management. The viewpoint taken here is that services management employs computer concepts, but its domain is by no means restricted to computer-based services and includes just about any service that a person can imagine.

Service Management Concepts

There are three forces operating in the sphere of service processes. The first is the use of ICT enablement in providing revenue growth, efficiency, and effectiveness for traditional and enhanced services, as well as for conventional business processes. This subject is commonly referred to as information systems. The second is the consulting services domain that provides IT services to external organizations. The third is the use of ICT to manage information systems and services, which is a field of endeavor known as IT Services Management. Briefly said, it is the use of computers to manage the enterprise and also to manage itself.

Domain of Service Management

Many people feel that what you see in the world depends on the lens through which you are looking. So if you adopt a service-centric point of view, most socially-developed phenomena can be viewed as services. It follows that if we are going to manage services, we should at least consider to whom services are applied and how the service delivery is achieved.

We are going to focus on an organizational setting consisting of people and everyday operational units. The *service provider*, in this instance, is a person acting in a service capacity or a group of persons, including support facilities, that has adopted a role of a service provider. The *service object* is another person or operational unit, usually referred to as a *business unit*. In the latter case, the service object need not be part of the same organization as the service provider. Some examples of service relationships are: (1) an accounting department in a manufacturing company; (2) a computer support person in an academic department; (3) a consulting group that services external customers; (4) an IT department that serves several business units in the same organization; and of course (5) a service professional serving several clients.

There are at least three different types of service arrangements:

Type I: The service provider delivers services to only one service object.

Type II: The service provider delivers services to more than one service object in the same organization.

Type III: The service provider delivers services to one or more service objects in external organizations.

Once a provider type is identified, in a particular instance, the next step is to determine who pays for the service and specifically how that support is organized. This process is known as *service provisioning*.

The internal processes of effective service management go through a cyclic process, known as the *service lifecycle* that includes service strategy, service design, service transition, service operation, and continual service improvement. The use of the methodology presented in this section is known as *best practices*. Most service organizations and all IT organizations would perform better if they adopted a set of best practices, and clearly, many of them do.

Service as a Business

The notion of service has its origin in ancient times and was understood to mean "one person doing something for another."

With the advent of civilization and industrialization, the definition of service was implicitly extended to encompass "one person doing something for an organization," usually in the form of employment. At this stage, specialization and entrepreneurship kicked in with all of their rights and privileges resulting in what we now recognize as the service organization.

Specialization has its roots in process efficiency, but has definite social overtones. Some jobs are more lucrative and have more prestige, and for a variety of reasons, people can do some tasks better than others. Specialization is not limited to individuals but applies to organizations and groups within organizations, as well. Specialization is commonplace, not only in service organizations. In conventional business processes, such as a sales group, certain tasks are performed more expeditiously by a single individual or group, as with credit checking, when the task is performed repeatedly. The degree of specialization needed in a service process is related to the amount of repeatability. Most production and service chains divide the process into individual tasks that are performed by a single unit, taken here to be a person, group, or machine, such that efficiency and effectiveness is achieved through specialization.

Innovation flourishes in a receptive service environment, so that effective service groups are commonly at odds with their parent organization. Service spin offs have resulted in a thriving service economy through entrepreneurship and innovation. Accordingly, it is important to recognize that *service is a business*, and that the principles given here apply equally well to internal and external service organizations.

Service Componentization

Services are ubiquitous, so practically everyone knows what one is. Well, maybe they can't exactly define it, but they recognize one when they see or experience it. What most people don't think about, unless they have to, is that a service is a process. Beneath the surface, there is usually a collection of activities to support that process. The activities are organized into components.

A *component* is an organizational entity for instantiating services. Some components provide more than one service and some services are comprised of more that one component. The operation of a simple restaurant is used to clarify the concept of componentization. (Adapted from Hurwitz, Bloor, Baroudi, and Kaufman (2007).)

We go to a restaurant for a meal. The meal is the service we are seeking. We grab a table, look at the menu, and give our order to a waiter or waitress. Subsequently, the meal is delivered. We consume the meal, pay the tab, and leave. In our interaction with the waiter or waitress, we exchange information, so in a very general sense, we co-produce the service event, although we do not experience the meal preparation. This is not a pure service, since the food is a product. However, the service part of the meal is a service.

On the other hand, we all know that the restaurant is a collection of interacting components that provide a meal service to one or more guests. The components of the restaurant are the server (i.e., the waiter or waitress), the kitchen (that prepares the food), a cleaning component, a food-ordering component, an accounting component, a facility-management component, and a restaurant management component that orchestrates the services supplied by the components. The *service orchestration*, which is an explicit or implicit specification of the interactions between components, is a necessary element in the design of a managed service system.

Collectively, the arrangements of components that make up a service offering constitute its architecture. In service architecture, some components are internal persons or units, some components are outsourced, and some components are business partners. One aspect of service management is the choreography of components in a specific business process – that is, how information or tasks are passed between components without explicit direction.

Another important aspect of service management is keeping track of the components and their attributes. When a service organization gets complicated, a service repository is required to keep track of the services that are provided by each component, and what components are needed for a particular service process. Usually, a computer database is used. From a strategic viewpoint, a component is an asset that must be managed just as any other asset.

IT Services Sourcing

There are several aspects of IT services that can vary between organizations. Examples are commonplace: computer operations, network management, hardware and software acquisition, system analysis and design, software design, software development, information systems integration, and call center and help desk operation and management. This is a representative set of tasks necessary for sustaining an IT services organization. You can do them yourself; you can have another business entity help you do them; or you can have a business entity do them for you. In the latter two cases, the business process is known as *IT service outsourcing*.

Most IT services reflect an underlying set of IT assets, such as hardware, software, users, and systems. The IT services organization has three possible roles regarding these assets: develop or acquire, operate, and manage. For each of the IT assets, role adoption can differ. For example, hardware can be acquired internally and operated by an outside contractor.

The entity that provides the service, that is, the external business unit, need not be an independent business entity in a foreign country. It can be a separate business unit in the same enterprise, located locally, in the same country, or offshore. Alternately, it can be an independent professional services business entity in the same country – a service usually regarded as *IT consulting*. In many cases, however, the organization providing the outsourced service *is*, in fact, an independent business entity operating out of and located in a foreign country.

IT Services Management

It would seem that a person's view of IT services management would be different, depending on whether your organization is the service provider or the service client, and indeed, it is. The common denominator between the various perspectives is the set of common issues that business and IT managers have to deal with, some of which are strategic planning, IT and business alignment, measurement and analysis, costs and investment, business partners and relationships, sourcing, continuous improvement, and governance. The issues are repetitive, recurring, and ongoing, and constitute a *service lifecycle*. The elements of the lifecycle are generic and do not necessarily apply to all service systems. Differences lie in the adoption and deployment of the lifecycle elements.

At the heart of IT services management is a set of tasks that involve "keeping track of things," and there are a lot of things to keep track of. We will call them *service elements*. Some of the service elements are obvious, such as users, hardware, software, network components, office facilities, and configurations. There are other service elements, mostly related to enterprise operations that can offer a challenge, such as categorization of services, to whom those services are supplied or alternately, from whom those services are obtained – contractors, outsourced projects, outsourcers, and business partners. A *service directory* is needed for this type of record keeping. Lastly, with regard to business alignment and service operations, there is a whole host of service operational elements that collectively possess business value that should not be ignored. Three of many such service operational elements are incident management, problem management, and change management. It is through the integration of service operational elements that an enterprise can achieve significant business value. The subject is covered in a later section.

Elements of the Service Lifecycle

The service lifecycle consists of five important elements, listed as follows: Service Strategy, Service Design, Service Transition, Service Operation, and Continuous Improvement. This sequence represents the waterfall model that suggests how the requirements process goes from strategy to continuous improvement, implementing a feedback process as required. Each element of the service lifecycle is considered separately.

Service Strategy

The most important element in the service lifecycle is service strategy. Successful service operations are not sustainable over long periods, because of environmental turbulence affecting resources, competition, and requirements. Accordingly, a service strategy is needed. A *strategy* is a long term plan, based on objectives, that allows an organization to adapt to changing conditions.

Since service is a client based endeavor, it is necessary that a service delivers perceptible value. A service strategy based on client needs is necessary for successful service operations. A service strategy, recorded in s *strategy document*, should reflect whether the strategy is intended for a provider or a client. How an organization uses a service strategy is an individual matter. A service document should reflect major items, such as whether services are managed internally or outsourced, who the key collaborators are, and what service management functions, such as problem and incident management functions, are needed.

Service Design

Service design refers to the synthesis of services to satisfy enterprise objectives. This stage has general applicability, even though it appears, on the surface to reflect IT services. Service design incorporates service architecture, processes, policies, and requisite documentation. Even though the service strategy phase identifies services, the service design phase is where they are established to satisfy business objectives. Even though a computer-based service is developed offshore, it is usually developed by the parent organization during this phase. Risks, quality, measurement, and infrastructure requirements are specified in this stage. Also, this stage involves capacity management, availability management, security management, and key organizational responsibilities.

Service Transition

Service transition concerns the implementation of services in the sense of putting them into a production environment. As such, service transition is an organizational bridge between the design and the operations stages. In many instances, the service transition phase involves a change to existing services involving limited functionality and operational procedures. As such, a service transition requires the establishing of or adhering to a formal policy for the implementation of required changes and the development of a framework for the integration of the changes. When additional training and help desk support is needed, it is established in the service transition stage, which may also include system validation and testing.

Service Operation

The function of the service operation stage is to manage and deliver the services established in the design stage. Business value to the enterprise is delivered in the operation phase, and event monitoring is of prime importance. A *service event* is a change of state during the delivery of a service that requires attention, such as an unplanned interruption of service. Two service management functions are commonly involved: incident management and problem management. *Incident management* is primarily concerned with resolving the situation and getting the system back up and running.

Problem management focuses on determining the root cause of an event and interfaces with change management to insure that the problem is not a recurrent event.

Continuous Improvement

Continuous improvement, or more properly, *Continuous Service Improvement*, refers to the process of maintaining value to the enterprise of a service or set of services. Practically all enterprises, subscribing to services, engage in continuous improvement to some degree, to protect their investment. The output of continuous improvement, known as *Service Reporting*, feeds back into the other four stages, on an as needed basis, constituting the service lifecycle.

This stage consists of seven steps, listed as follows:

1. *Define what you should measure*
2. *Define what you can measure*
3. *Gather the data*
4. *Process the data*
5. *Analyze the data*
6. *Report the information*
7. *Implement corrective action*

Continuous improvement is an excellent management tool as it suggests a means of prioritizing ongoing strategy and design activities.

EVOLUTION OF SERVICE MANAGEMENT

This section covers three topics relevant to effective service management: value nets, the pull model, and E-services. The subject of service management is constantly evolving, because the modern enterprise has a dynamically changing boundary based on a diverse portfolio of services.

Value Nets

A *value net* is a means of capturing business value from the integration of strategy, process, workforce, and technology. Business value is created by shifting from the traditional value-chain model to the value-net model in service systems. In the value-chain model, an organization creates value by adding elements to the finished product at each stage of a production process. In a general sense, raw materials are converted to value in a step-by-step production line. The modern competitive environment, however, requires faster turnaround time and more choices, especially with regard to service management.

Successful enterprises currently use value nets, in which suppliers and business partners interoperate through information over networks on a demand basis. The relationships between organization, suppliers, business partners, and customers are dynamic and adjust to changing requirements. Value nets are efficient because of the real time combination of services supplied by the key participants – the business, buyers, suppliers, and business partners.

The Pull Model for Service Agility

Hagel and Brown have identified the pull model as a means of mobilizing business resources for the upcoming generation of business activities based on mass communications and the Internet. The characteristics of the *pull model* are succinctly summarized in the following sentence from the Hagel/Brown web report. "Rather than 'push,' this new approach focuses on 'pull' – creating platforms that help people to mobilize appropriate resources when the need arises." Push models are "script oriented" and thrive in stable environments with little uncertainty. Forecasting, as in demand forecasting, is key in push environments and allows high levels of efficiency to be developed in business processes. Pull models are more amenable to uncertain business conditions that require compressed development times for new goods and services. The pull model represents service architecture at the enterprise level, and could properly be viewed as *enterprise service architecture.*

The pull model is a profound concept, since most services are client initiated.

E-Services

Every year, businesses spend millions of dollars on their IT infrastructure, consisting of hardware, system software, applications, networks, people, and other organizational assets. With "on demand" computing, they can plug into the wall, figuratively, speaking, and only pay for the IT services they use. The concept is called *utility computing* that is accessed as are most public utilities. We are going to refer to the utility computing concept as *E-services.* An E-service utility is a viable option for the provisioning of computing services.

The concept of E-services is the packaging of computer services as a metered facility without up-front costs for IT infrastructure and is commonly used for large-scale computations or peak demands. In the current view of things, an E-services utility is network based and is dependent upon the Internet as a transport mechanism. In recent years, computing has become the operational medium for business, government, and education and part of everyday life for most people. As with electric utilities, computing utilities have evolved from being a luxury to an everyday necessity.

An E-service utility is characterized by four key factors: necessity, reliability, usability, and scalability. *Necessity* refers to the idea that a preponderance of users depend on the utility to satisfy everyday needs. *Reliability* refers to the expectation that the utility will be available when the user requires it. *Usability* refers to the requirement that the utility is easy and convenience to use – regardless of the complexity of the underlying infrastructure. *Scalability* refers to the fact that the utility has sufficient capacity to allow the users to experience the benefits of an expandable utility that provides economy of scale.

Certainly, modern Internet facilities for search operations that engage thousands of servers satisfy these characteristics.

The notion of "paying for what one uses" is a compelling argument for using E-services for special or all computing needs. However, the proof of the pudding may, in fact, be in the details. The key question is whether the service should be based on a metered model or a subscription model. With the *metered model*, the usage is easily measured, monitored, and verified and lends itself to managerial control on the part of the user. In addition, metering can be applied to differing levels of service. With the *subscription model*, usage is difficult to control and monitor, and its adoption is favored by managers more concerned with convenience than with resource control.

For example, water and electricity service commonly use metered service while the plain ordinarily telephone system "usually" provides subscription service for local service and metered service for long distance. In the area of computer networks, broadband cable and telephone digital-subscriber line (DSL) rates are normally based on the subscription model. With cable TV, on the other hand, there are usually differing levels of subscription service along with "pay per view" for special services.

One can readily conceptualize a scheme for a typical E-service customer – nominally assumed to be a small-to-medium-sized business. Office services, such as word and spreadsheet processing, could be subscription-based service and special applications, such as integrated enterprise systems, would be metered service.

The difference between application services and multi-tenant services may very well be the deciding factor in determining whether metered or subscriber service is the way to go. With *multi-tenant service*, several clients may share the same software with separate data – as in the case of office processing. With *application service*, the service provider supplies one instance of the software per client, thereby lending itself to a form of metered service.

SERVICE BUSINESS CONCEPTS

The new enterprise business model is based on services. The complexity of the modern work environment is perhaps the key factor, as well as the changing demands of a networked economy. The increased level of worldwide incomes has added to the desire for enhanced business and social services. The dependence on information and communications technology (ICT) has been an enabler of the complexity and growth of services by facilitating the connection between suppliers and consumers of services.

Business Model

A *business model* is a representation of a business, emphasizing its purpose, strategies, organization and operational practices, and capabilities. It typically covers the following: core capabilities, partner network, value proposition, customer base, distribution methods, cost structure, and revenue base. One of the functions of a business's organization and operational structures is to translate the business model into an objective reality.

The point of view taken here is that an operational service model is a business model.

Strategy and Mission

A *strategy* has been defined as "A long term plan of action designed to achieve a particular goal," and *governance* as "The set of processes, customs, policies, laws, and institutions affecting the way an endeavor is directed, administered, or controlled." The two subjects command our attention, because much of the economy and workforce are engaged in services; but, as we have alluded to before, we seem to know the least about what we do the most.

The basic tenet underlying strategy is that a principal entity desires to accomplish something worthwhile called a *mission*. A mission is required so the entity, be it a business, government agency, educational unit, or person, knows where it is going, and a strategy is needed so it knows how to get there. The mission is a service participant's goal, and the strategy is the roadmap for achieving that goal. A *strategy* is a plan of action.

Service Ecosystem Characteristics

Before the revolution in ICT services, the exchange of information was a supporting element in most aspects of economic activity. Through advanced technology, information is now an important component in the value proposition of most services.

The modern enterprise can now exploit informational resources on a demand basis from remote locations and without necessarily owning them. Moreover, the facilities necessary to sustain those resources may be shared, creating innovative opportunities for service provisioning.

Through web sites, mobile computing, and kiosks, self-service channels are currently available to support informational interchange. Business functions, such as billing, payments, ordering and order processing, reservations, online service support, and information management, are currently available without regard to time or distance.

Through innovation and entrepreneurship, new business opportunities are available on an on-demand basis, frequently constructed from existing services.

Strategic Assets

A *strategic asset* is a resource that provides the basis for core competencies, economic benefit, and competitive advantage, thereby enabling a service business to provide distinctive service in the marketplace. Because services are labor intensive, investments in people, processes, knowledge, and infrastructure are directly analogous to investments in resources for production and distribution in capital intensive businesses.

Strategic assets permit a service enterprise to achieve a competitive advantage through service differentiation, cost advantage, and superior customer response. *Service differentiation* involves providing a high degree of uniqueness in the service experience and also in the quality of service provided. *Cost advantage* refers to efficiency in the use of facilities, as in an airline terminal, and with 24/7 operations to maximize the use of infrastructure. *Customer response* involves flexible, reliable, and timely solutions to customer requirements.

Service Context

A *service context* supports the efficacy of service provisioning. The development of a service context involves the asking of tough questions to examine the strategic goal and objectives of a service organization in order to identify and establish a service portfolio. Here are some questions a service organization might want to ask of itself: (ITIL, p.9)

- What services should we offer?
- To whom should the services be offered?
- How do we achieve competitive advantage?
- What is our customer's value proposition?
- How do we establish value for our stakeholders?
- How do we define service quality?
- How do we allocate strategic assets to our service portfolios?
- What are the bottlenecks to growth and effective service provisioning?

The questions apply in differing degrees to whether services are provisioned for one organization (or department), one of more units within the same parent organization, or to units in different organizations. Moreover, the services apply within the following contexts: do them yourself, another business entity helps you do them, and have another business entity do them for you.

Service Perspective

Every reasonable business model demands a context, and the one presented here is no exception. Our service model is based on a service management concept for providing value to customers in the form of capabilities that translate resources into valuable services.

The objective of service provisioning – regardless of whether the service involves people processing, possession processing, or information processing – is to provide value to customers through an intrinsic knowledge of customer needs obtained by preparation, analysis, usage patterns, and the application of best practices. Within this perspective, a *service* may be alternately defined as a means of delivering value to customers by facilitating outcomes customers want to achieve without the ownership of specific costs and risks. (Clark. p. 5)

SERVICE FACTORS

Three factors determine the need for services and the realization of those services. They are: value, flexibility and control, and risk. With regard to the value factor, it is not just value, per se, but value versus cost. When costs are reduced through internal or external outsourcing, for example, there should be concern over whether the value of the service to the client is the same as or greater than before the outsourcing. Using resources and capability as inputs to a service, is the resulting value to the client commensurate with the cost? Similarly, when internal or external outsourcing is implemented, there is concern over operational flexibility and management control. Some organizations have experienced the "tail wagging the dog" syndrome and have had to bring major services, such as IT outsourcing, back into the parent organization. It is very difficult to modify strong service level agreements, so the parent organization is effectively constrained by the very services that were supposed to provide them with business agility. Also, successful outsourcing, in some instances, has been diluted through mergers and acquisition, whereby competing services have been assimilated into a parent organization, effectively comprising the original benefits. Lastly, there is risk inherent in relying on services, even though there is a customary risk to be expected in everyday affairs. The uncertainty in the application of service level agreements works contrary to the expectation on the part of clients to receive a positive effect with the utilization of assets.

Injecting a bit of reality into the analysis, there is always the headache factor. The possibility always exists that outsourcing or calling in a consultant, is a means of relieving an organizational headache – regardless of the cost. Similarly, living with a third party in the form of outsourcing may be too much for some organizations to handle.

Service Creationism

In most views of service theory, there would appear to be service creationist forces at work. Through some unknown process, an enterprise comes to life and ostensibly needs service of some kind. (An *enterprise* for this discussion is a business organization, a governmental department or agency, an educational unit, or almost any other form of profit-or-non-profit socially constructed organization.)

A service organization enters the scene and identifies certain processes associated with the enterprise that it can use to make a profit. It's clear that the target enterprise is the service client, and the service organization is the service provider. The activity on the part of the provider that identifies candidate processes for the proposed benefit of the client is sometimes called service innovation. Usually, service innovation amounts to very little more than an elementary form of observational research. (At this point, we are only considering service innovation.) Product innovation involves other factors, although we can easily make the case that all products are actually services. In general, however, the tasks involved with creating and sustaining a service business usually constitute a rational process. The provider may possess superior capability, as is commonly the case with an IT consulting company that provides a variety of services to less experienced clients who choose to take advantage of the opportunity. The client's resources may be inadequate to effectively perform a particular set of tasks, as in the case of an enterprise that doesn't possess the needed people or technology to solve a particular problem or venture into a new area of endeavor. The client, in either of the cases, may choose to focus on core competency. In this instance, a core competency is a set of activities that affect the mission of the client. The use of services may be purely economic, which is usually the basis for most outsourcing.

Service Evolutionism

On the other hand, a service evolutionist might view the subject of service acquisition in a different manner. With client-side service provisioning, the process of obtaining and deploying services evolves through several identifiable stages of organizational dynamics, based on the three factors presented above, namely value, flexibility, and risk.

Most enterprise processes are comprised of two kinds of activities: core functionality and supporting functionality. In a bank loan department, for example, the lending function is core, and credit checking is supporting. Similarly, in a pension writing department, the synthesis of a pension plan is core, and the back-office computer operations are supplementary. When multiple departments demand the same services, it is a common management decision to combine the service operations and in the process, possibly enhance the level of service. "Kick it up a notch" is the usual justification. This is the first stage, referred to here as the *service recognition stage*.

At this point the emphasis changes from operating a service to using a service on the part of the core departments. The core department is avoiding the risks and costs associated with the supplementary function, since service costs are shared. Let us call this the *risk/cost avoidance* stage.

After the need for non-core services is realized and instantiated, there is a universal tendency to reduce costs – because after all, the services are not core to the mission of the organization – or endeavor to make a profit on the service operation. A decision can be taken at this point to spin off the service department as a self-standing internal or external organization, or outsource the total operation to an outside service firm. It would appear that this is either the *spin off stage* or the *outsource stage*, as the case may be.

There are additional considerations, based on infrastructure and management control. Here are some options:

- Outsource the total operation, including infrastructure, people, and management control
- Retain infrastructure and management control and outsource the people and operations
- Retain infrastructure, management control, and operations and outsource the people
- Outsource certain tasks within any of the above options

Task-oriented outsourcing is perhaps the end game in the relationship between enterprise dynamics and service science. It is commonplace in modern business to have professional and technical tasks, such as engineering, software development, and design, outsourced to specialist firms in much the same way that architectural services have existed for many years.

Service evolutionism represents a client–side view of service provisioning.

SERVICE UNDERPINNINGS

A *service business* is a collection of organizational assets that provide value to clients in the form of services by exploiting inherent capability on two levels: the client level and the provider level. Effective service provisioning permits the client to focus on core competencies.

Value Creation

The value of a service is determined by a client's expectation of service and the client's perception of the service that is experienced. Expectations are developed by word of mouth, personal needs, and past experience. The service that is delivered is a complex combination of five attributes: reliability, responsiveness, assurance, empathy, and tangibles. *Reliability* refers to the consistency of service. *Responsiveness* reflects the perception that the provider is willing to provide service. *Assurance* is a measure of the competence of the service provider. *Empathy* is a reflection of the personal attention afforded to clients. *Tangibles* refers to the infrastructure as it is related to the service experience. The five attributes of service quality reflect a traditional setting and do not take into account the complications associated with technology driven service provisioning.

To this important list, we are going to add availability, capacity, continuity, and security.

Availability, Capacity, Continuity, Security, and Risk

Availability reflects the degree to which services are available for use by clients under terms and conditions agreed upon in a service-level agreement. Clearly, a service is available only if the client can take advantage of it. Accessibility and expectations are major considerations from the user's perspective. The method of access should be made explicit in the service-level agreement and the user's expectations should be managed by the client. (The use of the terms *client* and *user* is intentional. Using the principal/agent model, the client is the principal and the user is the agent.)

Capacity is the ability of the service and the service provider to support the requisite level of business activity of the client. Demand for service must be available within a specified range and the service provider must be able to supply service provisioning during peak periods in a shared environment.

Continuity refers to the ability on the part of the service provider to support capacity during disruptive and catastrophic events. Continued service is not the only consideration. Alternate and backup facilities in the form of services must be in the service landscape.

Security refers to controls to assure that client assets will be safe from intrusion, disclosure, and physical destruction. Security refers to operational security *and* to the physical safeguard of client assets.

Availability, capacity, continuity, and security collectively determine the client's risk in acquiring services and assist in differentiating between service providers. When comparing the cost and value of services, risk should be factored into the equation.

Service Assets

Engaging in a business service would appear to be quite straightforward on the surface, but is actually a complex arrangement of business units, service units, services that connect the two, and provider types. The abstract term *business units* refers to the provider assets that give value to the client when applied. Similarly, *service assets* refer to the functions that the provider can perform. It follows that a *business service* is a mapping between the provider and the client, in much the same way that we ordinarily conceptualize the physician/patient relationship.

Service Portfolio

A *service portfolio* is a conceptual collection or list of services. Use of the term is intended to be analogous to a financial portfolio of investment instruments. However, there are major differences depending upon the *raison d'etre* of the portfolio.

A financial portfolio is ordinarily thought to be a collection of assets synthesized so that when the value of one asset goes down, another goes up. This is a bit of a simplification, but it's the idea that counts. The best case is when the value of all of the assets goes up, and the worst case is when the value of all of the assets goes down. Normal life is somewhere in between. With a service portfolio, there shouldn't be a downside, but some service firms do some things better than others.

With services, the *raison d'etre* of the portfolio depends on whether you are talking to a provider or a client. A provider portfolio might be a simple list of services – something an accounting firm might have as part of their marketing collateral. An IT consulting business, for example, could list items such as strategy formulation, service programming, and operations management.

From the client perspective, however, a service portfolio in indispensable, because it provides a central source of services agreed to in conjunction with the service provider, along with terms, conditions, and service metrics. A related concern is a database of potential suppliers of services.

OPERATIONS FRAMEWORK

An *operations framework* is a set of service management functions (SMFs) established as best practices that assist in providing business value to a client. They should be organized and staffed by internal and external providers involved in IT-based or non-IT-based service operations. The service functions definitely have an IT flavor to them but apply to all provisioning in the services domain. Collectively, the SMFs agree with the ITIL compendium of best practices. ITIL stands for Information Technology Infrastructure Library. It is a set of best practices for IT Services Management (ITSM). Each of the generic SMFs is briefly summarized.

Service-Level Management

A service-level agreement (SLA) is a formal and signed agreement between the service provider organization and the business unit to document expectations and requirements of a service delivered to the business unit from the service provider. The agreement aligns business needs with delivery of services and facilitates delivery of solutions to business requirements at acceptable cost. It involves a definition of requirements, an agreement on specifications, operations management expectations, and a review clause. The tasks include the creation of a service catalog, the development of internal procedures, the ability to monitor and respond to operational conditions, and the ability to perform regular service-level reviews. The service catalog delineates the priority of service-level tasks, the expected effect on employees, a description of users, a listing and description of service assets, and the organization's business partners and suppliers. Service-level monitoring is a key issue. The major service metrics are availability, responsiveness, performance, integrity and accuracy, and security incidents. In order to perform the service-level monitoring, the following steps are required: the identification and criteria for monitoring, establishing thresholds, the definition of alert, the specification of alert management, and essential response definition.

Service-level determination and management is the key element in a service package.

Availability Management

Availability management is the service management function that insures that a given service consistently and effectively delivers the level of support required by the customer. Continuity of service is the key objective. The usual risks to availability relate to technology, business processes, operational procedures, and human error. Countermeasures that have proven to improve availability are testing of business processes, effective release procedures, and employee training. The areas most affected by availability issues are the implementation of new IT services, critical business functions, supplier behavior, and internal organizational factors, such as policies, procedures, and tools.

Capacity Management

Capacity management is the service management function that optimizes the capability of the service infrastructure and supporting organization to deliver the required level of customer service in the established time domain. Capability of service is the key objective. This SMF is most affected by people, infrastructure, and technology.

Service-Desk Management

The service desk ia a single point of contact for customers and service technicians with the intent of delivering responsive solutions to service needs. The major service desk functions are to handle single incidents and individual service requests. Service desk scheduling has historically been a concern, and the current trend is to have self-managed teams that utilize service triads or peak period scheduling. A *triad* consists of a three person team, with two people on and one off at any time.

Incident Management

The objective of incident management is to detect events that disrupt or prevent execution of critical or normal IT services, and to respond to those events with methods of restoring normal services as quickly as possible. An *incident* is any event that is not part of the standard operation of a business process that causes, or may cause, an interruption to, or reduction in, the quality of service. In this context, a *problem* is the root cause of an incident; a *solution* is a method for resolving an incident or problem that resolves the underlying cause; and a *workaround* is a means of restoring a specific incident without resolving the underlying cause.

Problem Management

The objective of problem management is to investigate and analyze the root causes of incidents and initiate changes to service assets to resolve the underlying problem. The key function of problem management is to reduce the impact of incidents, problems, and errors on the organization by applying methods of root cause and trend analysis.

Change Management

The objective of change management is to provide a formal process for introducing changes to the service environment with a minimal amount of disruption to normal service operations while insuring the integrity of critical business functions. Change management preferably goes through several distinct steps: change initiation, change request, change classification, change authorization, release management, and review by a change board.

Relationship of Key Processes

Incident management is focused on restoring normal service and identifies resolution actions; problem management is focused on the identification and resolution of underlying problems and their root causes; and change management deploys changes developed by incident or problem management.

Directory-Services Management

The service directory is a database of service assets. Directory services is essentially a database from which users can obtain information on service assets through a secure and organized process that is accessible through appropriate information and communications technology (ICT) facilities. The major directory service functions are to record change events, describe connectivity, track service objects, and identify assets in the service landscape.

GOVERNANCE

A typical organization has a group of stakeholders who have something to gain if the organization is successful and something to lose if the organization is not successful. The gain could be financial in nature, as in the case of investors, or qualitative in nature, as in the case of non-profit or social organizations. Success or failure is a relative assessment, as is the concept of gain or loss on the part of the stakeholders. The stakeholders, often referred to as the *principles*, give the right to manage the organization to *agents*, ostensibly qualified to do so, and who are rewarded accordingly, through the application of policies and rules that represent the principle's best interests. The process is generally known as governance, a word derived from the Latin verb "to steer." Agents are often high-level or middle-level managers and administrators that derive short and long-term monetary gains that are directly related to the organization's success. There are as many forms of governance as there are organizations to control. Even though the words are similar, governance does not imply local, regional, or central government.

The principles of effective corporate governance are well-defined and usually implemented through "boards of directors" and other governing bodies. Governance is usually related to consistent management, cohesive policies, and effective decision rights. Information technology (IT) governance is generally regarded as a subset of corporate governance, as it relates to the operational management of IT systems. IT governance deals primarily with the connection between business focus and IT management and often involves the organization's IT application portfolio. IT governance is an important consideration in corporate governance because of the typically large budgets for IT infrastructure. *Service governance* is a subset of IT governance that assures the principals that the development and use of services are executed according to best practices.

Two important factors relate to service governance. The first factor involves the high-level of outsourcing of IT functionality and infrastructure. The main concern is the loss of control to an external service provider, and also the long-term loss of capability in critical areas of competence. The second factor is in the evolution to service-oriented architecture for the development of business/enterprise applications. The synthesis of applications from components accessed over the Internet from external service providers constitutes a long-term dependency with which many principals are not comfortable. In this case, the principals may want to use service governance as a means of protecting the long-term interest and possibly the intellectual capital of the parent organization.

QUICK SUMMARY

The main objective of this paper is to present an overview of the dynamically changing boundary of the modern enterprise, based on a portfolio of services. The overview is summarized in the following entries.

1. There are three forces operating in the sphere of service processes. The first is the use of ICT as an enabler in providing revenue growth, efficiency, and effectiveness for traditional and enhanced services, as well as for conventional business processes. This subject is commonly referred to as information systems. The second is the consulting services domain that provides IT services to external organizations. The third is the use of ICT to manage information systems and services, which is a field of endeavor known as IT Services Management. Briefly said, it is the use of computers to manage the enterprise and also to manage itself.

2. The notion of service has its origin in ancient times and was understood to mean "one person doing something for another." With the advent of civilization and industrialization, the definition of service was implicitly extended to encompass "one person doing something for an organization," usually in the form of employment. At this stage, specialization and entrepreneurship kicked in with all of their rights and

privileges, resulting in what we now recognize as the service organization.

3. Information is a critical asset in the operation of an enterprise and in the everyday lives of individuals. In a figurative sense, information is the grease that allows the components to work together. IT is employed to handle the information needed to manage the operations of an enterprise and to aid in making effective decisions. Thus, IT is a service to the enterprise, regardless if that enterprise is concerned with production processes, service operations, government reporting, professional services, scientific services, technical services, or personal services.

4. There are several aspects of IT services that can vary between organizations. Examples are commonplace: computer operations, network management, hardware and software acquisition, system analysis and design, software design, software development, information systems integration, and call center and help desk operation and management. This is a representative set of tasks necessary for sustaining an IT services organization. You can do them yourself; you can have another business entity help you do them; or you can have a business entity do them for you. In the latter two cases, the business process is known as *IT service outsourcing*.

5. The service lifecycle consists of five important elements, listed as follows: Service Strategy, Service Design, Service Transition, Service Operation, and Continuous Improvement.

6. Service quality is a complex arrangement of client expectations, client education, business value, and business utility. It is elusive because clients usually cannot assess quality until after a service event has been completed. Service providers present quality as adherence to standard operating procedures. Service clients view service quality based on expectations and value creation.

7. Every year, businesses spend millions of dollars on their IT infrastructure consisting of hardware, system software, applications, networks, people, and other organizational assets. With "on demand" computing, they can plug into the wall, figuratively speaking, and only pay for the IT services they use. The concept is called *utility computing* that is accessed as most public utilities. We are going to name the utility computing concept as *e-Services*.

8. A *business model* is a representation of a business emphasizing its purpose, strategies, organization and operational practices, and capabilities. It typically covers the following: core capabilities, partner network, value proposition, customer base, distribution methods, cost structure, and revenue base.

9. A *strategy* has been defined as "A long term plan of action designed to achieve a particular goal," and *governance* as "The set of processes, customs, policies, laws, and institutions affecting the way an endeavor is directed, administered, or controlled."

10. A *strategic asset* is a resource that provides the basis for core competencies, economic benefit, and competitive advantage, thereby enabling a service business to provide distinctive service in the marketplace. Because services are labor intensive, investments in people, processes, knowledge, and infrastructure are directly analogous to investments in resources for production and distribution in capital intensive businesses.

11. The objective of service provisioning – regardless of whether the service involves people processing, possession processing, or information processing – is to provide value to customers through an intrinsic knowledge of customer needs obtained by preparation,, analysis, usage patterns, and the application of best practices. Within this perspective, a *service* may be alternately defined as a means of delivering

value to customers by facilitating outcomes customers want to achieve without the ownership of specific costs and risks.

12. The objective of a service business is to assist in making resources available to the client as services, and in the process, creating value for both provider and client. The value of a service is determined by a client's expectation of service and the client's perception of the service that is experienced. Expectations are developed by word of mouth, personal needs, and past experience. The service that is delivered is a complex combination of five attributes: reliability, responsiveness, assurance, empathy, and tangibles.

REFERENCES

1   Carter, S., The *New Language of Business*, Upper Saddle River, NJ: IBM Press, 2007.

2   Cherbakov, L., et al, "Impact of service orientation at the business level", *IBM Systems Journal*, Vol. 44, No. 4, 2005.

3   Clark, J., *Everything you ever wanted to know about ITIL® in less than one thousand words! Connect Sphere Limited, www.connectsphere.com,* 2007.

4   Collier, D. and J. Evans, *Operations Management: Goods, Services, and Value Chains*, Mason OH: Thomson Higher Education, 2007.

5   Fitzsimmons, J.A. and M.J. Fitzsimmons, *Service Management: Operations, Strategy, Information Technology* (6th Edition), New York: McGraw-Hill/ Irwin, 2008.

6   Ganek, A. and K. Kloeckner, "An overview of IBM Service Management," *IBM Systems Journal*, Vol. 46, No. 3, 2007.

7   Hagel, J. and J.S. Brown, *From Push to Pull: Emerging Models for Mobilizing Resources*, www.edgeperspectives.com, 2007.

8   Heizer, J. and B. Render, *Operations Management* (8th Edition), Upper Saddle River, NJ: Pearson Prentice-Hall, 2006.

9   Hurwitz, J., Bloor, R., Baroudi, C., and M. Kaufman, *Service Oriented Architecture for Dummies*, Hoboken, NJ: Wiley Publishing, Inc., 2007.

10 ITIL, *Service Strategy*, London: The Stationary Office, 2007.

11 itSMF, *An Introductory Overview of ITIL® V3*, itSMF Ltd,, 2007.

12 Katzan, H., *A View of Services Science*, Southeast Decision Science Institute, Savannah, GA, February 21-23, 2007.

13 Katzan, H., "Foundations of Service Science: Management and Business" *Journal of Service Science*, 1(2): 1-16, 2008.

14 Katzan, H., *Service Science: Concepts, Technology, Management*, New York: iUniverse, Inc., 2008.

15 Krafzig, D., Banke, K., and D. Slama, *Enterprise SOA: Service-Oriented Architecture Best Practices*, Upper Saddle River, NJ: Prentice Hall, 2005.

16 Metters, R., King-Metters, K., Pullman, M., and S Walton, *Successful Service Operations Management* (2e), Boston: Thomson Course Technology, 2006.

17 *Microsoft Operations Framework (MOF)*, TechNet publication, Microsoft Corporation, www.microsoft.com/MOF, 2008.

18 Nichols, M., "Quality Tools in a Service Environment," www.ASQ.org, 2007.

19 Rappa, M.A., "The utility business model and the future of computing services," *IBM Systems Journal*, Vol. 43, No. 1, 2004.

20 Wikipedia, *Business Models*, www.wikipedia.com, 2008.

21 Wikipedia, *Corporate Governance*, www.wikipedia.com, 2008.

22 Wikipedia, *Governance*, www.wikipedia.com, 2008.

23 Wikipedia, *Information Technology Governance*, www.wikipedia.com, 2008.

24 Wikipedia, *Software as a Service*, www.wikipedia.com, 2008.

25 Wikipedia, *Strategy*, www.wikipedia.com, 2008.

26 Wikipedia, *Thinking Processes*, www.wikipedia.com, 2008.

27 Woods, D. and T. Mattern, *Enterprise SOA: Designing IT for Business Innovation*, Sebastopol, CA: O'Reilly Media Inc., 2006.

***** End of Chapter 7 *****

8

SERVICE TECHNOLOGY

SERVICE TECHNOLOGY CONCEPTS

The basis of service technology is really straightforward. Clients and providers communicate with one another through the use of messages and contracts, and in many areas of service, the communication involves information and communications technology (ICT). A client and a provider can be tightly coupled, as when a patient is sitting in front of the doctor and they are having a give-and-take conversation, or loosely coupled, as when you send a request to someone via email and receive a response at some undetermined time in the future. In the former case, the client and provider are communicating in a *synchronous mode* without technology, and in the latter case, they are communicating in an *asynchronous mode* with the use of technology. The *contract* is a formal or informal agreement that delineates the service in which the client and provider are engaged. The contract can be a formal document, an informal agreement, or be implicit in the activity under consideration. Another view of a contract is that it is a specification of how to use a service and what to expect from a service. This essay is quite technical and can be omitted, based on the needs of the individual reader.

Messaging Basics

Each service event requires at least one message, and each message requires a context, which gives meaning to the interaction. Entities that participate in a service-oriented message are called the message sender, the message intermediary, and the message receiver. When you fire up your Internet browser, for example, and enter a World Wide Web address, such as www.ibm.com, the browser sends a message to the IBM server somewhere out in cyberspace. The browser, acting on your behalf, as the client of the Web service, is the message sender. The IBM web site is the message receiver. When IBM sends its home page back to be rendered for you by your browser, the roles are reversed; it is the sender and your browser is the receiver, and the Internet is the message intermediary. The *message* is the glue that ties a service together.

Conceptual Model of Service Processing

The most profound aspect of service science is that a *service is a process*, as suggested by the following message pattern:

1. A client sends a message to a service provider.
2. The provider performs the required action and returns a message to the client.

The focus is on the data that is transmitted and not on the communications medium, which can take the form of a human interaction or a computer-based message. The context for the message can be embedded in the message or it can be inherent in the way that the service provider is addressed. The importance of context is suggested by the cartoon floating around where two dogs are seated in front of a computer screen. One dog says to the other, "On the Internet, no one knows you're a dog." Two good rules of thumb are that in face-to-face services, interpersonal communication provides the context. In human-to-computer services, the context must be inherent in the message. For example, entering "Boston Red Sox" into your browser to get the score of the last World Series game is probably going to generate a lot of miscellaneous information in which you are not interested, because you provided no context.

Initially, it is useful to recognize that we are operating at two levels: the service level and the message level. At the *service level*, the message entity that receives the message is the service provider and is regarded simply as the **service**. At the *message level*, there is some choreography involved with providing a service, as demonstrated by the above two-step interaction. In fact, a service may involve the interchange of several messages.

Enterprise Service Technology

Many modern enterprises (i.e., business, government, education) provide computer support to internal users, clients, business partners, and other enterprise entities. The facilities are usually integrated into administrative, product development, supply chain, or customer relationship operations. Because those services, consisting of computer applications and associated procedures, are tried, tested, and dependable, it would be prudent to use them as building blocks for new enterprise applications.

The concept that underlies service orientation is that it is simply more efficient and reliable in identifying the bundled services and packaging them as reusable components than it would be to rewrite them. Bundled services could then be used by other services, so that information system applications could be developed more rapidly and enable the enterprise to be more responsive to external conditions. This practice is the basis of web services that are covered in this paper.

A typical business function that lends itself to componentization is to perform a credit check on a prospective customer before confirming a large order. Such a check is normally performed in different operational systems in an enterprise. After restructuring, the credit check software is packaged as a single business component and exposed as an enterprise service for use by other enterprise service applications.

SERVICE MESSAGING

When two service entities are engaged in communication, they are regarded as being *connected*. An enterprise has two options for developing a service connection:

1. Message entity to message entity (ME→ME)
2. Message entity to enterprise entity (ME→EE)

The first option, denoted by ME → ME, refers to either a client-to-provider or a provider-to-client communication. The second option denoted by ME →EE refers to a client-to-many-provider communication. The notion of connectedness is needed for an appreciation of message patterns and topologies, covered in the next section. For example, the ME→ME option may represent the case where an order-processing application sends a message to a shipping application to have an item shipped to a customer. The ME→EE option might represent the case where an airline's flight operations application sends a message to other involved computer applications, such as scheduling and reservations, when a plane has taken off.

Message Patterns

A *message pattern* is a model of service communications that represents a single connection between one sender and one receiver. There are three basic patterns representing message traffic that can go only one way, both ways but only one way at a time, and both ways simultaneously.

The one-way message flow is regarded as a "fire-and-forget-it" send, also known as *simplex* and *datagram* communications service in the computer community. The second model is the request/

reply model, known as *half duplex*, wherein only one participant communicates at a time as with the walkie-talkie type of interaction. In the final model, called *full duplex*, both messaging participants can send messages at the same time, as in an ordinary telephone conversation. Clearly, messaging can take on different patterns depending upon the operational environment used for technical support.

Message Structure

In its simplist form, a message is a string of characters encoded using standardized coding methods commonly employed in computer and information technology. Messages have a uniform format consisting of a header and a body. The *header* primarily concerns addressing and includes the addresses of the sender and the receiver. In the request/reply message pattern, the return address is picked up from the message header for the response portion of the transaction. The *body* of the message contains the information content of the message, and because it is intended only for the receiver, is not usually regarded during message transmission.

The manner in which messages are structured is similar to the way that letters are handled by the postal service. The outside of the envelope contains addressing information and the insides are handled as private information.

Message Topology

Message topology refers to the manner in which messages are sent between messaging participants, and not necessarily to the communication techniques used to send them. The most widely used form of communication is known as *point-to-point* using any of the message patterns given above. Usually, point-to-point implies the request/reply message pattern where the reply address is picked up from the message header. A variation to point-to-point is *forward-only point-to-point* where a message reply is not expected.

Message Interactions

In most cases of messaging, the sending participant needs to know that the receiving participant is listening before the real message is transmitted. It is something like the following:

> Sender: Are you listening?
> Receiver: Yes.
> Sender: Are you Gregory Charles Cabot?
> Receiver: Yes.
> Sender: You've just won one million dollars.

OK, it's a bit contrived and also, it's messaging at the service level. There is also handshaking going on at the message level, which we are going to cover in the next section.

The following example demonstrates message interaction through instant messaging at the service level. It demonstrates message interactions. (This example is adapted from Van Slyke and Bélanger, p. 110.) For this instance, **User A** is sending an instant message to **User B** who responds to **User A.** The interaction consists of four distinct messages, delineated as follows:

> Message 1: User A logs on to the instant messaging (IM) server. The expected response is that the IM server will return a message from the users in A's group that are currently logged on. The message goes from User A through the Internet to the IM server.

> Message 2: The IM server sends a message to User A with the members that are logged on. The message goes from the IM server to User A.

> Message 3: User A sends a message, such as "Hi User B," to User B. The message goes from User A through

the Internet to the IM server. The IM server then sends the message through the Internet to User B.

Message 4: User B responds with a message, such as "Hi yourself," to User A. The message goes through the Internet to the IM server. Then the IM server sends the message through the Internet to User A.

Most people would regard this interaction sequence in which User A sends an instant message to User B as a service and B's response to A as another service. Popping up a level, the service provider is the instant messaging server and users A and B are clients.

SERVICES ON THE INTERNET AND THE WORLD WIDE WEB

A service that takes place on the Internet and the World Wide Web is called a *web service*. A web service is a process in which the provider and client interact to produce a value; it is a pure service. The only difference between a web service and medical provisioning, for example, is that in the former case, the client and provider are computer systems. Ordinary email is a web service. Requesting a home page from a provider's web site is a web service. Sending an instant message over the Internet is a web service. Almost anything you can think of doing on the web would be called a web service. However, there is another category of service known as a Web Service. Note that Web Service is a proper noun. It is a formal process, developed by organizations such as Microsoft, Apple, and others, for conducting business over the Internet. It is covered separately.

Simple Mail Model

The most pervasive web service computer application on the Internet is electronic mail, commonly known as email. It is used in two ways: (1) To communicate between email clients; and (2) To provide a record that communication has taken place – or at least, to show that an attempt at communication has taken place. Clearly, email is designed to be a person-to-person endeavor. There are two scenarios that are relevant to web services.

In the first scenario, we have a desktop personal computer (PC) operating as an email client – referred to as a PC running an email client – from which the end user sends and receives email. The email client is connected to incoming and outgoing email servers through a local-area network or a dial-up, broadband cable, or DSL connection to an Internet service provider (ISP) that is in turn connected to the mail servers. Email messages are normally managed locally, which means they are downloaded and stored on the end user's computer. When the end user decides to access email messages, he or she presses a receive button and incoming messages, stored on the incoming email server, are transferred to the local email client. Similarly, when the end user constructs a message for sending, a send key is pressed to transfer it to the outgoing email server for subsequent forwarding over the Internet. An email client uses push technology to send email messages and pull technology to receive email messages.

In the second scenario, we again have an email client for message management. The email client, however, is connected to an email-service server via the Internet through a local browser. The service access point is an account set up on an Internet service portal. A web based email account is used in the same manner as in the local scenario, except that the email server is remote.

The concept of a remote service server is also a platform for other web applications, such as word processing and spreadsheet operations. A remote service server that provides application functionality is known as an *application service provider*, and exists as an alternative to purchasing infrequently used software.

Service Model for the World Wide Web

When addressing a web service, there is a certain way that most people go about doing things. It's not entirely clear whether the web service architecture determines how people use the web or, the other way around, whether the architecture of the web reflects how people use it. We are calling it a generic web services model.

Imagine the following scenario. You're interested in purchasing a pair of running shoes and don't know any brands or web sites. So what do you do? You point your browser to a search engine, such as Google™, enter the words "running shoes" in the search window and click the "search" button or press the enter key. Your message is sent to Google's web server that searches an index of key words, created beforehand, and makes a list of appropriate web sites, just for you. The web server then prepares your list in a language called HTML and sends it back to your browser over the Internet. The browser then renders the HTML statements into a readable form. This is an example of the first element in the web services model. It's known as *discovery*. The service process was accomplished without regard to time, distance, or the kind of hardware and software.

Each of the entries (known as a "hit") on the resultant running-shoe list gives a brief description and a *hyperlink* with which to obtain more definitive information. This process reflects the second element in the web services model, and it is known as *description*. Various enterprises have web sites and associated web pages containing descriptive information of interest. In a separate operation, the organization behind the search engine searches the web sites in cyberspace and prepares indexes for fast retrieval.

If your goal is information, then this is perhaps as far as you will go with this example. If you are going to make a purchase over the web using an appropriate site, then the next step is to *bind* to that web site and go through an interactive process for selection, payment, and delivery. Each step in the bind process requires additional web services, so that a web service is essentially a cascading series of other web services.

A variety of tools and techniques are required for a successful implementation of web services architecture. Whenever there is a service, there is communication; and whenever there is communication, there are messages. Whenever there is a message, there is a context so that the intent of the service can be sustained. These elements are present in one form or another in all services, ranging from the more straightforward human interaction to the operation of a sophisticated enterprise computer application.

HyperText Transfer Protocol

HyperText Transfer Protocol (HTTP) is a collection of rules and procedures for transferring messages between computers over the World Wide Web. Without HTTP, the web would not be the revolutionary phenomena that it is today. When you make a service request over the web, your entry goes through your browser before it goes over the Internet. Here's how.

When you fire up your browser, you are initiating the execution of a program that runs on your personal computer, workstation, personal digital assistant (PDA), cell phone, terminal – or whatever you choose to use. Now that computing device is performing a service for you in the sense that you can now do things you could not possibly do without it. In fact, you could run all manner of programs, such as productivity software that does word processing, without any information leaving or entering your local environment. As far as the Internet is concerned, however, essentially nothing has happened. You type a URL into your browser window and press the enter key, and then things start to happen. This is when HTTP gets into the act.

Your browser prepares a message called a HTTP request, such as

GET /index.html HTTP/1.1
Host: www.example.com

and sends it over the Internet to the web server of the "example.com" web site somewhere out in cyberspace. The web server responds in turn to the return address obtained from your message header with

> HTTP/1.1 200 OK
> Date: Mon, 02 Dec 2007 12:38:34 GMT
> Server: Apache/1.3.27 (Unix) (Red-Hat/Linux)
> Last-Modified: Wed, 08 Jan 2003 23:11:55 GMT
> Etag: „3f80f-1b6-3e1cb03b"
> Accept-Ranges: bytes
> Content-Length: 155
> Connection: close
> Content-Type: text/html; charset=UTF-8

This response message is followed by a blank line and then the requested information that represents the contents of the file (usually the default file, such as index.html) from the site specified in the HTTP get request. The information content of the response message might take the form (highly unlikely but possible):

```
<html>
  <head>
    <title>Hello World</title>
  </head>
  <body>
    <h1>Hello World</h1>
    <par>
    Greetings from Cyberspace
    </par>
  </body>
</html>
```

that would be rendered by your browser and displayed on your screen. The text is transmitted in a well-known language peculiar to the web and known as HyperText Markup Language (HTML). It is introduced in the next section.

The *HyperText Transfer Protocol* has additional verbs, such as POST, PUT, and DELETE, that facilitate the transfer of messages between a client computer and a server computer.

HYPERTEXT MARKUP LANGUAGE

Aside from the Internet information super highway and the idea of linking information pages together (i.e., the World Wide Web), probably the coolest thing that has ever happened in the over-hyped world of computers, is the realization that it is possible to send a document from one computer to another and have that document displayed on the receiving end in a reasonable form without regard to the brand and model of computer, kind of software, time of day, and location. This amazing feat – and it is truly that – is possible because of hypertext markup language (HTML), as introduced in the previous section. We are interested in HTML for two important reasons. First, it is a useful thing to know something about, as long as you don't get hung up in the details. Secondly, HTML is a forerunner to Extensible Markup Language (XML) that is a technology for sending messages between services.

HTML Documents

To start off, an HTML document is nothing more than a bunch of characters that someone has entered into a text editor or a word processor and saved as a file on a computer employed as a web server. When you request an answer from a web site, such as the one and only www.ibm.com, the corresponding web server goes to a default file named index.html, retrieves the HTML file, and sends it back to your browser for rendering on your computer's display. It is someone's job to put the right stuff into index.html, and that stuff should be written in HTML. Now the file named index.html might have links to other pages that are returned in a similar manner when you click on them.

Those links are referred to as *hot links,* because we get some action when we click on them – as we just mentioned. You can even put programs into an HTML document. These programs are executed by your browser resulting in some visual or audio activity on the receiving end. The active behavior can result in a wide variety of audio, video, and data-oriented interactive forms.

Tags

The basis of an HTML is a tag, such as <html>, that provides information to the receiving browser. In the case of <html>, for example, the tag indicates the beginning of an HTML document. Actually, a tag is only a strong suggestion, since each browser has a mind of its own. Most tags have an enclosing tag, such as </html>, that delineates a section of a document, such as in the following HTML snippet:

```
<html>
  <head>
    <title>University of the United States</title>
  </head>
  <body>
    •
    •  ←--- The content goes here
    •
  </body>
</html>
```

Tags give an HTML document structure and information on page rendering; they do not give meaning. We will use XML for that.

Discovery

One of the key aspects of web page design is to facilitate discovery, whereby clients can find services. Search engine companies use a technique known as "web crawling" in which a program called a *web crawler* or a *bot* (for robot) crawls through web pages following hyperlinks to build indexes for subsequent search operations. Without additional information, all words in a web page are treated the same. You can add additional information to the "head" section to increase the fidelity of searching and increase the chances that a user will navigate to your web site.

This is where the <meta> tag comes in. With the meta tag, web page designers commonly supply three types of descriptive items: a list of keywords, a description, and the name of the web page owner – sometimes the name of an organization and sometimes an author. Search bots use this information when building indexes. The following example depicts the use of meta tags:

```
<html>
  <head>
    <title>Savannah Motor Works</title>
    <meta name="keywords" content="Porsche, Mercedes, BMW">
    <meta name="description" content="The south's most prestigious
          performance car dealership">
    <meta name="author" content="Gregory Cabot">
  </head>
  <body>
    •
    •
    •
  </body>
</html>
```

Actually, there are no predefined meta tags in HTML, so a web page designer can create them to satisfy a particular need. The meta tag demonstrates a tag without an enclosing tag.

Document Elements

The HTML language has an extensive vocabulary that is a subject in its own right. A brief subset of HTML features is covered here as a forerunner to Extensible Markup Language (XML) that is used to construct messages between clients and service providers. Some of the most commonly used document elements are <h1> through <h6>, <p>, <b>, <i>, <br>, and <hr>, which represent headings, paragraph, bold face, italics, blank line, and horizontal rule, respectively. Several of these elements are depicted in the following script:

```
<html>
  <head>
    <title>My First Novel</title>
  </head>
  <body bgcolor="yellow">
    <h1 align="center">The Car</h1>
    <p align="center"> <i>by</i> </p>
    <p align="center"> <b>Gregory Cabot</b></p>
    <p> My uncle gave me my first car. It was a 1939 Chevy
    with fluid
    drive. It had a flat tire and the brakes didn't work. It
    also had a
    broken window.
    </p>
    <p> My father taught me how to do the repairs and I
    had to do them.
    Afterwards, I didn't like the car and sold it for $50.
    </p>
    <hr>
    <p align="center">The End</p>
  </body>
</html>
```

Of course, complete comprehension is not necessary or even expected. However, the key point has been made that HTML is a powerful tool in the construction and communication of web-based documents.

EXTENSIBLE MARKUP LANGUAGE

To put the virtues of HTML and XML into perspective, we can properly say that HTML is used to describe web pages and XML is used to describe information. XML stands for eXtensible Markup Language. Both languages use markup, a term that ostensibly is intended to imply that someone prepares a document and then incorporates descriptive elements to suggest how the document should look when displayed *or* to communicate the intended meaning of the document. With XML, markup gives semantic information as suggested by the following script:

```
<?xml version="1.0" ?>
<library>
  <library_name>Pleasure Books</ library_name>
  <book>
    <title>The DaVinci Code</title>
    <author>Dan Brown</author>
  </book>
  <book>
    <title>The Secret Servant</title>
    <author>Daniel Silva</author>
  </book>
</library>
```

We will call the semantic information "tags" as we did with HTML, even though XML specialists refer to them as "element type names." An XML document must contain a prolog and at least one enclosing document element. In the above example, the following statement is the prolog:

<?xml version="1.0" ?>and the enclosing document element is:

<library>

•

•

•

</library>

This is an example of a main element that must be present in all XML documents. It is often referred to as the *root element*, and it is the characteristic that gives an XML document a hierarchical structure. All opening tags in XML, such as <book>, must have closing tags, such as </book>. With XML, we can make up our own tags, since we are using the language to describe information that has a specific meaning.

Rendering an XML Document

Even though an XML document, by definition, is intended for communication, we can display the contents in a particular form by using a stylesheet. To use a stylesheet, we have to extend the prolog with a statement of the form:

<?xml:stylesheet href="library.css" type="text/css" ?>
and develop a stylesheet description file, named library.css in this example, that would have descriptive content, such as the following:

library_name {
        display: block;
        font: bold 24pt;
}

```
title {
        margin-top: 20px;
        display: block;
        font: italic 18pt;
}
author {
        display: block;
        font: 12pt;
}
```

A rendering of the penultimate XML document would be achieved with the library.css stylesheet file.

Additional XML Features

There is a lot more to the XML language, such as a formal means of defining data types and stylistic structures for XML documents along with a whole host of operational facilities. If it would take one book to totally describe HTML, it would take two books to fully give the features in XML. For a basic knowledge of service science, complete comprehension of XML is not needed – only an idea of what it is all about.

At this point, we have enough knowledge of service tools and techniques to proceed with Web Services, introduced in the next section. We are going to start with a specification of the XML grammar for a form of web messaging known as SOAP, which was initially an acronym for Simple Object Access Protocol.

WEB SERVICES

A Web Service has been defined as any service that is available over the Internet, uses a standard XML messaging system, and is not dependant upon any one particular operating system. (See E. Cerami, *Web Services Essentials* (Selected Reading), for much of the subject matter in this section.) This statement has the makings of something different from the "web service" that was presented earlier when discussing HTTP. Well, it is. Earlier, we described the human web wherein an end-user sends an informational request via HTTP to a web server, and the requested information is returned, also via HTTP, to the user's browser for visual display. In this section, we are going to cover the automated web, in which one computer sends information, in the form of an XML document, to another computer over the Internet, and the intended result is to initiate a service of some kind. The latter form is a well-defined web service model such that the name Web Service is a proper noun. It is important to mention that XML is used for things other than Web Services. In just so happens that they grew up together, so that they are naturally associated with one another.

Web Service Concepts

There are two general approaches to using a Web Service. The first is to have one computer (*the sender*) send a simple message to a second computer (*the receiver*) to have the receiver execute a procedure for the sender and return the result. The procedure is known as a *method* and the process is referred to as an XML-RPC, which stands for *XML-Remote Procedure Call*. A frequently used example to demonstrate the concept is the weather service application: a requester sends a zip code to the weather service program and the program (i.e., the method) returns the temperature. The initial request message can be written in XML as:

```
<?xml version="1.0"?>
<weatherRPC>
    <weatherMethod>getTemperature</weatherMethod>
    <parameters>
       <zip_code>29909</zip_code>
    </ parameters >
```

```
        </weatherRPC>
```

The example is conceptual and the message headers and other information are omitted. The response from the weather service would take the form:

```
<?xml version="1.0"?>
<weatherResponse>
  <parameters>
    <value><int>75</int></value>
  </parameters>
</weatherResponse>
```

XML-RPC can be implemented via an HTTP request/response or by embedding the informational content of the transaction in a SOAP message, which is the second approach.

SOAP is a protocol for exchanging information between computers where the structure of the information is represented in XML. The basic idea underlying SOAP messaging is to make sure that programs running on two communicating computer platforms have the capability of understanding each other. Accordingly, the XML element definitions from several namespaces need to be specified in a standard manner and also be accessible over the Internet. We are not going to include the definitions, per se, in the SOAP message, but instead, include a reference to the definitions, so that if things change, every message in the world does not have to change.

A simplex (i.e., one-way) message from a client to a server or from a server to a client is called a *SOAP message* and consists of a SOAP envelope in which is placed a message header and a message body. The optional header is intended to allow the inclusion of application-specific information, such as security and account numbers. The required message body contains the references and informational content of the SOAP message. Here is what the SOAP envelope looks like:

```
<SOAP-ENV:Envelope
  xmlns:SOAP-ENV="http://schemas.xmlsoap.org/soap/
  envelope/"
  xmlns:xsi="http://www.w3.org/2001/XMLSchema-instance"
  xmlns:xsd="http://www.w3.org/2001/XMLSchema">
  •
  • ←----- The message body would go here
  •
</SOAP-ENV:Envelope>
```

and a sample message body is

```
<SOAP-ENV:Body>
  <ns1:getTemp
  xmlns:ns1="urn:xmethods-Temperature"
  SOAP-ENV:encodingStyle="http://schemas.xmlsoap.
  org/soap/encoding/">
    <zipcode xsi:type="xsd:string">29909</zipcode>
  </ns1:getTemp>
</SOAP-ENV:Body>
```

Again, comprehension is not required or expected. The scripts are exceedingly detailed, but one point is clear, even from this simple example. Once the structure of SOAP messaging is developed, the addition of the content can be quite straightforward.

To sum up this section, SOAP messaging is straightforward. All one SOAP client has to do to send a message to another SOAP client is to put the content document into a predetermined SOAP message structure and send it through the Internet. It doesn't matter if the sender is a client or a server, as long as the sender and the receiver are both SOAP clients. The message itself is not important to the messaging process. It could be a request to have a method executed, or it could be a document, such as a financial report or a script representing a computer graphics procedure.

Web Service Model

In order to request a service over the Internet, a person must go through a standard procedure. We covered this earlier. There are three roles: the service provider, the service requester, and the service registry. The *service provider* makes a service available over the Internet. The *service requester* consumes a service by sending an XML message to the service provider over the Internet. The *service registry* is a centralized repository of information about services that are available, serving as a computer-oriented version of the traditional "yellow pages."

Associated with the three roles are three activities. The service provider publishes available services in the service registry. The service requester finds out about services by accessing the service registry. The service requester invokes a service (called *bind*) by sending an XML message, referred to above, to the service provider. A familiar example of publish, find, and bind is an online book service. The prospective buyer consults the company's online catalog to find a suitable book. The buyer then finalizes the purchasing process by providing the requisite information, and the seller handles the billing and the physical transportation of the item purchased.

There is more to it, of course. When a service provider publishes service information, it must be described in a form that the service requester can understand. XML is used for this task by employing a document structure known a UDDI, which stands for *Universal Description, Discovery, and Integration.* When a service requester invokes a service, XML is again used in a form of descriptive language known as WSDL, which stands for *Web Services Description Language.*

Web Service Goal

The goal of Web Services was, and still, is the process of having computers talk to each other to arrange for a service without human intervention. At this stage, the Internet community has done a commendable job of establishing the requisite technical infrastructure, but the process still requires client interaction at the service-requester end. The focus is currently on building a service-oriented architecture to support future developments.

SERVICE ARCHITECTURE CONCEPTS

Service architecture is a collection of design patterns for constructing services from building blocks that can be shared between service systems. Most business processes already incorporate a form of service architecture, since the principles are derived from ordinary common sense. For example, many accounting departments include component services, such as credit checking and invoicing. When the objective is to align information services with business processes, however, the design gets more complicated and has given rise to a field of study known as *service-oriented architecture* (SOA). The basic idea behind service architecture is that you have a collection of components, representing business functions or computer applications, and you want to fit them together to make a business process or an information system. Components encapsulate services so that a service-oriented application or a business process is assimilated from multiple components that achieve the desired functionality by collectively orchestrating the operation of the needed services. The guiding principle behind service-oriented architecture is that once a component is established, it can be reused in other applications or business processes. Eventually, an organization runs out of components to build so that the synthesis of an application or a business process becomes a matter of piecing the components together – much like the manner in which an aircraft manufacturer or automobile company assembles relatively complicated products from off-the-shelf or specially-designed components. There are two aspects to the idea of building functionality with components; the first is putting the components together, and the second is making the inherent services interact in such a way that a desired state of business process engineering (BPE) is achieved.

Solution Life Cycle

An effective solution sequence for any development project incorporates a set of well-defined steps, such as the following: requirements analysis, modeling, architectural design, detailed design, construction, and testing. In the modern view of development, incorporating service architecture principles, these steps are divided into two phases: the *preproduction phase*, wherein a set of packaged components are collected, and the *production phase*, consisting of assembly and deployment.

It is important to recognize that the term "production" in the context of service life cycle refers to the synthesis of a business process or the development of an information system, and not to the actual utilization of the process or system, as in everyday operations. So, in a sense, we are producing a solution and not using a solution. Once we have the wherewithal to assemble a solution from components and do not have to develop those components from scratch, then we can spend our resources making sure that the eventual solution to whatever problem we are dealing with actually satisfies business needs – and is developed in a reasonable time frame. This is where the term *agility* comes from. The management of an enterprise, for example, perceives that it needs an IT solution to an e-commerce opportunity, and the IT department can expeditiously deliver that solution.

On Demand

The term "on demand" seems to have navigated its way into the business literature in at least three ways. In the first instance, on demand refers to the access of information, such as from the World Wide Web or any other information repository, from wherever the end user may be and whenever the interaction takes place. In the second instance, on demand refers to access to computer application programs without specifically having to purchase them. Also known as *utility computing*, this form of on demand would allow end user to pay only for the use of software, rather than having to purchase it, as is typically the case with traditional office software. Finally, the third instance of on demand and the one in which we are interested refers to the techniques for the rapid development of business processes and computer information systems to support enterprise services.

The flexibility inherent in on demand services provides a payback for most enterprises that is greater than the value of the processes and applications for which the services were originally intended. Overall, on demand processes developed through service orientation can deliver innovation, flexibility, shorter time to market, and they also serve as a vehicle for rethinking industry structures. (Cherbakov, et al., 2005) In fact, the business value of service architecture is perhaps best summarized by the following quotation from the same paper by Cherbakov, Galambos, Harishankar, Kalyana, and Rackham: (op cit. p. 654):

> What is described here is a business that is able to recognize change as it is occurring and react appropriately, ahead of the competition, and keep pace with demands of its customers, value-net partners, and employees alike. In trying to achieve this state, the business will need to leverage technology to the fullest. We call such a business an "on demand business." Fundamentally, becoming an on demand business is equivalent to achieving total business flexibility. Two important enablers contribute to the realization by an enterprise of this vision of on demand – componentization and service orientation.
>
> Components are related to functions – or to be more specific, business components are related to business functions. In a real sense, therefore, service architecture refers to the deconstruction into

components of an existing business system, and subsequently, its reconstruction into an operational network of cooperating and integrated elements needed for synthesizing responsive enterprise-wide systems.

Components, Services, and Functions

It's all relatively straightforward: most components encapsulate one or more services; many complex services require more than one component; enterprise processes are constructed from components; and enterprise functions are an amalgamation of corresponding services. The notion of putting components together to achieve some enterprise function is called *composability,* and in order to do this, the methodology demands severe constraints on the manner in which the components are constructed and packaged for reuse. Components must fit together in order to operate as intended; this requirement is known as *interoperability.*

Service Orientation

Many people are going to say that dealing with a collection of interacting components is just going to increase the complexity of their everyday life. After all, they say, why not buy an application program or adopt an established business process and be done with it? On the other hand, there is something to be said for building systems out of packaged components. If a component fails, replace the entire assembly and let the customer – or should be say client – pay for it. After all, that perspective has some merit with products and is widely adopted. The point to remember is, "What's good for products is not necessarily good for services." Here are some of the reasons.

Because services are heterogeneous and involve client interaction, most service interactions are essentially different, so that the unrestricted use of packaged facilities does not automatically contribute to efficiency. With both products and services, features sell packaged facilities, so that if you obtain two related packages, there would normally be a duplication of functionality. In other words, organizations that produce packages, in the most general sense, include as many features as possible to optimize marketability. Most of us THINK products and DO services. Moreover, there is no guarantee that similar components in different packages operate – or interoperate – in exactly the same manner.

Another consideration is that in the area of professional, scientific, and technical services, the operant process is to construct a flexible system, perhaps for a client, in which components can be replaced on a demand basis to satisfy business conditions. In this instance, one would want each component to be designed as granular as possible with a well-defined interface.

SERVICE DEVELOPMENT

One of the basic tenets of service science is that service providers can participate in a service experience by applying knowledge, skill, ingenuity, and experience, without having to invest in the usual encumbrances of product development. In this section, we are going to cover *service development*, without having to necessarily develop each and every service resource. The subject matter primarily concerns "legacy systems," and the methodology applies to just about any kind of service an ordinary person can imagine.

Legacy Systems

Many, if not most, information systems used in business, education, and government are known as *legacy systems* and continue to be the core of enterprise technology. For example, the "grunt" work underlying heavy duty data processing is performed behind the scenes, often during the wee hours of the night by mainframe computers. Linking these systems to modern Web services has been difficult, because they are difficult to change without running the risk of upsetting the applecart of good performance. The programs are written primarily in the COBOL programming language and precise specifications are not always available, adding another dimension to the problem.

Information systems that are cumbersome to change are referred to as being "brittle" and limit an enterprise's ability to respond to changing business requirements. On the other hand, legacy systems are serious assets to an organization and typically represent considerable investments. In many cases, organizations achieve a level of competitive advantage through the use of legacy systems. Legacy systems support day-to-day operations and incorporate the business logic inherent in all areas of the business model.

Service architecture purports to leverage legacy systems by unlocking the business functionality through loosely-coupled, but well-structured, service components abducted from legacy systems. The service components can then be choreographed to adapt or extend business processes to satisfy current needs. This can be achieved in two ways: leveraging or repurposing. With *leveraging*, the functions in legacy systems are exposed without rewriting the system. With *repurposing*, the programs are rewritten for the modern world with a modern language, such as Java, for use on servers designed for the Internet and the World Wide Web. Clearly, leveraging is the way to go with legacy systems, because of the risk involved with rewriting large programs and getting it right the first time.

Exposing Functionality in Legacy System

Exposing business services by leveraging legacy systems is not a simple matter, and it requires good strategic planning, time, and considerable resources. Typically, the work is outsourced to IT consulting companies, because a high level of expertise is required, but not otherwise needed, to sustain enterprise operations.

Although the task is exceedingly complex, the idea is relatively simple: put a software wrapper around the legacy code and expose what you want to expose through well-defined interfaces. The conceptual software wrapper is known as an *adapter*.

Here's how it works. One component needs the services of another component, which may reside locally or be available over the Internet residing somewhere out in cyberspace. The needy component sends an XML message to the servicing component requesting a service of some kind. What this means is that the serving component does something and returns the result as an XML message to the requestor. The messages adhere to an agreed-upon format so that the programs can understand each other.

The overall process is not much different from when one person asks another person for the time. The requestor issues the request in a socially agreed upon language in a well-defined format. The responder accesses a time resource and returns the time in the same language and in a related but different format. If another person asks for the time, the process is repeated.

There are some hidden components in the messaging scenario. The requestor needs information on who would know the actual time. So an internal registry of "people who know about time" is implicitly consulted before the initial message is sent by the requester to the responder. With service architecture, a registry of components is needed to know which components to call upon when a particular service is needed. Part of the registry process could very well involve a search process to determine which registry contains the needed information. Then, perhaps, the requestor might engage a local registry to store pertinent information from non-local registries to facilitate subsequent operations.

SERVICE REFERENCE ARCHITECTURE

A certain amount of structure among components is required for the capabilities, mentioned above, to function together as a coherent whole. It is commonly known as the *SOA Reference Architecture*. The reference architecture is essentially a stack of functionality, implying that service messages flow upward and downward in the stack.

Loose Coupling

The basic principle of service architecture is that synthesis involves composition. A business process or a computer application is created by combining independent components that are loosely coupled. *Loose coupling*, in this instance, simply means that components – that is, the components providing the services – pass requests and data, in the form of messages, between each other in a standard manner without the need for underlying assumptions that would compromise component operational interdependence. Thus, a small change in the functioning of one component would not require a change to other components that rely on the changed component. With component architecture of this sort, it is important to recognize that components normally relate to enterprise-level processes spanning people, systems, and information.

Services

Services can be created or exposed. In the former case, an organization creates the business process or a computer application from scratch. In the latter case, an existing service is insulated with a logical container and its functionality is explicitly described so that other entities can use it. It's entirely possible that a service developed for another generation doesn't exactly fit in with what you are doing. In this instance, an adapter is needed to make whatever adjustments are necessary to use the service. It's like using your spouse as an adapter to your mother-in-law to arrange for babysitting service. In the world of computers, an *adapter* is a software module that permits access to a service through a standard messaging interface, usually created through the XML language.

Combining diverse services and exposing them as a single service is commonplace in everyday life. Consider, for example, a delivery service that combines three capabilities: dispatcher, driver, and accountant. The dispatcher interacts with the customers and makes the arrangements for the deliveries. The driver organizes his or her delivery route and makes the deliveries. The accountant records transactions, sends bills, and records payments. Yet, to the customer, there is only one service interface, which, in fact, is the point where the package is submitted for transportation. The delivery service has been composed from the three component services and the total process is called *composition*. Facilities, sometimes called *tools*, are needed to put references to components and corresponding services in the registry so that system designers can find them. All of this points to why the subject of web services is so important. Web services with its associated XML, SOAP, UDDI, and WSDL facilities, provide a convenient means of establishing a reference architecture.

Messaging

The messaging layer of the service reference architecture provides the means for the components to interact and emphasizes the need for in-between functionality to provide the requisite level of independence required by SOA Reference Architecture. Consider, for example, an investment firm that supports a database of up-to-the-second stock prices. An investment advisor with a client on the line would like the latest price of AT&T stock. So he or she enters the stock exchange code for AT&T, namely 'T', and presses a key on the advisor's workstation. In a flash, the current stock price is returned. Some in-between hardware and software, known as *middleware*, is required to make it all happen. Clearly, many other services within the investment firm would also utilize the same stock price service. It's a simple example but gives evidence that the component-based approach to system development has some definite merit.

A messaging service would normally use *asynchronous messaging*, which means that the requestor sends the message to the service and the result is returned as soon as possible. While the person may be waiting for a response operating in a synchronous mode, the underlying hardware and software goes along its merry way sending messages back and forth asynchronously. Because of the great difference in processing speeds of humans and computers, it appears as though the computer is sitting there waiting for a request and responds immediately. In reality, that request may be put on a queue and processed in order of arrival, recognizing that different methods for queue management may be used.

Registry

The concept of a registry was introduced previously in the context of legacy systems and web services. With web services, the registry is a general facility for storing service information that can be retrieved through XML messaging. It's more complicated but that's the idea. With service architecture, as in the present context, the registry is a repository for information on components, intended for persons synthesizing a composite service, and additionally contains tools to assist in achieving that synthesis. *The registry is a data base of components and the services they supply.*

The registry should also contain facilities for convenient search, the import and export of entries, and change management. In the latter instance, it is necessary for users to be informed of updates that might affect their performance.

The registry should additionally reflect business policy as it refers to distribution, security, and ownership.

Architecture Services Management

In the present context, services management refers to the operation and management control over business processes constructed with a service orientation. The efficacy of service operations is always of concern as it relates to service-level agreements as they relate to performance and quality of service. In the former case, performance encompasses the availability and reliability of individual services. In the latter case, quality of service refers to the statistical analysis of specific service events.

Management control reflects governance concepts as they apply to the operations mission, previously mentioned. Governance should reflect the fact that service architecture is a methodology for using services to construct services and has two major focuses: (1) The creation of processes, operating in the form of services, to support both IT-enabled and non-IT-enabled business activities; and (2) The control and support of the business services through a formal process for managing services. To summarize, governance provides support for empowering people to do what they do in line with organizational objectives.

Orchestration

Orchestration refers to the dynamic linking of services together to achieve a business purpose. The business processes are layered on top of the services, so in a sense, the services are anchored into the processes. In IT-enabled processes, the business process is a script written in a "business process execution language" that successively calls the needed components in order to invoke the services constituting the business function. This combinatory operation was earlier referred to as composition and can be conceptualized as the workflow of services. In a non-IT enabled process, the composition is achieved through management directed policies, procedures, and business rules.

Actually, the term "orchestration" has two meanings in the context of service science. Let's take a computer application as an example. The first meaning has to do with setting up the structure as a controlling module that successively invokes services to achieve a business objective. The components do not have some form of inherent stickiness that enables operational affinity among loosely-coupled components in a meaningful order. That is where the business process execution language (BPEL), referred to just above, comes in. The application designer has to set up the service chain beforehand.

The service bus effectively connects the registry, workflow, composition, and the underlying system (called the *platform*) as pieces that do the work to construct function from components viewed as services. The second meaning of the term "orchestration" refers to the actual running of the application. The BPEL script is actually executed by an operational entity, intermediate data is stored in an operational database (not shown), and the business result is achieved.

Analysis

One of the facets of the service domain is that service quality is directly related to client interaction and involvement. This requires constant tweaking, otherwise known as continuous improvement (i.e., *kaizen* in operations management). Business performance is constantly monitored – there is nothing new about this. With service systems, however, the raw operational data is frequently embedded deep down in independently constructed loosely-coupled components. Getting this data out for analysis is a task that should be addressed at the design level.

User Interaction

On the surface, the end-user interface development model seems simple. All that needs to be done is to construct a prototype, test it, improve it, and then have the end-user group sign off on it. With service-oriented architecture, however, the *user interaction* is with a business process, which is a notch up from what normally is construed as the end-user interface. The term "user," therefore, refers to the user of a service, and not necessarily to the user of an application. As in the restaurant example, the user of a service doesn't have to be the customer.

The user of a service can be another service, which leads to the notion of a service architecture in which components can be assembled without the use of special adapters.

SERVICE ARCHITECTURE PRINCIPLES

The use of design principles is paramount to the construction of a successful service project. Otherwise, service systems development is another "random walk down Wall Street." Here is a set of service architecture principles.

> **Service Abstraction.** The key benefit of service abstraction is that "inside" information about a component is effectively hidden from the outside so that a component can be used by other diverse services. This principle is sometimes referred to as information hiding. Often, internal operational details are superfluous to a referencing service where only a result is needed. Take the credit checking service as an example. An outside user of that service is usually only interested in the credit worthiness of a subject and not in the procedures and file processes necessary to ascertain that rating. In fact, operational details may change without the requester knowing or caring about them. The concept of abstraction applies to other organizational functions and computer modules, as well.
>
> **Service Encapsulation.** Service encapsulation enables a service – often bundled as part of a larger operational entity – to be referenced via an adapter to preserve and take advantage of previously developed functionality. As with the preceding principle, encapsulation may apply to organizational as well as informational components.
>
> **Service Loose Coupling.** This principle simply demands that components are not implicitly

dependent upon one another, such that use by a non-coupled component is prohibited. Another way of expressing the concept of loose coupling is one component does not require that another component be in a particular state at the time of invocation.

Service Contract. The concept of a service contract reflects that it is necessary that a complete specification be made of the precise services provided by a service component and exactly how those services are to be addressed. A service contract describes how two components are to interact. With Web services, the contract refers to a WSDL (Web Services Definition Language) definition and a specification of the XML schema definition of precisely how messages between a requester and the repository are to be formatted.

Service Reusability. Service reusability simply refers to the practice of designing a component so that it can be used in more than one place. In general, the intention is to provide services that can be used by more than one business process.

Service Composability. Service composability refers to the combining of services to form composite services. This practice implicitly imposes a restriction on the component services so that they adhere to the specifications in the service contract. Service composition is usually performed to synthesize a business process.

Service Autonomy. Service autonomy is conceptually modeled after the human nervous system and refers to a component's capability to self-govern its own operational behavior. Autonomy reduces the complexity of business processes composed from self-regulating components. Autonomy allows a business process to provide a higher level of productivity by being able to manage itself. This is a tricky principle, because the implication is that a component just operates on its own as some artificial intelligence robot. For most services, this principle simply means that a service invoked through some form of "service bus" takes its input parameters and performs its functions, as specified in its service contract, without requesting additional input or operating instructions.

Service Discoverability. Service discoverability is a complex arrangement of being describable, via the service contract, and being accessible via a registry and a description language. Essentially, this means that the description of a service, found through a search process, additionally provides information on how to use a service.

SERVICE ARCHITECTURE
STRUCTURE AND OPERATION

A business process is composed of one or more business services frequently implemented through information and communications technology (ICT). Krafzig, Banke, and Slama state the modern dependence on ICT in the following way. "… enterprises heavily depend on the IT backbone, which is responsible for running almost all processes of modern enterprises, be they related to manufacturing, distribution, sales, customer management, accounting, or any other type of business process." This section introduces the concept of enterprise systems and then presents definitive information on the structure and operation of service architecture in an enterprise environment.

Enterprise Systems

An enterprise system cuts across the total organization and encompasses inter-departmental dependencies and relationships with suppliers and business partners. Accordingly, the enterprise software should be tightly coupled with the organization, but not with itself, based on the component model. This reflects the agility and incremental change that we referred to earlier. We require a structure that promotes loose coupling through messaging and platform interoperability.

Service Architecture Structure

The key structural elements in a service system are the services, a service repository, the service broker, the service bus, the service manager, and the interface elements. The interface elements can be to end users or to application programs.

From a structural viewpoint, the *service* provides business logic and consists of an implementation and a service contract. The *service repository*, operating as a virtual library, exists as a place to store service information and how to retrieve that information. The service repository certainly has a computer flavor to it, but that need not be the case. Many service firms have manual lists of the services they offer. In the computer version of a service repository, however, the storage facility could be accessed manually during development and dynamically during the execution of a component. The *service broker* connects services together by accessing the service repository for information about services and providing the linkage to connect components. The *service bus* is the nerve center in an enterprise system and is covered separately, as is the service manager, which is the mechanism by which enterprise processes are constructed. The interface elements are the input and output to the system.

The term "interface" normally implies an end-user interface with which most persons are familiar. In the case of enterprise systems, however, an interface can be to another computer application, a database, or a legacy system.

Enterprise Service Bus

An *enterprise service bus* (ESB) is a collection of ICT facilities for routing messages between services, or more specifically between components. The bus metaphor is apt in this case. The message gets on, goes to its destination, and gets off. The metaphor ends there, because there are different kinds of busses and unique things happen on different busses.

The most straightforward kind of service bus is a high-speed data link between services, as alluded to earlier in the stock broker example. The stock broker needs the current price of a stock for an ongoing transaction. The stock symbol is entered into a workstation and a button is pressed. In a fraction of a second, the current price is returned by a service connected to the other end of the service bus. The service bus in this instance, is a combination of hardware and software, often referred to as middleware. In this model of bus, the service bus could also be a specially constructed data link between business partners or between organizational units, termed electronic data interchange (EDI).

The most general form of ESB, however, uses the Internet with all of its inherent requirements for interoperability. In this instance, a message, perhaps requesting a service, may go through a necessary protocol conversion in its route from sender to receiver. Another possible function performed by an ESB is *context mediation*, which refers to a change in value based on contextual differences. An example would be the change of a price from Yen to Dollars during message processing.

Another related topic is *web based intermediary*, or WBI for short. A WBI is a program that runs in concert with a client's browser and acts as a form of software assistant, filtering and preparing information to satisfy particular needs.

Service Manager

The most prevalent use of service architecture is to construct computer applications. The service manager ties everything together and runs the show. Clearly, this is an operational function, but a structural component is needed to do it. In a sense, the service manager is the "main program" of an application. The service manager could be a specially written component in an enterprise system, or it could be a vendor-supplied package that successively calls upon required services.

Service Architecture Operation

An enterprise system is sometimes referred to as an "end to end" operation that represents a business process. Another means of conceptualizing an enterprise system is that it is controlled process flow. As covered above, the service manager controls the process flow through a process called *orchestration*. The conductor of an orchestra controls the activity of a set of musicians through minute actions termed orchestration. The same concept can be applied to the execution of an enterprise system.

Orchestration is different than choreography. Choreography refers to what a collection of services can do, and orchestration refers to precisely when and how they actually do it.

A business process can be scripted in a language, such as BPEL, or written in a computer programming language. Business Process Execution Language (BPEL) is an XML-based scripting language for orchestrating service applications.

QUICK SUMMARY

The purpose of this overview is to present a bird's eye view of service technology and architecture. The principles inherent in this viewpoint are summarized in the following quick summary.

1. Services are ubiquitous but require messages to communicate information between client and provider. A client and a provider can be tightly coupled, as when a patient is sitting in front of the doctor, and they are having a give-and-take conversation, or loosely coupled, as when you send a request to someone via email and receive a response at some undetermined time in the future. In the former case, the client and provider are communicating in a *synchronous mode* without technology, and in the latter case, they are communicating in an *asynchronous mode* with the use of technology.

2. The focus is on the data that is transmitted and not on the communications medium, which can take the form of a human interaction or a computer-based message. The context for the message can be embedded in the message or inherent in the way that the service provider is addressed. It is useful to recognize that we are operating at two levels: the service level and the message level. At the *service level*, the message entity that receives the message is the service provider, and in the case of a computer, it is regarded simply as the service. At the *message level*, there is some choreography involved with providing a service, as demonstrated by the above two-step interaction. In fact, a service may involve the interchange of several messages.

3. In its most simple form, a message is a string of characters encoded using standardized coding methods commonly employed in computer and information technology. Messages have a uniform format consisting of a header and a body.

The *header* primarily concerns addressing and includes the address of the sender and of the receiver. In the request/reply message pattern, the return address is picked up from the message header for the response portion of the transaction. The *body* of the message contains the information content of the message, and because it is intended only for the receiver, it is not usually inspected during message transmission.

4. A service that takes place on the Internet and the World Wide Web is called a *web service*. A web service is a process in which the provider and client interact to produce a value; it is a pure service. The only difference between a web service and medical provisioning, for example, is that, in the former case, the client and provider are computer systems. The most pervasive web service computer application on the Internet is electronic mail, commonly known as email. The most widely used application on the World Wide Web is to find information. The major web technology tools and techniques are HTTP, HTML, and XML.

5. *HyperText Transfer Protocol* (HTTP) is a collection of rules and procedures for transferring messages between computers over the World Wide Web. Without HTTP, the web would not be the revolutionary phenomena that it is today.

6. It is possible to send a document from one computer to another and have that document displayed on the receiving end in a reasonable form without regard to the brand and model of computer, kind of software, time of day, and location. This feat is possible because of hypertext markup language (HTML).

7. Extensible Markup Language (XML) is a language and a standard for service messaging. Whereas HTML describes how a document will be rendered on the receiving end of a message, XML gives the semantics (or meaning) of a document.

8. A Web Service is any service that is available over the Internet, uses a standard XML messaging system, and is not dependant upon any one particular operating system.

9. *Service architecture* is a collection of design patterns for constructing services from building blocks that can be shared between service systems. The basic idea behind service architecture is that you have a collection of components, representing business functions or computer applications, and you want to fit them together to make a business process or an information system.

10. Components encapsulate services so that a service-oriented application or a business process is assimilated from multiple components that achieve the desired functionality by collectively orchestrating the operation of the needed services. The guiding principle behind service-oriented architecture is that once a component is established, it can be reused in other applications or business processes. Eventually, an organization runs out of components to build so that the synthesis of an application or a business process becomes a matter of piecing the components together.

11. The term "on demand" seems to have navigated its way into the business literature in at least three ways. In the first instance, on demand refers to the access of information, such as from the World Wide Web or any other information repository, from wherever the end user may be and whenever the interaction takes place. In the second instance, on demand refers to access to computer application programs without specifically having to purchase them. Also known as *utility computing*, this form of on demand would allow an end user to pay only for the use of software, rather than having to purchase it, as is typically the case with traditional office software. Finally, the third instance of on demand and the one in which we are interested refers to the techniques for

the rapid development of business processes and computer information systems to support enterprise services.

12. It's all relatively straightforward: most components encapsulate one or more services; many complex services require more than one component; enterprise processes are constructed from components; and enterprise functions are an amalgamation of corresponding services. The notion of putting components together to achieve some enterprise function is called *composability*, and in order to do so, the methodology demands severe constraints on the manner in which the components are constructed and packaged for reuse. Components must fit together in order to operate as intended; this requirement is known as *interoperability*.

13. An enterprise is service oriented if it can be properly viewed as a set of services connected to produce a specific result. Similarly, a computer application or information system is service oriented if is constructed from interacting components running on the same platform or accessible from different platforms via networking facilities.

14. Service architecture purports to leverage legacy systems by unlocking the business functionality through loosely-coupled but well-structured service components abducted from legacy systems. The service components can then be choreographed to adapt or extend business processes to satisfy current needs. This can be achieved in two ways: leveraging or repurposing. With *leveraging*, the functions in legacy systems are exposed without rewriting the system. With *repurposing*, the programs are rewritten for the modern world with a modern language, such as Java, for use on servers designed for the Internet and the World Wide Web. Clearly, leveraging is the way to go with legacy systems, because of the risk involved with rewriting large programs and getting it right the first time.

15. A certain amount of structure among components is required for the capabilities, mentioned above, to function together as

a coherent whole. It is commonly known as the *SOA Reference Architecture*.

16. The use of design principles is paramount to the construction of a successful service project. A set of service architecture principles includes the following elements: service abstraction, service encapsulation, service loose coupling, service contract, service reusability, service composability, service autonomy, and service discoverability.

17. An enterprise system cuts across the total organization and encompasses inter-departmental dependencies and relationships with suppliers and business partners. Accordingly, the enterprise software should be tightly coupled with the organization, but not with itself, based on the component model. The key structural elements in a service system are the services, a service repository, the service broker, the service bus, the service manager, and the interface elements. The interface elements can be to end users or to application programs. An *enterprise service bus* (ESB) is a collection of ICT facilities for routing messages between services, or more specifically between components.

18. An enterprise system is sometimes referred to as an "end to end" operation that represents a business process. As covered above, the service manager controls the process flow through a process called *orchestration*. Orchestration is different than choreography. Choreography refers to what a collection of services can do, and orchestration refers to precisely when and how they actually they do it.

REFERENCES

1   Carter, S., The *New Language of Business*, Upper Saddle River, NJ: IBM Press, 2007.

2   Cerami, E., *Web Services Essentials*, Sebastopol, CA: O'Reilly Media, Inc., 2002.

3   Cherbakov, L., Galambos, G., Harishankar, R., Kalyana, S., and G. Rackham, "Impact of service orientation at the business level," *IBM Systems Journal*, Vol. 44, No. 4, 2005, pp. 653-668.

4   Dykes, L. and E. Tittel, *XML for Dummies* (4th Edition), Hoboken, NJ: Wiley Publishing, Inc. 2005.

5   Erl, T., *Service-Oriented Architecture: A Field Guide to Integrating XML and Web Services*, Upper Saddle River, NJ: Prentice Hall, 2004.

6   Erl, T., *SOA: Principles of Service Design*, Upper Saddle River, NJ: Prentice Hall, 2008.

7   Ernest, M. and J.M. Nisavic, "Adding value to the IT organization with the Component Business Model, *IBM Systems Journal*, Vol. 46, No. 3, 2007, provider.387-403.

8   Gottschalk, K., Graham, S., Kreger, H., and J. Snell, "Introduction to Web services architecture," *IBM Systems Journal* (Vol. 41, No. 2), 2002, pp 170-177.

9   Hagel, J. and J.S. Brown, *The Only Sustainable Edge*, Boston: Harvard Business School Press, 2007.

10   Hurwitz, J., Bloor, R., Baroudi, C., and M. Kaufman, *Service Oriented Architecture for Dummies*, Hoboken, NJ: Wiley Publishing, Inc., 2007.

11   IBM Corporation, *Extend the value of your core business systems: Transforming legacy applications into an SOA framework*, Form G507-1950-00, September 2006.

12   Katzan, H. "Foundations of Service Science: Technology and Architecture," *Journal of Service Science*, 2(1): 11-33, 2009.

13   Krafzig, D., Banke, K., and D. Slama, *Enterprise SOA: Service-Oriented Architecture Best Practices*, Upper Saddle River, NJ: Prentice Hall, 2005.

14   Margolis, B. with J. Sharpe, *SOA for the Business Developer: Concepts, BPEL, and SCA*, Lewisville, TX: 2007.

15   McGrath, M., *XML in Easy Steps*, New York: Barnes & Noble Books, 2003.

16   Musciano, C. and B. Kennedy, *HTML: The Definitive Guide*, Sebastopol, CA: O'Reilly Media, Inc., 1998.

17   Potts, S. and M. Kopack, *Web Services in 24 Hours*, Indianapolis: Sams Publishing, 2003.

18   Smith, J., *Inside Windows Communication Foundation*, Redmond, WA: Microsoft Press, 2007.

19   Spohrer, J., *Service Science, Management, and Engineering (SSME): State of the Art – service science*, IBM Nordic Service Science Summit, Helsinki, Finland, February 28, 2007.

20 Van Slyke, C. and F. Bélanger, *E-Business Technologies: Supporting the Net-Enhanced Organization*, New York: John Wiley and Sons, Inc., 2003.

21 Watt, A., *Teach Yourself XML in 10 Minutes*, Indianapolis: Sams Publishing, 2003.

22 webMethods, *SOA Reference Architecture: Defining the Key Elements of a Successful SOA Technology Framework*, www.webMethods.com, 2006.

23 Wikipedia, *HTTP*, www.wikipedia.org, 2007.

24 Woods, D. and T. Mattern, *Enterprise SOA: Designing IT for Business Innovation*, Sebastopol, CA: O'Reilly Media Inc., 2006.

***** End of Chapter 8 ****

9

IDENTITY AS A SERVICE

INTRODUCTION

Identity is a major issue in the security of modern information systems and the privacy of data stored in those systems. Security and privacy concerns are commonly associated with behavioral tracking, personal-identifiable information (PII), the relevance of private data, data repurposing, and identity theft. We are going to approach the subject from a cloud computing perspective, recognizing that the inherent problems apply to information systems, in general. Cloud computing is a good delivery vehicle for underlying security and privacy concepts, because data is typically stored off-premises and is under the control of a third-party service provider. When a third party gets your data, who knows what is going to happen to it? The main consideration may turn out to be a matter of control, because from an organizational perspective, control over information has historically been with the organization that creates or maintains it. From a personal perspective, on the other hand, a person should have the wherewithal to control their identity and the release of information about themselves, and in the latter case, a precise determination of to whom it is released and for what reason. Privacy issues are not fundamentally caused by technology, but they are exacerbated by employing the technology for economic benefit. After a brief review of cloud computing, security, and privacy to set the stage, we are going to cover identity theory, identity requirements, and an identity taxonomy. This is a working paper on this important subject.

Cloud Computing Concepts for Identity Services

Cloud computing is an architectural model for deploying and accessing computer facilities via the Internet. A cloud service provider would supply ubiquitous access through a web browser to software services executed in a cloud data center. The software would satisfy consumer and business needs. Because software availability plays a major role in cloud computing, the subject is often referred to as *software-as-a-service* (SaaS). Conceptually, there is nothing particularly special about a cloud data center, because it is a conventional web site that provides computing and storage facilities. The definitive aspect of a cloud data center is the level of sophistication of hardware and software needed to scale up to serve a large number of customers. Cloud computing is a form of service provisioning where the service provider supplies the network access, security, application software, processing capability, and data storage from a data center and operates that center as a utility in order to supply on-demand self service, broad network access, resource pooling, rapid application acquisition, and measured service. The notion of measured service represents a "pay for what you use" metered model applied to differing forms of customer service.

The operational environment for cloud computing supports three categories of informational resources for achieving agility, availability, collaboration, and elasticity in the deployment and use of cloud services that include software, information, and cloud infrastructure. The *software category* includes system software, application software, infrastructure software, and accessibility software. The *information category* refers to large collections of data and the requisite database and management facilities needed for efficient and secure storage utilization. The *category of cloud infrastructure* is comprised of computer resources, network facilities, and the fabric for scalable consumer operations.

Based on this brief description, we can characterize cloud computing as possessing the following characteristics: on-demand self service, broad network access, resource pooling, rapid elasticity, and measured service. (Nelson 2009) The benefit of having lower costs and a less complex operating environment is particularly attractive to small-to-medium-sized enterprises, certain governmental agencies, research organizations, and many countries. In this paper, cloud computing is used as a delivery vehicle for the presentation of identity services.

Information Security and Identity

The scope of information security is huge by any objective measure. One ordinarily thinks of information security in terms of identity, authentication, authorization, accountability, and end-to-end trust.

Identity is a means of denoting an entity in a particular namespace and is the basis of security and privacy – regardless if the context is digital identification or non-digital identification. We are going to refer to an identity object as a *subject*. A subject may have several identities and belong to more than one namespace. A pure identity denotation is independent of a specific context, and a federated identity reflects a process that is shared between identity management systems. When one identity management system accepts the certification of another, a phenomenon known as "trust" is established. The execution of trust is often facilitated by a third party that is acknowledged by both parties and serves as the basis of digital identity in cloud and other computer services.

Access to informational facilities is achieved through a process known as *authentication*, whereby a subject makes a claim to its identity by presenting an identity symbol for verification and control.

Authentication is usually paired with a related specification known as authorization to obtain the right to address a given service.

Typically, *authorization* refers to permission to perform certain actions. Users are assigned roles that must match corresponding roles associated with a requisite computer application. Each application contains a set of roles pertinent to the corresponding business function. Access is further controlled by business rules that specify conditions that must be met before access is granted. The role/business-rule modality also applies to information storage, and this is where the practice of privacy comes into consideration.

In general, the combination of identification and authentication determines who can sign-on to a system – that is, who is authorized to use that system. Authorization, often established with access control lists, determines what functions a user can perform. Authorization cannot occur without authentication. There are two basic forms of access control: discretionary access control, and mandatory access control. With discretionary access control (DAC), the security policy is determined by the owner of the security object. With mandatory access control (MAC), the security policy is governed by the system that contains the security object. Privacy policy should, in general, be governed by both forms of access control. DAC reflects owner considerations, and MAC governs inter-system controls.

Accountability records a user's actions and is determined by audit trails and user logs that are prototypically used to uncover security violations and analyze security incidents. In the modern world of computer and information privacy, accountability would additionally incorporate the recording of privacy touch points to assist in managing privacy concerns over a domain of interest. Although the Internet is a fruitful technology, it garners very little trust, because it is very cumbersome to assign responsibility for shortcomings and failure in an Internet operational environment. Failure now takes on an additional meaning. In addition to operational failure, it is important to also include "inability to perform as expected," as an additional dimension.

Trustworthy computing refers to the notion that people in particular and society as a whole trust computers to safeguard things that are important to them. Medical and financial information are cases in point. Computing devices, software services, and reliable networks are becoming pervasive in everyday life, but the lingering doubt remains over whether or not we can trust them. Expectations have risen with regard to technology such that those expectations now encompass safety, reliability, and the integrity of organizations that supply the technology. Society will only accept a technological advance when an efficient and effective set of policies, engineering processes, business practices, and enforceable regulations are in place. We are searching for a framework to guide the way to efficacy in computing.

It is generally felt that a framework for understanding a technology should reflect the underlying concepts required for its development and subsequent acceptance as an operational modality. A technology should enable the delivery of value rather than constrain it, and that is our objective with identity service

Privacy Concepts

Information systems typically process and store information about which privacy is of paramount concern. The main issue is identity, which serves as the basis of privacy or lack of it, and undermines the trust of individuals and organizations in other information-handling entities. The key consideration may turn out to be the integrity that organizations display when handling personal information and how accountable they are about their information practices. From an organizational perspective, control over information should remain with the end user or the data's creator with adequate controls over repurposing. From a personal perspective, the person should have the wherewithal to control his or her identity as well as the release of socially sensitive identity attributes. One of the beneficial aspects of the present concern over information privacy is that it places the person about whom data are recorded in proper perspective. Whereas such a person may be the object in an information system, he or she is regarded as the subject in privacy protection – as mentioned earlier. This usage of the word *subject* is intended to imply that a person should, in fact, have some control over the storage of personal information.

More specifically, the *subject* is the person, natural or legal, about whom data is stored. The *beneficial user* is the organization or individual for whom processing is performed, and the *agency* is the computing system in which the processing is performed and information is stored. In many cases, the beneficial user and the subject are members of the same organization.

The heart of the issue is *privacy protection*, which normally refers to the protection of rights of individuals. While the concept may also apply to groups of individuals, the individual aspect of the issue is that which raises questions of privacy and liberty

Privacy Assessment

The Federal Bureau of Investigation (U.S.A.) lists several criteria for evaluating privacy concerns for individuals and for designing cloud computing applications: (FBI 2004)

- *What information is being collected?*
- *Why is the information being collected?*
- *What is the intended use of the information?*
- *With whom will the information be shared?*
- *What opportunities will individuals have to decline to provide information or to consent to particular uses of the information?*
- *How will the information be secure?*
- *Is this a system of records?*

Since privacy is a fundamental right in the United States, the above considerations obviously resulted from extant concerns by individuals and privacy rights groups. In a 2009 Legislative Primer, the following concerns are expressed by the Center for Digital Democracy: (CDD 2009, p. 2)

- Tracking people's every move online is an invasion of privacy.
- Online behavioral tracking and targeting can be used to take advantage of vulnerable consumers.
- Online behavioral tracking and targeting can be used to unfairly discriminate against consumers.
- Online behavioral profiles may be used for purposes beyond commercial purposes.

We are going to add to the list that the very fact that personal data is stored online is a matter of concern and should be given serious attention. Based on these issues, this paper is going to take a comprehensive look at the subject of identity in computer and human systems.

IDENTITY THEORY

The notion of identity is an important subject in philosophy, mathematics, and computer information systems. In its most general sense, identity refers to the set of characteristics that makes a subject definable. Each characteristic can be viewed as a single point in a three-dimensional Cartesian coordinate system where the axis are *subject, attribute,* and *value.* (Katzan 1975) Thus, the fact that George is twenty-five years old could be denoted by the triple <George, age, 25>. A set of characteristics over a given domain can uniquely identify a subject. This simple concept is the basis of privacy and identity in cloud computing, information systems, and everyday life. The notion of identity applies to organizational subjects as well as to person subjects.

Knowledge and Power

The phrase "knowledge is power" is a popular means of expressing the value of information. So popular, in fact, that one would think its origin is the modern age of computers and information technology. That assumption, however, is not correct. The first reference that could be found is credited to the famous Sir Francis Bacon is his book published in 1605 entitled *Advancement of Learning*, quoted as follows: (Bacon 1605)

> *But yet the commandment of knowledge is yet higher than the commandment over the will: for it is a commandment over the reason, belief, and understanding of man, which is the highest part of the mind, and giveth law to the will itself. For there is no power on earth which setteth up a throne or chair of estate in the spirits and souls of men, and in their cogitations, imaginations, opinions, and beliefs, but knowledge and learning.*

Knowledge, in the sense that it is information concerning a thing or a person, can be used to further one's endeavors or it can be used to control a subject, thus diminishing its freedom and liberty. The protection of personal privacy is a Fourth Amendment right, and identity is the basis of privacy. The following sections give a philosophical view of identity.

Knowledge, Attributes, and Identity

Identity is primarily used to establish a relationship between an attribute or set of attributes and a person, object, event, concept, or theory. The relationship can be direct, based on physical evidence, and in other cases, the relationship is indirect and based on a reference to other entities. In a similar vein, the relationship can be certain or uncertain, and in the latter case, based in deduction or inference. The relationship determines an element of knowledge. For example, the knowledge element "you are in your car" is a statement in which "you" and "your car" are things that exist and the "in" is a relationship. Direct knowledge is known by *acquaintance* and is evidenced by a physical connection. Indirect knowledge is determined through a reference to a particular with which the analyst is acquainted. The form is known as knowledge by *description*. (Russell 1912) *Direct knowledge* is determined through sense data, memory, or introspection. *Indirect knowledge* is determined through a reference to another particular, as in "the person who ran for congress in 2004" or through a form of self-awareness where what goes on in subject's mind, for example, is estimated by an analyst's interpretation based on experience or self-evaluation.

Synthetic knowledge reflects certainty based on evidence inherent in the attribute values at hand. *Analytic knowledge* reflects a degree of uncertainty and is determined by deduction, as in "he is the only person with that 'attribute value'," or by inference based on known particulars, such as "all terrorists have beards." Inference, in this case, could be regarded as a form of derivative knowledge. The value of analytic knowledge is that it enables the analyst to exceed his or her limit of private experience. (Kant 1787)

Numerical and Qualitative Identity

Identity refers to the characteristics that make a subject the same or different. We are going to establish two forms of identity: numerical and qualitative. Two subjects are *numerically identical* if they are the same entity, such that there is only one instance. Two subject (or objects in this case) are *qualitatively identical* if they are copies or duplicates. In the popular movie *The Bourne Identity*, for example, the characters *Jason Bourne* and *David Web* are numerically identical, and the number of subjects is one. So it is with *Superman* and *Clark Kent* in another domain. On the other hand, a set of animals with the same biological characteristics – e.g., a species – are regarded as being qualitatively identical. The notion of qualitative identity is remarkably similar to the modern definition of a *category* informally defined as a collection of entities with the same characteristics, having the same values for the same attributes.

Theory of the Indiscernibles

An important aspect of identity theory is that subjects exhibit features of permanence and change, analogous to sameness and difference mentioned previously. We are going to discuss the concept of temporal identity in the next section. The notion of change implies a subject that undergoes a transformation and also a property that remains unchanged. Both Locke and Humehave proclaimed that change reflects the idea of unity and not of identity. Leibnitz proposed the *Theory of Indiscernibles* suggesting that subjects (i.e., objects or entities) that are indiscernible are identical. (Stroll 1967) The subject of indiscernibles has implications for cloud computing, information systems, and change. To what extent a change in a characteristic denotes a change in identity is an open item at this time and implies that there is a probabilistic aspect to identity.

Russell approaches the subject of identity from an alternate viewpoint, analogous to definite and indefinite articles. Russell proposes that a description may be of two sorts: definite and indefinite. A definite description is a name, and an indefinite description is a collection of objects x that have the property ø, such that the proposition øx is true. (Russell 1919) In the phrase *Dan Brown is a famous author*, for example, 'Dan Brown" is a name and the indefinite description is obvious, leading to the probabilistic link between a subject and a characteristic.

Temporal Identity

There is a rich quantity of philosophical literature on the change of identity over time. Are you the same person you were yesterday? Are there persistent attributes that allow for positive identity between time periods? As alluded to previously, entities in everyday life exhibit features of permanence and change. In the domain of personal identity, address attribute is a primary candidate for change. For example, John Smith lives at 123 Main Street. He moves out and another John Smith moves in. This is distinct possibility in a crowded city. In there a concept in identity theory for this phenomena? Should an identity system take this eventuality into consideration?

There is a form of *attribute duality* between a person subject and an object subject. A subject – an object, such as a residence, in this case – is characterized by who lives there. For example, rich people live on Sutton Place in New York. The discussion leads to four related concepts: endurant identity, perdurant identity, endurant attribute, and perdurant attribute. Clearly, the term *endurant* refers to a noun that does not change, where perdurant refers to one that does. Thus, the identity problem is essentially translated to an operant problem of "recognizing identity."

IDENTITY PRINCIPLES

It would appear that there are two essential problems in identity theory: protection of identity and recognition of identity. Protection refers to the safeguarding of one's identity from unwanted intrusion into personal affairs. Recognition refers to the use of identity measures to detect wanted persons. This characterization of the identity problem reflects two sides of the same sword.

It is generally regarded that effective identity governance should be based on a set of principles to guide the professional activities of IT managers, security officers, privacy officers, and risk management. (Salido 2010, OECD 2010) As delineated, the principles would be based on efficacy in governance, risk management, and compliance with the following objectives:

Governance. Assurance that the organization focuses on basic issues and who is responsible for actions and outcomes.

Risk Management. Assurance that procedures are in place for identifying, analyzing, evaluating, remdying, and monitoring risk.

Compliance. Assurance that actions are within the scope of social and legal provisions.

In accordance with the stated objectives, we can delineate the eight core principles of effective and efficient identity management. (OECD op cit., p.3)

Principle #1. Collection Limitation Principle – there should be prudent limits on the collection of personal data with the knowledge or consent of the subject.

Principle #2. Data Quality Principle – personal data should be relevant to stated purposes and be accurate, complete, and up-to-date.

Principle #3. Purpose Specification Principle – the purpose of the data collection should be specified beforehand.

Principle #4. Use Limitation Principle – data should be used only for the use specified and not be repurposed.

Principle #5. Security Safeguards Principle – personal data should be safeguarded by reasonable and state-of-the art security facilities.

Principle #6. Openness Principle – the technical infrastructure for protecting personal data should be open as to development, practices, and policies.

Principle #7. Individual Participation Principle – the subject should have the right to definitive information concerning the personal data collected, methods used, and safeguards employed and have the right to challenge the procedures employed.

Principle #8. Accountability Principle – social, business, educational, and governmental data controllers should be required by legal or regularity means to abide by principles 1-8 and be accountable for violations of their provisions.

The eight principles of identity agree in part and parcel to Cavoukian's "7 Laws of Identity, listed as follows without unneeded detail: (Cavoukian 2010) Personal control and consent; Minimal disclosure for limited use; "Need to know access;" User-directed identity; Universal monitoring of the use of identification technology; Human understanding and involvement; and Consistent access and interface to personal data.

Cloud computing hasn't caused the identity problem, but it clearly has exacerbated it, because of limitless flexibility, Internet service provisioning, enhanced collaboration, portability, and easy access. Some of the features that support identity protection are multiple and partial identities, single sign-on, third-part trust relationships, and audit tools that can be used by individuals.

Clearly, there are aspects of cloud computing that need to be addressed.

REFERENCES

1   Bacon, Sir Francis. 1605. *Advancement of Learning*. (Republished in the *Great Books of the Western World*. Volume 30, Robert Maynard Hutchins, Editor in Chief, Chicago: Encyclopedia Britannica, Inc., 1952).

2   Black, M. 1952. Identity of Indiscernibles. *Mind* 61:153. (Secondary reference.)

3   ACLU of Northern California. 2010. *Cloud Computing: Storm Warning for Privacy?* www.dotrights.org, (downloaded 3/11/2010).

4   Cavoukian, A. 2009. *Privacy in the Clouds*. Toronto: Information and Privacy Commission of Ontario (www.ipc.on.ca).

5   Cavoukian, A. 2010. 7 Laws of Identity: The Case for Privacy-Embedded Laws of Identity I the Digital Age." Toronto: Information and Privacy Commission of Ontario (www.ipc.on.ca).

6   Center for Digital Democracy (CDD). 2009. *Online Behavioral Tracking and Targeting: Legislative Primer September 2009*. www.democraticmedia. org/privacy-legislative-primer. (downloaded 3/11/2010).

7   Federal Bureau of Investigation. 2004. *Privacy Impact Assessment*. www. fbi.gov/biometrics.htm. (downloaded 2/20/2010).

8   Kant, I. 1787. *Critique of Pure Reason*. (Republished in *Basic Writings of Kant*. Allen W. Wood, Editor, New York: The Modern Library, 2001).

9   Katzan, H. 1975. *Computer Data Management and Data Base Technology*, New York: Van Nostrand Reinhold Co.

10 Katzan, H. 2010. On the Privacy of Cloud Computing. *International Journal of Management and Information Systems,* (accepted for publication).

11 Nelson, M. 2009. Cloud Computing and Public Policy. *Briefing Paper for the ICCP Technology Foresight Forum*. JT03270509, DATI/ICP(2009)17.

12 OECD 2010. OECD Guidelines on the Protection of Privacy and Transborder Flows of Personal Data. www.oecd.org. (downloaded 3/23/2010).

13 Russell, B. 1912. *The Problems of Philosophy*. (Republished by Barnes & Noble, New York, 2004).

14 Russell, B. 1919. *Introduction to Mathematical Philosophy*. (Republished by Barnes & Noble, New York, 2005).

15 Salido, J. and P. Voon. 2010. A Guide to Data Governance for Privacy, Confidentiality, and Compliance: Part 1. The Case for Data Governance. Microsoft Corporation,

16 Stroll, A. 1967. *Identity.* (Entry in *The Encyclopedia of Philosophy*, Volume 4, Paul Edwards, Editor in Chief, New York: Macmillan Publishing Co., 1967).

***** End of Chapter 9 *****

10

PRINCIPLES OF SERVICE SYSTEMS: AN ONTOLOGICAL APPROACH

SERVICE PRINCIPLES

The basic concepts of service, service systems, and service science have been well-developed. (Sampson and Froehle 2006, Maglio and Zysman 2007, and Katzan 2008b) To fully benefit from the service perspective, however, an ontological foundation is required to facilitate communication among researchers and assist with the ongoing theoretical and pragmatic development of the discipline. To some extent, an ontology is dependant upon a particular point of view, and this paper seeks to identify a set of rigid descriptors that link to the various underlying concepts. We are going to take the view that a comprehensive depiction of the application domain is as important in service ontology as is the taxonomy used to describe it.

Service

In a widely distributed paper on the science of service, Spohrer and associates (Spohrer 2007b) give several characteristics of an elementary service event: customer participation, simultaneity, perishability, intangibility, and heterogeneity. *Customer participation* refers to the co-production of the service experience and the co-creation of service value. *Simultaneity* denotes the fact that a service is produced and consumed simultaneously. *Perishability* refers to time perishable capacity from the provider's viewpoint and opportunity loss from the client's perspective. *Intangibility* normally denotes the obvious fact that goods are not produced by a service event. Lastly, *heterogeneity* refers to the variation in a service from client to client and from provider to provider, along with the recognition that a service system is a complex system that can be mediated by information technology. This seemingly simple definition belies the complexity of the situation, since there is a multiplicity of service definitions, based on existential considerations. A service is a socially constructed temporal event, and within that domain, an objectivist view of the subject matter is adopted. Service exists and possesses an implicit lifecycle comprised of design, development, analysis, and implementation, similar in nature to most technical innovations. Specificity will be added to the service lifecycle model in a later section. Moreover, a service evolves and is subject to descriptive and nominative modalities. As with traditional social activities, a service can be analyzed and measured. In fact, a service is an economic entity that possesses demonstrable value to the participants, in particular, and to organizations and society, as a whole.

Services are indigenous to the existence of modern society. In fact, if one replaces the concept of labor with that of service, the principles of service science can be derived from the essential work of Adam Smith (Smith 1776), most pointedly in his notions of "value in use" and "value in exchange."

Social Constructivism

Social constructivism is a theory of knowledge (epistemology) based, at least in part, on the social and material setting in which a belief is produced or maintained. In social constructivism, individuals and groups participate in a perceived reality, and create an element of knowledge, as espoused by the philosophical doctrine of Equal Validity. (Boghossian 2006, Bergquist 1993) Equal validity suggests the notion that other means of knowing exist in addition to the factual predominance of scientific investigation. Consider an example of a simple wooden chair developed in antiquity and regarded as a place to sit and pile books. A chair is made from a type of wood that we as a society have discovered as being useful to the purpose. Wood exists as a natural phenomenon independently of chairs and the social setting in which it exists. The precise form and substance of a chair, however, is a socially constructed form of knowledge that none but the hardened skeptic would deny is a valid form of knowledge. Service systems are socially constructed forms of interaction wherein entities exchange beneficial forms of action through the combination of people and technologies that adapt to the changing level of information in the system. As such, reality constructed through social mechanisms is a dynamic process replicated and maintained by social interactions within a service and between services.

Service systems are actual social phenomena that existed, in part, before the development of service science and are analogous to economic systems that existed before the development and study of economics. Both types of systems are governed by events in their operational environments and are continually being created, modified, and retired. A service is neither synthetic (like synthetic rubber or various chemical compounds) nor artificial (like artificial intelligence in the computer field). Services are observable, and through a process of shared reality, concepts are developed that lead to classes of service and subsequently instances of that service. We are going to apply epistemological concepts to develop a service ontology that adheres to the hypothetico-deductive modality of scientific research. (Sutherland 1975)

Service Universe

A *service universe* is a collection of services under consideration at a given point in time by a person, group, organization, or even a society. A service universe is typically a set of services, organized in some fashion to achieve a discernable purpose. However, that need not necessarily be the case, and could be a disparate collection of temporal service events, or even a combination of the two categories. The notion of a service is problematical, because there are differing points of view on exactly what constitutes a service, even though most persons could reliably identify a service when confronted with one. Professional, technical, and scientific people are service providers, even though they do not normally think of themselves in that fashion. Call centers, consulting companies, and utilities also do service, but dry cleaners and fast-food restaurants do them, as well. The subject is important because 80-90% of the working population in developed countries is engaged in services, and they are also consumers of services.

A simple question on this subject, such as "What is a service?' can yield a surprisingly large number of different answers. Here are a few instances that would immediately come to mind:

1. An action performed by one person or group on behalf of another person, organization, or group.
2. A generic type of action, such as a medical service or a web service.
3. The process of performing some action classified as a service.
4. The result of an action – typically a change affecting an object or person.
5. The utility of a change affecting a person or object – the value proposition.
6. An organization behaving in a prescribed way to benefit or operate in the best interests of a person or group.
7. A promise, contractual agreement, or obligation to perform a specified action in the future as a response to a triggering event.

8. The deployment of service assets for the benefit of service participants, commonly regarded as provider and client.

There are two fundamentally different points of view: the global view and the local view. The *global view* refers to the notion of a system comprised of interacting and complementary services. One could consider the global view as an external service description, useful for determining how a collection of services functions in order to benefit various people, organizations, and business processes. This view is analogous to macroeconomics. The *local view* describes and delineates the steps in a distinct service process, emphasizing the service participants and the complementary roles they play in the service event. This view is analogous to microeconomics. A discrete service fits nicely into one of several mutually exclusive categories based on service characteristics that can be distinguished with a service DNA. (Katzan 2008a) In this paper, we are going to adopt global and local viewpoints and structure the ontology according to that dichotomy. Between the global and local points-of-view, we are going to develop a consistent set of underlying concepts, relationships, and language elements.

Service Systems

A singular service event is a form of social organization in which two or more resources interact to achieve an agreed-upon purpose, where a resource can be a person, organization, or an element of technology. The service is the unit of exchange in the interaction that is established to produce value for each of the participants. (Spohrer 2007b) The resources are commonly referred to as service entities or entities. Based on this assessment, we can propose the following definition:

Definition of Service Two entities collaborate and what is produced from the interaction is a service, *if and only if*

- Both parties participate in the exchange
- Both parties benefit from the exchange such that value is co-created in a complementary form
- The action of the service is complementary
- The parties assume complementary but differing roles
- The roles are commonly known as *provider* and *client*.

The provider role is regarded as a serving activity, and the client role is, likewise, regarded as a receiving activity. Moreover, the collaboration adapts to the win-win model of economic exchange, since value is co-created for both participants. The complementary form of activity is intended to distinguish it from a supplementary form in which participants operate as partners to perform a stated function. For example, a physician and a patient exhibit complementary roles in a service, whereas a scenario in which two masons work together to build a structure represents a supplementary form of behavior. A singular service event is the most elementary form of a service system. (Spohrer 2007)

A unified service is a process that takes input and produces output. In between the input and the output, there exists one or more steps that constitute the service process. (Sampson and Froehle 2006, Katzan 2008b) The steps in a service process often include other services leading to the concept of a service system.

A *service system* is a collection of resources, economic entities, and other services capable of engaging in and supporting one or more service events. Services, i.e., service processes, may interact or they may be included in a service value chain. This is a recursive definition of a service system that would support the following modalities of service operation: *tell me, show me, help me, and do it for me.* Service systems are inherently multidisciplinary, since a service provider may not have the knowledge, skill, time, resources, and inclination to perform all of the steps in a service process and require the services of an external service provider.

As introduced above, service systems are social constructs that commonly encompass other services and are components of a larger reality. An organizational structure of this particular genre could be regarded from either of two points of view: as an economy or as an adaptive social structure. As an *economy*, it is a system of relationships that govern the availability of scarce resources and operate under conditions of efficiency and effectiveness. As an *adaptive social structure*, the efficacy of a service event depends upon the dynamic environment in which an organization operates. (Selznick 1948) A service system is a cooperative dynamically changing formal system, with a porous boundary so that the environment it which it resides has a deterministic effect on its behavior.

A unified service system requires some sort of organizational entanglement so that an enterprise can invest prudently and produce predictable outcomes. Accordingly, research into the mechanics of service systems requires three things: an appropriate operational platform, a design theoretic formulation, and an ontology of service and service systems, which is introduced in subsequent sections.

Service Science

With regard to academic disciplines, there is an old saying that goes somewhat as follows: "If it has the word 'science' in its title, then it isn't science." It would appear that service science is an exception. There are two fundamental questions: "What is science, anyway?" and "What does a conceptualization of science have to do with service?"

In an earlier debate concerning computer science, Newell, Perlis, and Simon (Newell 1967) state, "Wherever there are phenomena, there can be a science to describe and explain those phenomena." Further, Kuhn (Kuhn 1962) states, "Science is the agreed upon methods and standards of rigor used by a community to develop a body of knowledge that accounts for observable phenomenon with conceptual frameworks, theories, models, and laws that can be empirically tested and applied within a world view or paradigm." Moreover, since service systems are an observable and evolving phenomena, subject to the dynamics of the economic world, the development of a science of service, replete with its own frameworks, models, and theories, is an essential element in a total world view. (Spohrer 2007a)

Epistemologically, there exists a conceptual service universe in which observable services and service systems operate. One can view this service universe in a manner similar to which we view the physical universe described by physics and chemistry. The modus operandi in those disciplines is to abstract a piece of that universe and study it as a sub-discipline. Mechanics, heat, and sound are elementary sub-disciplines that fall into the discipline of physics.

The services in the service universe can be viewed metaphorically as entities floating around in a service space waiting for the chance to be called upon to execute as a singular event, as a component of a service system, or as a chance to be called upon interactively. Some services are used in more than one service system. *Service science* is a collection of models of sub-disciplines abstracted from the service universe, in much the same manner that the physical sciences are collections of sub-disciplines. The procedure in all cases is to take a piece of an existing system and put it under the microscope of academic scrutiny. Thus, a particular service or a service system is an abstraction of service science, as with the physical universe, and a service theory is a means of tying the various models together. On the other hand, if one views the entire amorphous service space as a service system, then service science could be alternately viewed as a basic abstraction of service systems, realizing, of course, that the ultimate objective is to study categories of service systems.

There are, of course, additional considerations regarding the phenomena of service and service systems. Services evolve and are continually being developed and modified. Service systems are affected through their porous boundaries by stakeholders, laws, and social customs. They also require formalization as important aspects of the discipline of service science.

ONTOLOGY

Ontology is a specification of "what is." In philosophy, use of the term reflects the study of being (or existence) and describes and delineates a collection of basic categories, and defines the entities and classes of elements within a category. In service science, ontology is a specification of a conceptualization used to enable knowledge sharing. Since ontology concerns existence, an ontological definition of a subject – perhaps a service category – reflects a materialization of a concept obtained through a shared reality, and not what it is called or how it is made or used. In this paper, the definition of ontology, as "a set of representational primitives with which to model a domain of knowledge or discourse," will be adopted. (Gruber 2008, Wikipedia 2009a) More specifically, ontology can be viewed as a data model that describes objects, classes, attributes, and relations. In his ground-breaking book on knowledge representation, John F. Sowa gives an appropriate definition for our purposes:

> The subject of *ontology* is the study of the *categories* of things that exist or may exist in some domain. The product of such a study, called *ontology*, is a catalog of the types of things that are assumed to exist in a domain of interest **D** from the perspective of a person who uses the language **L** for the purpose of talking about **D**. The types in the ontology represent the *predicates, word senses,* or *concept and relation types* of the language **L** when used to discuss topics in the domain **D**. (Sowa 2000)

One common approach to the delineation of ontological elements is to divide the extant entities into groups called "categories." These lists of categories can be quite different from one another. It is in this latter sense that ontology is applied to such fields as theology, service science, and artificial intelligence. (Wikipedia 2009)

Ontological Naming

In the naming of ontological elements, it is important to note that there are two approaches to the use of nouns. In one philosophical school, nouns should refer to existent entities. In the alternate school, nouns are used as a shorthand as reference to a collection of object or events. For example the word *mind* would refer to a collection of mental states, and society would refer to a collection of people.

Ontological Engineering

Ontological engineering encompasses a set of activities conducted during conceptualization, design, implementation, and deployment of ontologies. (Dedvedzic 2002) Ontological engineering seeks to achieve the following goals in a given domain:

Definition of terms

Establishment of a body of domain knowledge
Specification of coherent and expressive knowledge bases

In short, ontology defines the vocabulary of a problem domain and a set of constraints on how terms are related. It also gives data types and operations defined over the data types.

Most forms of ontology are expressed in an ontology language and share structural similarities, such as individuals, classes, attributes, relations, function, restrictions, rules, axioms, and events. The basic idea behind ontology languages is to allow software agents to communicate in a knowledge intensive computer-based environment: We are going to concentrate on the following components: (Guarino 1995, Wikipedia 2009)

Individuals referring to instances and objects

Classes expressed as sets, collections, and kinds of things

Attributes giving features and characteristics of individuals and classes

Relations that determine ways that individuals and classes relate

The components determine whether a specific ontology is a domain ontology or an upper ontology. In a *domain ontology*, a specific type would be relevant to particular category, such as in a medical or household category. In an *upper ontology*, a type would be applicable to all ontologies in the universe of discourse. In the service ontology, presented in the following section, we are going to be developing an upper ontology for service systems.

UPPER ONTOLOGY FOR SERVICE SYSTEMS

The ontology of service systems is a developmental artifact for the study, design, analysis, and application of services. Essentially, a framework is needed to tie the elements together, so that they are applicable to a wide range of operational scenarios. (Alter 2008) The primary measure of an ontological determination is how it assists in delineating the value chain for services, comprised of people, technology, and organizations, and its relevance to education, government, business, and other social phenomena.

Service Systems Lifecycle

Service science is one of the few disciplines in which the basic principles and resultant theory apply to both small-scale and large-scale operations. We are going to proceed with that assumption. In its most basic form, a service is a value producing interaction between a service provider and a service client, consisting of a process conceptualized as a layered set of activities. (Ferrario and

Guardino 2008) It is useful to conceptualize the layers according to the following global service system lifecycle:

> Service commitment
> Service production
> Service availability
> Service delivery
> Service analysis
> Service termination

Initially, we are going to be looking at services from a global view, where the lifecycle pertains to a set of generic services supplied by an economic entity, such as a governing body, a business, an institution, or an individual acting in a service capacity. *Service commitment* refers to the formal agreement to provide a class of services to a service audience by a principal or trustee with the proper administrative control over the service environment. The agreement to provide fire service by a municipality and the founding of a health clinic are common examples. *Service production* pertains to service provisioning, infrastructure, availability, quality management, and back-office processing. The producer is the agent of the principal in a prototypical principal-agent scenario. The principal and agent may be the same economic entity or different economic entities depending upon the scope of the service domain. The manager of a chain of restaurants and the medical director of a clinic are examples. *Service availability* is the time during which a service is available. Commitment does not necessarily imply availability, because of a variety of spatiotemporal events. *Service delivery* is the class of actions usually regarded as the service and is the layer where the service client comes into the picture. The doctor/patient relationship is a good example of this layer. The service provider, who could have a dual role as producer, is an agent of the producer as the primary source of service revenue and the primary provider of a service. *Service analysis* refers to measurement activities and the determination of value propositions needed to sustain service operations. *Service termination* reflects the inevitable consequence of a dynamic and evolving economic environment where a total service operation has to be retired, because of insufficient activity or realigned opportunities. The global lifecycle represents a provisioning perspective of service systems.

Service Entities

We are looking at five service entities: the *service principal*, functioning as a trustee of a service or a service system; the *service producer*, responsible for the availability, infrastructure, service provisioning, and back-office processing; the *service provider*, charged with the application of resources for the benefit of another service entity: the *service client*, who has a complementary service relationship with the service provider; and the *service object* that may be the direct recipient of the result of the service process.

A *service entity* need not be a person, but can be a group, organization, business, governing body, educational institution, or a physical object, such as a possession or an element of computer software.

Service Commitment

Service commitment is a guarantee by a principal to provide a set of actions that constitutes a service. A common example might be the promise of a mayor of a town to provide fire service to his constituents. (Ferrario and Guardino 2008) The principal can be an organization, such as a government, a medical group, an educational institution, a private service business, a consulting firm with a service-level agreement, and an ad hoc entity that provides service to other service entities. A service commitment may result from an explicit declaration, such as "I agree to provide said service to a receiving agent" or be implicit in a legal charter or understanding, such as a medical practice or financial institution. A service commitment may apply to all constituents in the principal's domain – perhaps to all families moving into a community or entering a service facility.

The committed service may not, and probably will not, be performed by the principal, who may rely on a service producer and an ensuing service provider known as a *service agent* to actually execute the service process. Thus, a service agent provides a service to the principal and to the service object. The service principal, producer, and provider may coincide or be distinct to some degree.

Service Production

Service production supports a service commitment by establishing service parameters, such as time, location, availability, infrastructure, provisioning, record keeping, and legal compliance and certification. Time and location are key factors in service delivery that are summarized through a service DNA, which partitions the service domain into mutually exclusive service categories. (Katzan 2008a) The principle element in service production is maintenance of the service infrastructure, consisting of physical facilities, operational procedures, satisfaction of legal requirements, competent provider provisioning, and dependable auxiliary service provisioning.

Service Availability

The *availability* of a service is dependent upon the inherent nature of the service commitment. The access to and duration of medical provisioning, banking, insurance, product warranties, and household service, as examples, probably differ in most cases. It is important to additionally note the significance of service commitment with regard to service availability. What a service principal commits to is the *service content* and not to its associated service process, scheduling, and other operational considerations.

Service Delivery

In order for a service provider and a client to co-create a service event, there must be some degree of locality to the situation, in the sense that the client travels to the provider, the provider travels to the client, the client and provider execute the service event in a third-party location, or they communicate via some form of interactive device and its corresponding media. Location is basic to service provisioning. When the client travels to the provider site, the location is termed a *service factory* and the client or the service object remain in the service factory for the duration of the service transaction. When the service object is left in the provider's facilities, the location is known as a *service shop*. The provider may travel to *client facilities*, as in the cases of custodial work or nursing home care. With information service, the provider may reside in a remote facility and provide access through a service portal.

A related consideration is the distinction between *discrete service* and *continuous service*. There are many edge cases. Insurance is commonly regarded as a continuous service, as is banking – except in the cases where the customer visits a bank branch. Medical provisioning, automobile maintenance, and household service are usually regarded as discrete services. In the latter case, when a service event is over, it's over. A follow-on service is regarded as another service event.

Service Analysis

To some extent, all services consist of the application of resources, and the success of those services is dependent upon how efficiently and effectively those resources are applied in a normative manner to a specific problem domain. (Spohrer 2007a) Thus, measurement and analysis is required to assess both individual service interactions and the cumulative result of a set of service interactions. The basic tenet of service delivery is the following. *The client starts out with expectations, and a service deliverer should start out off by assessing what those expectations are.* However, not all service events are successful, so that a risk analysis should be performed by the providers and the client prior to a service engagement. In service analysis, the success of a service event is dependent upon how accurately the service providers and the client assess their roles.

Measurement and analysis are often the modus for judging service and service quality, and in an organizational setting, is achieved through service level agreements between complementary economic entities. For instances where implicit agreements persist, service analysis involves responsiveness, timeliness, and completeness – traditional metrics that have evolved through informal agreement.

Service Termination

In order for a service system to be successful, it must *exist* and *persist*. To exist, that service must satisfy the economic goals of provider, client, producer, and trustee in due consideration of the needs surrounding its competitors, partners (business or operational), employees, and investors. (Spohrer 2007a) The economic goals are known as the *value proposition* of the service consisting of the provider's sacrifice, the client's sacrifice, provider's exploitation, and the client's exploitation, from both short-term and long-term perspectives. (Alter 2008) Accordingly, a discrete service offering can be unsuccessful in either of four ways: (Spohrer op cit.)

> The client does not accept the provider's value proposition in light of its own.
> The client decides to engage in "self service'
> The client decides to accept service from an alternate source
> The client decides to forgo service

Thus, cumulative service decisions from within the *client domain* essentially determine the persistence of a service commitment.

DOMAIN ONTOLOGY FOR SERVICE

A discrete service event entails the commitment of resources for the benefit of a client. Each service event – frequently referred to as a service interaction – consists of a series of steps called *the service process* intended to achieve a particular goal. Within a given service category, the various service processes are similar within acceptable limits of variability.

Basic Service Categories

A *service* is a provider/client relationship (Katzan 2008b) that captures value for both participants that can be individuals, organizations, software, or a complex arrangement of the three, given as follows:

$$
\begin{aligned}
\text{<service-participant> ::=} \quad & \text{<individual> | <organization>} \\
& \text{|<software-as-a-service>|} \\
& \text{<service-participant> +} \\
& \text{<individual> |} \\
& \text{<service-participant> +} \\
& \text{organization>}
\end{aligned}
$$

Service operations are customarily grouped into three classes: people processing, possession processing, and information processing. Within each domain, it is therefore important to view the client/provider relationship along the following dimensions:

Tangible vs. intangible
Primary vs. secondary
    Facilitating vs. auxiliary

This approach focuses on the fact that a service event is a process consisting of primary and secondary services. (Sampson and Froehle 2006)

TANGIBLE AND INTANGIBLE SERVICE A *tangible service* is a provider/client event that results in demonstrable values to the service participants. With an individual service participant, this is a left-brain function (LBF). In retailing, it is the acquisition of a product including attendant activities that change the ownership attribute of the associated product. However, the value proposition for a product may be determined from the service it provides, rather than from the intrinsic value of its specific components. In pure service, such as a people and possession processing service, value is created through the work performed on behalf of the client by the provider. With information service, the service's value is derived from the transfer of information from service provider to the client. An *intangible service* provides value for a service participant through the perspective of a right-brain function (RBF). Certain products, such as premium automobiles (Rosengarten 2006), special jewelry, and elegant real estate, for example, are typically associated with a high-level of intangible service. As mentioned previously, the intangible value of a product may exceed its tangible value.

PRIMARY AND SECONDARY SERVICE A *primary service* is the core service for which the provider and the client interact to produce demonstrable value. Simple examples are a dental appointment or a lawn care service. A *secondary service* is a service that does not exist separately as a primary service and plays a supportive role to a primary service. Common examples are the weigh in and blood pressure checks associated with a doctor's visit and the acceptance and delivery of garments at a dry cleaning establishment.

Secondary service can also exist as a supplementary or referral service.

FACILITATING AND AUXILIARY SERVICE A *facilitating service* is disjoint from a primary or secondary service and enables a client to obtain utility from a tangible service. Usability service, commonly associated with automobiles and computers, is a common example of a facilitating service. Another common example of a facilitating service is the purchase of an event ticket. In this instance, the event – be it a visit to the theatre, sporting match, or an amusement park – is the tangible service and the ticket is the intangible service.

An *auxiliary service* is independent from a core service and may be experienced before or after the primary service. A blood test taken prior to a doctor's appointment and a medical referral are examples of auxiliary services.

SERVICE FUNCTIONS Many service functions relate to satisfaction models for consumer judgments regarding service interactions. One of two possible viewpoints is selected: expectation confirmation or rational utility assessment. With the expectation confirmation approach, the psychological distance between expectation and realization is measured. The tangible aspects of service are emphasized. With the rational utility approach, the tangible factors of service delivery, as well as the intangible factors, are taken into consideration. *Tangible assessment* is a means of referring to the demonstrable attributes of service delivery, such as product characteristics, skills of the service provider, and explicit service results as they pertain to people, possession, and information processing service. Tangible service results are utilitarian and measurable. *Intangible assessment* is a means of referring to the feeling that one experiences from a service interaction or the ownership of a product. Intangible service results are affective and hedonistic. The level of intangible service is normally a function of the feelings that one derives from ownership of a premium product or the participation in a service event with a particular service provider. The service functions are summarized in the DNA of a category of service, presented in the appendix and covered below.

Service Process Lifecycle

It is necessary to identify the key events in the operational service lifecycle and the major entities involved. The *service lifecycle* can be viewed as those activities that exist between service acquisition and service termination – from both structural and operational viewpoints. From the *structural* point-of-view, the set of layered activities incorporate the service commitment, service infrastructure, service availability, service delivery, and the eventual termination of a service, as delineated previously for the upper service ontology. From an *operational* point-of-view, the layered activities describe service events and incorporate those transactable actions that constitute the essence of service.

Based on the above definitions, the lifecycle of a service process consists of a loosely defined set of steps intended to co-create value for complementary service participants. It is useful to conceptualize a generic lifecycle for a domain ontology as consisting of the following steps:

Service acquisition
Service invocation
Service execution
Service termination

Service acquisition refers to the process of identifying a service provider with the requisite infrastructure, and its corollary, the process of attracting clients. *Service invocation* involves the scheduling and logistics part of the service process. *Service execution* entails the actual steps in the service process including supplementary services. *Service termination* incorporates referral, warranty, and archiving activities. The requisite infrastructure for sustaining the service process lifecycle is referred to as the *service platform* and is related to the activities of the producer in the upper ontology, covered previously. The service process lifecycle can be viewed as a set of layered events. We are going to supplement the service process lifecycle with service analytics that are descriptive of the end state of a service event.

Service Acquisition

The generic steps that comprise service acquisition represent the handshaking needed to establish a service relationship. From the client perspective, acquisition consists of an awareness that some form of service is needed, known as *service awareness*, followed by the discovery of a suitable delivery vehicle, called *service discovery*, perhaps using Web Services, and finally the development of a service level agreement, usually known as *service negotiation*. From the provider perspective, service acquisition is fueled by a service commitment, service availability, and a variety of service conditions incorporated in the DNA of that service category. Prototypical examples of service acquisition are finding a doctor in a new town or locating a shop for automobile repair.

In a discrete service, the service provider assumes the role of the "service producer" and the service client assumes the role of the "service requestor," in the sense that the client takes the initiative in the acquisition process. In professional and technical services, the service provider often assumes the role of the requestor by directly approaching from a business perspective or through direct advertising.

Service Invocation

An exogenous condition is needed to initiate a service process by the service provider on behalf of a service client. (Ferrario 2008) It is termed a *triggering event* that can take one of a variety of forms, such as:

- An independent event requiring attention, such as a medical situation or a fire
- A request by the client, or its representative, to have a service performed that the client doesn't want to do, can't do, or the provider can do more efficiently
- A required service, perhaps by law or convention, initiated by the client or a governing body

The triggering event is typically followed by a *service scheduling* process that establishes a spatiotemporal location for service delivery. Some service providers use appointments to manage demand as a means of achieving service efficiency. The steps that facilitate core or primary service invocation are customarily regarded as a secondary service.

Service invocation involves back-office administrative record keeping and coordination, such that the provider and client can interact on a planned basis. The service delivery, availability, and demand dimensions of the service DNA sequence reflect the dynamics between provider and client in a service event. Appointments with professional service providers are formally scheduled, whereas arrangements with nonprofessionals are commonly scheduled on an informal basis.

Service Execution

Service execution is the phase of the service process lifecycle where the service provider engages the service client to achieve a goal state that reflects both provider and client perspectives. Alternately, the service object may be a service entity over which the client has legal or social responsibility. In general, the service object can be a person, a possession, information, or an abstract entity such as a financial investment. We are going to refer to the provider, the client, and the service object as *service participants*.

The primary objective of a service event is referred to as the *core service* that has tangible value to the service participants. The core service is conventionally comprised of primary, secondary, and auxiliary services, as described earlier under Basic Service Categories. We are going to establish five categories with which the execution of a service event, per se, can be determined:

Category	Alternative
Modality	discrete, continuous
Diversity	heterogeneous, homogeneous
Temporality	active, passive
Complexity	low complexity, high complexity
Duration	short, long

Modality denotes whether the texture of the service takes place as a single interaction (*discrete*), such as a doctor's visit that is over when it is over, or it takes place over an extended period of time (*continuous*), such as an insurance policy. *Diversity* refers to whether the service can be performed by a specific provider (*heterogeneous*), such as particular attorney or accountant, or any one of a group of providers (*homogeneous*), such as a bank teller. *Temporality* specifies whether the service is one in which the provider and client actively participate (*active*), such as a dentist's visit, or one in which the service participants are not actively engaged (*passive*) until a triggering event occurs, such as an insurance policy or a municipality's fire service. *Complexity* refers to whether the service is completed in a few similar steps (*low complexity*), or many different steps (*high complexity*). A hospital procedure or a home remodeling would reflect a high complexity; an appointment at the eye doctor's or a car detailing would exhibit low complexity. *Duration*, not to be confused with modality, refers to whether the service execution takes place in a few hours or less (*short duration*), or whether it takes place over a few days or longer (*high duration*). In medicine, a doctor's visit would have short duration, and a hospital stay would have long duration. In transportation, a ferry ride would have short duration, and a trans-Atlantic cruise would have long duration. Clearly, the collection of categories is generic and reflects the underlying difficulty in attempting to be specific with a ubiquitous social phenomena, such as service.

It is important to state the difference between DNA dimensions (see the *Appendix*) and categories of service execution. DNA dimensions are intended to describe and delineate the total service environment from the standpoint of upper and domain ontology. The categories of service execution are simply intended to provide specificity to the service process.

Service Termination and Analytics

Service termination and analytics encompasses follow-on activity, record keeping, archiving, and the financial aspects of service. Accordingly, this essential lifecycle element involves both front-office and back-office activities on the part of the provider and the client, leading to quality and value assessments.

The service value analysis involves four components: provider's costs, provider's revenue, client's cost, client's revenue – recognizing that cost and revenue are not necessarily monetary. The *fundamental theorem of service delivery* applies to service analytics such that the cost of service by the provider must equal the value of commensurate service to the client, represented as:

$$C_p = V_C$$

where C_p is the cost to the provider and V_C is the value to the client. Accordingly,

$$C_p = C_p + C_s + C_t$$

where C_p is the cost of primary core service, C_s is the cost of secondary service, and C_t are the transaction costs.

Similarly,

$$V_C = V_t + V_i$$

where V_t is the value of tangible service and V_i is the value of intangible service.

Analytics help the provider and the client answer fundamental questions, such as: Should we? (*business value*), Can we? (*technology*), May we? (*governance*), and Will we? (*business priority*).

TAXONOMY OF SERVICE SYSTEMS

This section delineates a taxonomy of service systems. A taxonomy essentially provides a prose glossary of a body of knowledge and a methodology for systems analysis and design. In this particular instance, the taxonomy of service systems supplies a lens into a collection of concepts, definitions, and relations that describe the complex subject of service science.

1. Service Identification
   1.1 Service name
   1.2 Sponsoring organization
   1.3 Service initiation date
2. Service Participants
   2.1 Service principal
   2.2 Service producer
   2.3 Service provider
   2.4 Service client
   2.5 Service object
3. Service System Lifecycle
   3.1 Service commitment
   3.2 Service production
   3.3 Service availability
   3.4 Service delivery
   3.5 Service analysis
   3.6 Service termination
4. Service Process
   4.1 Service acquisition
       4.1.1 Service awareness
       4.1.2 Service discovery
       4.1.3 Service negotiation
   4.2 Service invocation
       4.2.1 Triggering event
       4.2.2 Service scheduling
   4.3 Service execution
       4.3.1 Service participants
       4.3.2 Service categories
           4.3.2.1 Service modality
           4.3.2.2 Service diversity
           4.3.2.3 Service temporality
           4.3.2.4 Service complexity
           4.3.2.5 Service duration
           4.3.2.6 Service DNA

4.4 Service termination
    4.4.1 Provider costs
        4.4.1.1 Core service
        4.4.1.2 Secondary service
        4.4.1.3 Auxiliary service
        4.4.1.4 Transaction costs
    4.4.2 Client value
        4.4.2.1 Tangible value
        4.4.2.2 Intangible value

In using the taxonomy of service systems, a service analyst would necessarily supply entries for each of the ontological elements, as required by a particular service system under investigation.

SUMMARY

An ontological introduction to the principles of service systems has been presented with an emphasis on concepts, classes, objects, relations, and terminology. The paper introduces social constructivism, as a basis of service science, and continues with service concepts, service systems, ontology, and then on to upper ontology for services, domain ontology for service, and finally a taxonomy of service systems, as well as a short treatise on a DNA of service.

REFERENCES

Alter. S. 2008. Service system fundamentals: Work system, value chain, and life cycle. *IBM System Journal*, 47(1): 71-85.

Bergquist, W. 1993. Post Modern Thought in a Nutshell. [Published in *Classics of Organization Theory* (4th Edition – J. Shafritz and J. Ott, editors), New York: Harcourt Brace College Publishers, 1996. Adapted from Bergquist, W. 1993. *The Postmodern Organization: Mastering the Art of Irreversible Change*, Jossey-Bass Inc., Publishers, pp. 15-36.]

Boghossian, P. 2006. *Fear of Knowledge: Against Relativism and Constructivism.* Oxford: Oxford University Press.

Dedvedzic, V. 2002. Understanding Ontological Engineering. *Communications of the ACM* 45(4):136-144.

Ferrario, R. and N. Guardino. 2008. Towards an Ontological Foundation for Services Science. *Proceedings of the Future Internet Symposium,* Vienna Austria, 28-30 September 2008.

Fitzsimmons, J.A. and M.J. Fitzsimmons. 2006. *Service Management: Operations, Strategy, Information Technology* (5th Edition), New York: McGraw-Hill Irwin.

Gruber, T. 2008. Ontology. *Encyclopedia of Database Systems,* Liu, L. and M. Ozsu (Eds.), Springer-Verlag,

Guarino, N. 1995. Formal Ontology, Conceptual Analysis and Knowledge Representation. *International Journal of Human-Computer Studies,* 43(5-6):907-928.

IBM Almaden Services Research. 2006. "SSME: What are services?" Referenced from the following Web site: http://almaden.ibm.com/ssme.

Katzan, H. 2008a. Event Differentiation in Service Science. *Journal of Business and Economics Research,* 6(5): 141-152.

Katzan, H. 2008b. *Service Science: Concepts, Technology, Management.* New York: iUniverse, Inc.

Kuhn, T. 1996. *The Structure of Scientific Revolution* (3rd edition), Chicago: University of Chicago Press. [Secondary reference]

Maglio, P. and J. Zysman. 2007. Toward a Science of Service Systems. *Sofcon 2007.* Carnegie Mellon University, April 30, 2007, pp. 5-6.

Newell, A., Perlis, A., and H.A. Simon. 1967. Computer Science. *Science,* 157: 1373-1374. [Secondary reference]

Sampson, S. and C. Froehle. 2006. Foundations and Implications of a Proposed Unified Services Theory. *Productions and Operations Management,* 15(2): 329-343.

Selznick, P. 1948. Foundations of the Theory of Organization. *American Sociological Review* 13: 25-35. [Published in *Classics of Organization Theory* (4th Edition – J. Shafritz and J. Ott, editors), New York: Harcourt Brace College Publishers, 1996.]

Smith, A. 1776. *The Wealth of Nations,* published as "An Inquiry into the Nature and Causes of the Wealth of Nations" in London, England (1776).

Sowa, J. 2000. *Knowledge Representation: Logical, Philosophical and Computational Foundations,* Brooks Cole Publishing.

Spohrer, J., Anderson, L., Pass, N., Ager, T., and D. Gruhl. 2007a. Service Science. *Journal of Grid Computing* (Special Issue of Grid Economics and Business Models, August 2, 2007).

Spohrer. J., Vargo, S., Caswell, N., and P. Maglio. 2007b. The Service System is the Basic Abstraction of Service Science. IBM Almaden Research Center, http://www.almaden.ibm.com/asr.

Sutherland, J. 1975. *Systems: Analysis, Administration, and Architecture.* New York: Van Nostrand Reinhold Co.

Wikipedia. 2009. Ontology, www.wikipedia.org/ontology.

****** End of Chapter 10 *****

11

TOWARD A UNIFIED ONTOLOGY OF TRUSTED IDENTITY IN CYBERSPACE

INTRODUCTION

The nation's digital infrastructure is in jeopardy because of inadequate provisions for privacy, identity, and security. The "everyone is free to do everything" mentally that would appear to be prevalent in America and worldwide has resulted in an onslaught of identity theft, fraud, digital crime, and an unnecessary concern over cyber security by many individuals. It is patently necessary for careful participants to operate defensively in cyberspace in order to protect themselves from the evils just mentioned. Those that do not act responsibly do so at their own peril. In fact, digital crime has served as a precursor to and is associated with physical crime. (OECD 2008)

The computer security and Internet communities have been generally responsive but apparently ineffective, so it is time for a third party to step in, take charge, and provide an infrastructure to assist in protecting the citizens of the world. (White House 2010) Similar concerns prevail in other developed countries, since many cyber crimes are perpetrated from lesser-developed countries without cyber awareness from legal, political, economic, and technical perspectives.

Moreover, there are no good reasons why underdeveloped countries should get a free-ride in this regard. The nations and organizations that lend a blind-eye to its residents that commit cyber crimes against persons and organizations in other countries will change their tune when cyber benefits are subsequently denied to them through political, social, and technological processes.

This paper is a contribution to the domain of ontological commitment as it applies to a description of subjects, objects, actions, and relationships as they pertain to the National Strategy of Trusted Identity in Cyberspace initiative.

BASIC CONCEPTS

Identity is a major issue in the security of modern information systems and the privacy of data stored in those systems. Identity and privacy concerns are commonly associated with behavioral tracking, personal-identifiable information (PII), the relevance of private data, data repurposing, and identity theft. (Windley 2005) We are going to approach the subject from an information systems perspective, recognizing that the inherent problems also apply to societal systems. Information systems are a good conceptual vehicle for the underlying security, identity, and privacy models, because data is typically stored off-premises and is under the control of a third-party service provider. When a third party gets your data, who knows what is going to happen to it? The main consideration may turn out to be a matter of control, because from an organizational perspective, control over information has historically been with the organization that creates or maintains it. From a personal perspective, on the other hand, persons should have the wherewithal to control their identity and the release of information about themselves, and in the latter case, a precise determination of to whom it is released and for what reason. Privacy issues are not fundamentally caused by technology, but they are exacerbated by employing the technology for economic benefit. After a brief review of identity and privacy to set the stage, we are going to cover identity theory, privacy theory, and identity requirements. This is a working paper on this important subject.

Identity

Identity is a means of denoting an entity in a particular namespace and is the basis of security and privacy – regardless if the context is digital identification or non-digital identification. We are going to refer to an identity object as a *subject*. A subject may have several identities and belong to more than one namespace. An identity denotation is based on attributes as suggested by Figure 1.

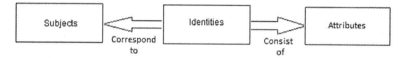

Figure 1. Conceptual relationship between subjects, identities, and attributes.

A pure identity denotation is independent of a specific context, and a federated identity reflects a process that is shared between identity management systems. When one identity management system accepts the certification of another, a phenomenon known as "trust" is established. The execution of trust is often facilitated by a third party that is acknowledged by both parties and serves as the basis of digital identity in information systems.

Access to computing facilities is achieved through a process known as authentication, whereby an entity makes a claim to its identity by presenting an identity symbol for verification and control. Authentication is usually paired with a related specification known as authorization to obtain the right to address a given service.

It is generally felt that a framework for understanding a technology should reflect the underlying concepts required for its development and subsequent acceptance as an operational modality. A technology should enable the delivery of value rather than constrain it, and that is our objective with this paper.

Privacy

Information systems typically process and store information about which privacy is of paramount concern. The main issue is identity, which serves as the basis of privacy or lack of it, and undermines the trust of individuals and organizations in other information-handling entities. The key consideration may turn out to be the integrity that organizations display when handling personal information and how accountable they are about their information practices. From an organizational perspective, control over information should remain with the end user or the data's creator with adequate controls over repurposing. From a personal perspective, the person should have the wherewithal to control his or her identity as well as the release of socially sensitive identity attributes. One of the beneficial aspects of the present concern over information privacy is that it places the person about whom data are recorded in proper perspective. Whereas such a person may be the object in an information system, he or she is regarded as the subject in privacy protection – as mentioned earlier. This usage of the word *subject* is intended to imply that a person should, in fact, have some control over the storage of personal information.

More specifically, the *subject* is the person, natural or legal, about whom data is stored. The *beneficial user* is the organization or individual for whom processing is performed, and the *agency* is the computing system in which the processing is performed and information is stored. In many cases, the beneficial user and the subject are members of the same organization.

The heart of the issue is *privacy protection*, which normally refers to the protection of rights of individuals. While the concept may also apply to groups of individuals, the individual aspect of the issue is that which raises questions of privacy and liberty

Privacy Assessment

The Federal Bureau of Investigation (U.S.A.) lists several criteria for evaluating privacy concerns for individuals and for designing computer applications: (FBI 2004)

- *What information is being collected?*
- *Why is the information being collected?*
- *What is the intended use of the information?*
- *With whom will the information be shared?*
- *What opportunities will individuals have to decline to provide information or to consent to particular uses of the information?*
- *How will the information be secure?*
- *Is this a system of records?*

Since privacy is a fundamental right in the United States, the above considerations obviously resulted from extant concerns by individuals and privacy rights groups. In a 2009 Legislative Primer, the following concerns are expressed by the Center for Digital Democracy: (CDD 2009, p. 2)

- Tracking people's every move online is an invasion of privacy.
- Online behavioral tracking and targeting can be used to take advantage of vulnerable consumers.
- Online behavioral tracking and targeting can be used to unfairly discriminate against consumers.
- Online behavioral profiles may be used for purposes beyond commercial purposes.

We are going to add to the list that the very fact that personal data is stored online is a matter of concern and should be given serious attention. Based on these issues, this paper is going to take a comprehensive look at the subject of identity in computer and human systems.

Harry Katzan Jr.

IDENTITY THEORY

The notion of identity is an important subject in philosophy, mathematics, and computer information systems. In its most general sense, identity refers to the set of characteristics that makes a subject definable. Each characteristic can be viewed as a single point in a three-dimensional Cartesian coordinate system where the axis are *subject, attribute,* and *value.* (Katzan 1975) Thus, the fact that George is twenty-five years old could be denoted by the triple <George, age, 25>. A set of characteristics over a given domain can uniquely identify a subject. This simple concept is the basis of privacy and identity in information systems and everyday life. The notion of identity applies to organizational subjects as well as to person subjects.

Knowledge, Attributes, and Identity

Identity is primarily used to establish a relationship between an attribute or set of attributes and a person, object, event, concept, or theory. The relationship can be direct, based on physical evidence, and in other cases, the relationship is indirect and based on a reference to other entities. In a similar vein, the relationship can be certain or uncertain, and in the latter case, based in deduction or inference. The relationship determines an element of knowledge. For example, the knowledge element "you are in your car" is a statement in which "you" and "your car" are things that exist and the "in" is a relationship. Direct knowledge is known by *acquaintance* and is evidenced by a physical connection. Indirect knowledge is determined through a reference to a particular with which the analyst is acquainted. The form is known as knowledge by *description.* (Russell 1912) *Direct knowledge* is determined through sense data, memory, or introspection. *Indirect knowledge* is determined through a reference to another particular, as in "the person who ran for Congress in 2004" or through a form of self-awareness where what goes on in subject's mind, for example, is estimated by an analyst's interpretation based on experience or self-evaluation.

Synthetic knowledge reflects certainty based on evidence inherent in the attribute values at hand. *Analytic knowledge* reflects a degree of uncertainty and is determined by deduction, as in "he is the only person with that 'attribute value'," or by inference based on known particulars, such as "all terrorists have beards." Inference, in this case, could be regarded as a form of derivative knowledge. The value of analytic knowledge is that it enables the analyst to exceed his or her limit of private experience.

Numerical and Qualitative Identity

Identity refers to the characteristics that make a subject the same or different. We are going to establish two forms of identity: numerical and qualitative. Two subjects are *numerically identical* if they are the same entity, such that there is only one instance. Two subject (or objects in this case) are *qualitatively identical* if they are copies or duplicates. In the popular movie *The Bourne Identity*, for example, the characters *Jason Bourne* and *David Web* are numerically identical, and the number of subjects is one. So it is with *Superman* and *Clark Kent* in another domain. On the other hand, a set of animals with the same biological characteristics – e.g., a species – are regarded as being qualitatively identical. The notion of qualitative identity is remarkably similar to the modern definition of a *category* informally defined as a collection of entities with the same characteristics, having the same values for the same attributes.

Theory of the Indiscernibles

An important aspect of identity theory is that subjects exhibit features of permanence and change, analogous to sameness and difference mentioned previously. We are going to discuss the concept of temporal identity in the next section. The notion of change implies that a subject undergoes transformation and also has a property that remains unchanged. Both Locke and Hume have proclaimed that change reflects the idea of unity and not of identity. Leibnitz proposed the *Theory of Indiscernibles* suggesting that subjects (i.e., objects or entities) that are indiscernible are identical. (Stroll 1967) The subject of indiscernibles has implications for information systems and attribute change. To what extent a change in a characteristic denotes a change in identity is an open item at this time and implies that there is a probabilistic aspect to identity.

Russell approaches the subject of identity from an alternate viewpoint, analogous to definite and indefinite articles. Russell proposes that a description may be of two sorts: definite and indefinite. A definite description is a name, and an indefinite description is a collection of objects x that have the property ø, such that the proposition øx is true. (Russell 1919) In the phrase *Dan Brown is a famous author*, for example, 'Dan Brown" is a name and the indefinite description is obvious, leading to the probabilistic link between a subject and a characteristic.

Temporal Identity

There is a rich quantity of philosophical literature on the change of identity over time. Are you the same person you were yesterday? Are there persistent attributes that allow for positive identity between time periods? As alluded to previously, entities in everyday life exhibit features of permanence and change. In the domain of personal identity, address attribute is a primary candidate for change. For example, John Smith lives at 123 Main Street. He moves out and another John Smith moves in. This is a distinct possibility in a crowded city. In there a concept in identity theory for this phenomena? Should an identity system take this eventuality into consideration?

There is a form of *attribute duality* between a person subject and an object subject. A subject – an object, such as a residence, in this case – is characterized by who lives there. For example, rich people live on Sutton Place in New York. The discussion leads to four related concepts: endurant identity, perdurant identity, endurant attribute, and perdurant attribute. Clearly, the term *endurant* refers to a noun that does not change, where perdurant refers to one that does. Thus, the identity problem is essentially translated to an operant problem of "recognizing identity."

PRIVACY THEORY

It has long been recognized that privacy is a two-edged sword, not only for individuals, but also for groups and organizations. Subjects have First and Fourth Amendment rights designed to protect against unwarranted disclosure of information with unlimited scope to unwanted parties without proper authorization by the subject. However, privacy considerations protect criminals and terrorists, in addition to ordinary citizens, groups, and organizations. Protections and other conventions used to safeguard trade secrets can also be employed to enable non-disclosure of design and manufacturing flaws from consumers and regulatory bodies.

Privacy has been in the news for at least forty years originating with Alan Westin's seminal book on the subject entitled *Privacy and Freedom*, published in 1967. Others have joined the struggle, namely (Westin 1977, Miller 1971, Katzan 1980, and Givens 2009) to reference only a few of many, with apologies to those not mentioned. One of the toughest problems facing the computer industry is data protection, summarized very well in 1971 by Arthur R. Miller: (Miller 1971, p.37)

> The new information technologies seem to have given birth to a new social virus – "data-mania." Its symptoms are shortness of breath and heart palpitations when contemplating a new computer application, a feeling of possessiveness about information and a deep resentment toward those who won't yield it, a delusion that all information handlers can walk on water, and a highly advanced case of astigmatism that prevents the affected victim from

perceiving anything but the intrinsic value of data. Fortunately, only some members of the information-handling fraternity have been stricken by the disease.

This quote was written over 39 years ago; what would the author think about today's environment?

Privacy and Data Protection

Data protection is given the most attention when the privacy of an individual or an organization is jeopardized. According to Alan F. Westin: (Westin 1967)

> Privacy is the claim of individuals, groups, or institutions to determine for themselves when, how, and to what extent information about them is communicated to others.

> Privacy is related to data protection, because it is an integral part of society and affects the behavior of its citizens. *Privacy is a service that a subject should expect from and be provided by society.* The physical state of being private has four primary attributes: solitude, intimacy, anonymity, and reserve, which supply group separation, group participation, group freedom, and personal protection, respectively. These states collectively provide the confidentiality required to participate in a civilized society. Concerns for privacy should be an integral part of a data protection program.

An organization requires privacy to achieve its basic objective – whether it is business, education, or government. The disclosure of private internal affairs affects "brand equity" and is detrimental to success.

Another consideration is personal surveillance – even though it may be socially or legally accepted. When a subject does not have control over its informational profile, there is no safeguard over its authenticity. Therefore, a double barreled approach, consisting of technology and regulation, is required for operating in a global economy. (Katzan, 1980, p. 44)

Information Control

Because of the widespread application of computer and communications technology, there has been a gradual trend among private institutions and government agencies to ignore the individual's need for privacy. Privacy safeguards are the individual's sole line of defense against the exercise of power through information control. Individuals can lose control of information about themselves in three ways:

1. Information obtained against the subject's wishes.
2. Information obtained from an agency against the wishes of the agency and of the subject.
3. Information willingly disclosed by the beneficial user or agency but against the subject's wishes.

Information obtained against a subject's wishes is an area in which privacy is normally expected. This category includes explicit attempts to obtain information and implicit methods where a subject is forced to disclose personal information. Typical actions are:

1. Searches and seizure
2. Compelled self-disclosure
3. Informers and secret agents
4. Participant monitoring
5. Public observation and recording of information
6. Consent for fear of reprisal
7. Disclosure for privilege

Some benefits are commonly associated with disclosure of private information, so the fine line between willing and unauthorized disclosure is frequently blurred. In the case of *Information obtained from an agency against the wishes of the agency and of the subject,* the conditions of privacy should apply to the agency as they do to the subject and are normally of concern because of computer security deficiencies and unauthorized access. In the case of *Information willingly disclosed by the beneficial user or agency but against the subject's wishes,* as in interagency transfers, accuracy and context are normally of concern. This is the prototypical *repurposing of information* that lies at the heart of most subjects' concerns over the disclosure of personal information.

Recordkeeping

Records typically fall into four classes: administrative, operational, intelligence, and statistical. In theory, *administrative records* are maintained by governmental agencies and give subjects their identity. For individuals, administrative records normally include birth certificates, diplomas, military discharge papers, driver's licenses, and immigration papers. For organizations, administrative records include certificates of incorporation and related documents. *Operational records* reflect tax and other certificates. *Intelligence records* are maintained by government agencies and represent security permissions and legal investigations. *Statistical records* can be obtained through an official questionnaire, as with the census, or from any of the other records that have been "cleansed" so as not to reflect personal information. Privacy safeguards are summarized in a far-reaching report by the Department of Health, Education, and Welfare (HEW 1973, pp. xx-xxi.):

1. There must be no personal data record-keeping systems whose very existence is secret.
2. There must be a way for an individual to find out what information about him is in a record and how it is used.

3. There must be a way for an individual to prevent information about him that was obtained for one purpose from being used or made available for other purposes without his consent.

4. There must be a way for an individual to correct or amend a record of identifiable information about him.

5. Any organization creating, maintaining, using, or disseminating records of identifiable personal data must assure the reliability of the data for their intended use and must take precautions to prevent misuse of the data.

The five principles are regarded as a Code of Fair Information Practice, emphasizing that privacy is a service that should be afforded to all citizens by other citizens, organizations, and the government in a free and open society.

Privacy Issues

The subject of privacy in all of its "multi-faceted dimensions" is of concern to many persons. Some individuals only wake up to the subject when their privacy is invaded and then quickly go back to sleep when the situation subsides, or they get tired of worrying about it. In the present context, Internet computing would seem to constitute a privacy threat to many persons and also organizations, because sensitive information is held by third-party service providers. However, having a third-party service provider is not a necessary condition for privacy invasion. The gang-of-three (government, employers, and education) would appear to be doing a good job with that. What are the specific issues about which we should be concerned? The topic has been addressed by the Privacy Rights Clearinghouse (PRC) in a document entitled "Privacy Today: A Review of Current Issues" developed by its director Dr. Beth Givens. (Givens 2009) The report lists twenty-three issues in privacy rights with a substantial description of each issue. The report highlights and summarizes the key issues and also contains links to special interest groups working on particular topics in that domain. We are going to concentrate on five subjects deemed relevant to the mission of this compendium:

o   Biometrics
o   Video surveillance and workplace monitoring
o   Data profiling
o   Behavioral tracking and targeting
o   Records on the Internet

A selection from the PRC list is also necessary because every privacy subject has its privacy point and twenty-three primary issues are more than we can usefully cover in this paper. Here is a simple straight-forward case of an individual personal privacy concern. "Joe Smith is a good runner and ran a local marathon in 3 hours and 20 minutes. The marathon organizer lists the name, age, finishing time, finisher's place, and home city and state of all finishers of the race on the Web. Joe has two concerns. He is a bit embarrassed, because a couple of years ago, he ran the same race in less than 3 hours. So, in this case Joe would prefer not to have the results published online for everyone to see – that is, if anyone besides runners would be interested. Joe's friend Al has a different opinion. Al says, 'That is a great time Joe. My father, who is about your age, ran it in 3 hours and 10 minutes.' The second concern is more serious. Joe is 57 years old and is looking for a good position, since he was recently laid off. He is concerned that a prospective employer can Google him and determine his age from the online list of finishers, since age discrimination is a major concern for many employers in this country." If the race were run in Canada or Europe, on the other hand, the same information would not be available to outside persons, because of privacy laws.

We are going to present a descriptive technique that will apply the five selected dimensions, placing each dimension in a privacy-identity continuum.

Biometrics

The term *biometrics* refers to the use of bodily characteristics for identification, which can be exact or probabilistic. If you have been in the ROTC, the military, law enforcement, possess a government security clearance, or have been born recently, you have an exact biometric identity consisting of your set of fingerprints on file in an official place. A person's DNA and retinal scan are also supposedly exact biometric identifiers. Clearly, an exact biometric marking does in fact identify a particular individual. However, the assignment of a name from an appropriate namespace is quite another thing. If the task is to link an individual with a specific name, then there is some probability involved. The picture on an official passport, driver's license, or government issued identification is also regarded as an exact identifier. But, how exact is exact? As mentioned before, there is some risk in linking name identification between two or more types of identity.

Less exact biometrics, such as facial recognition, has been employed in social situations to identify persons of interest – such as at sporting events. Using facial geometry and other visual clues, facial recognition technology has been very successful in criminal investigation. But, what about the identification and recording of persons in a lawful demonstration, guaranteed as a First Amendment right? Everyone knows there are at least two kind of demonstrators: those persons participating in the physical part of a demonstration because they genuinely believe in the cause, and those persons with nothing else to do on a Saturday afternoon. As Dr. Givens writes, "As a result, innocent people can be wrongly identified as criminal (false-positives), and known criminal and suspected terrorists can fail to be detected altogether (false-negatives).

Video Surveillance and Workplace Monitoring

Low-cost video surveillance systems are prevalent in modern society, and their use ranges from convenience stores to day-care centers. In fact, video surveillance is so pervasive that most people think nothing about being under the eye of the camera. In criminal investigation, video surveillance is a useful identifier, albeit within some probabilistic limits, and also as an investigative tool.

Collectively, video surveillance and workplace monitoring can provide information related to the following phenomena:

o   Facial recognition
o   Unproductive employment activity
o   Improper use of resources
o   Violation of conditions of service

Use of an employer's computer or other resources is a good case in point. There are other forms of surveillance, such as Radio Frequency Identification (RFID) chips embedded in employee identification cards that can be used as an employee locator by recording when he or she leaves one room and enters another.

Keystroke monitors are sometimes used to determine ineffective use of equipment. Most employees do not seem to mind employee monitoring when on premises – but what can they do about it? Off premises and off hours surveillance and monitoring are quite another thing and exist as an open issue in privacy.

Data Profiling

Most of us are well represented in a multitude of gang-of-three databases, such as the tax bureau, social security administration, state motor vehicles office, education records, employment files, insurance, and health records. Information of this type can be regarded as the operational part of the fabric of life. We can temper the intrusion but not totally eliminate it, because it is paramount to identity determination and service management. Identities are linked by numbers, such as the social-security number, name, date of birth, telephone number, address and ZIP code, mother's maiden name, and even mother's birthday. It is even possible to find the social security number of an unrelated deceased person on the Web. Immigration records are also easily obtainable. The Privacy Act of 1974 and its amendments generally cover governmental data protection and profiling.

There is another form of data that is involuntarily collected about individuals where there is some choice involved, such as personal expenditures, lifestyle, Internet activity, political activity and donations, and so forth. Supermarkets, bookstores, department stores, health stores, fitness centers, libraries, toll booths, big-ticket retailers, travel agencies, magazine publishers, and airlines – all contain personal data on individuals. An idea of interests, activities, and expenditures are available from credit card purchases, bank records, and operational files of business, governmental, and educational institutions. Thus, it is quite easy for an interested party to create a *data profile* of a person.

Pundits claim that profile data determines who or what we are. However, there is a tendency to interpret data based on the psychological perspective of the profiler. If you subscribe to "guns and ammo," does that indicate that you are a terrorist, member of the local shooting club, an Olympic athlete, worker in a sporting goods store that sells guns, or a medical professional who uses a service to provide magazines for the waiting room.

It has been reported that search providers turn over search queries of individuals to the agencies of the government. (Conti 2009, pp.259-298) This is a modern form of data profiling. A method, termed *chaffing,* is mentioned to widen the search domain and provide some protection. So, if you are going to search for a controversial person, you might also want to search for some non-threatening person to widen the search area.

Behavioral Tracking and Targeting

'Behavioral tracking and targeting is an area of privacy concern related to data profiling with emphasis on what a subject does.

Here is a typical scenario. A subject rents a car and drives that vehicle out of state or out of the country by accident or by intention. When the car is turned in to the agency, the renter is charged an enormous penalty. The fine print in the contract was not read, because the renter is usually out of his or her element or just in a hurry. How did the agency know of the unfortunate travel? The car rental agency used a global positioning system (GPS) device to track the path of the vehicle. In addition to GPS tracking, license plate tracking, implemented through highway cameras, is also widely used by state and local law enforcement officials. There is always a stated reason why organizations do things, but in the case of privacy, the main problem is the repurposing of collected data. Through data mining technology, computers can identify patterns based on happenstance, rather than purposeful activity. Here is another example: At the time this paragraph was written, the state of Arizona decided to take border control into its own hands. The federal government could do it and can do it, but we live in a large country with enough problems to go around. Getting the right person's or an organization's attention at the right time usually takes some up front planning. Demonstrations ensue for varying reasons, including the possibility that certain outside people want to stir up trouble. Proper officials are looking into persons flying into Arizona with recently booked tickets for travel lasting only a few days and are doing some data mining to identify those persons. Are identified persons demonstration instigators or grandparents attending a graduation ceremony. Regardless, they are prime candidates for behavioral tracking. In an era of supercomputing, piecing together a travel itinerary is not a major task. All that is needed is a subject to track.

The subject of behavioral tracking also includes the practice of collecting and compiling consumers' online activities, interests, preferences, and/or communications over time. (Givens 2009, 18 of 23) This form of behavioral targeting serves as the basis for advertising and other forms of marketing. Web browsing is a primary source of information in this regard.

There is also a growing trend by Internet service providers (ISPs) to use deep packet investigation (DPI) to look at email, Web sites visited, music, video sharing, and downloads by inspecting the data packets that constitute Internet traffic. This form of privacy intrusion is a major challenge to privacy advocates.

Records on the Internet

There is a tendency in society for persons in a political or geographical jurisdiction to be generally the same. This refers to attitudes, culture, psychological properties, and so forth. Between countries, however, there tend to be some differences between the two groups of people. People from Switzerland are different from people from England. The same idea holds true for people from Minnesota and Georgia, for example. We are referring to what is acceptable behavior, from a cultural viewpoint, or "would you like that person living next door."

The disclosure of public records in an open government is not sensitive to cultural differences, since the context for the information in government-managed files does not travel with the information. Citizens in one area may be more or less sensitive to the content of public information than persons from another – especially in a large country. The "one size fits all" mentality of public disclosure is a subject that frustrates privacy advocates.

Nevertheless, divorce records, criminal records, under-age convictions, bankruptcy proceedings, DIU convictions, motor vehicle records, and so forth, are all publically available through mailing list and information brokers. All an identity thief or stalker needs is a Social Security number and $19.95. The motivation for many, if not most, automobile breakins in modern times is an attempt to obtain personal information in the glove box, even thought the thief may also take a camera from the rear seat.

IDENTITY REQUIREMENTS

It would appear that there are two essential problems in identity theory: protection of identity and recognition of identity. Protection refers to the safeguarding of one's identity from unwanted intrusion into personal affairs, and is reflected in the identity principles that follow. Recognition refers to the use of identity measures to classify certain persons, based on the combination of evidence and abductive inference. This characterization of the identity problem reflects two edges of the same sword.

Identity Principles

It is generally regarded that effective identity governance should be based on a set of principles to guide the professional activities of IT managers, security officers, privacy officers, and risk management. (Salido 2010, OECD 2010) As delineated, the principles would be based on efficacy in governance, risk management, and compliance with the following objectives:

> **Governance.** Assurance that the organization focuses on basic issues and who is responsible for actions and outcomes.

> **Risk Management.** Assurance that procedures are in place for identifying, analyzing, evaluating, remdying, and monitoring risk.

> **Compliance.** Assurance that actions are within the scope of social and legal provisions.

In accordance with the stated objectives, we can delineate the eight core principles of effective and efficient identity management. (OECD op cit., p.3)

Principle #1. Collection Limitation Principle – there should be prudent limits on the collection of personal data with the knowledge or consent of the subject.

Principle #2. Data Quality Principle – personal data should be relevant to stated purposes and be accurate, complete, and up-to-date.

Principle #3. Purpose Specification Principle – the purpose of the data collection should be specified beforehand.

Principle #4. Use Limitation Principle – data should be used only for the use specified and not be repurposed.

Principle #5. Security Safeguards Principle – personal data should be safeguarded by reasonable and state-of-the art security facilities.

Principle #6. Openness Principle – the technical infrastructure for protecting personal data should be open as to development, practices, and policies.

Principle #7. Individual Participation Principle – the subject should have the right to definitive information concerning the personal data collected, methods used, and safeguards employed and have the right to challenge the procedures employed.

Principle #8. Accountability Principle – social, business, educational, and governmental data controllers should be required by legal or regularity means to abide by principles 1-8 and be accountable for violations of their provisions.

The eight principles of identity agree in part and parcel to Cavoukian's "7 Laws of Identity, listed as follows: personal control and consent; minimal disclosure for limited use; need to know access; user-directed identity; universal monitoring of the use of identification technology; human understanding and involvement; and consistent access and interface to personal data. (Cavoukian 2010)

Identity Analytics

An important aspect of identity theory concerns whether a certain subject is a member of a group of interest. The basis for this form of identity determination is that identity is a function of the subject's namespace and attributes. A subject belongs to a category if it possesses the attributes that define the category. Another approach is to employ a knowledge source to determine a subject's group membership. This is the method we are going to use in this section. A popular characterization of the problem would be, "Is suspect A a member of group T?" or in short form, "Is A a T?" Clearly, the methods would apply to most diagnostic systems, such as medical diagnosis, auto repair, and the analysis of aircraft failures. We are going to propose two methods of analysis: the combination of evidence (Shafer 1976, Katzan 2006, Katzan 2010) and abductive inference (Josephson 1996).

With the *combination of evidence,* a certain level of belief is afforded a knowledge source, as in the following scenario:

> We are trying to identify subjects that belong to a certain group G. We know about the group G and its attributes. We have a paid knowledge source K_1 that informs us that subject A is a member of G. However, K_1 is not always correct, and we know that. We have used K_1 enough to know that he provides us with information when he needs money. We have an intuitive belief of how often he is correct. Fortunately, we have another source K_2 that can supply similar information. K_2 is not as hungry for

money as K_1, and his opinion frequently runs contrary to K_1's. We would like to use analytics to combine the information from K_1 and K_2 so as to obtain a composite picture of the situation.

The relations between the knowledge sources and the subject are represented by the following mappings:

$$K_1 \to A$$
$$K_2 \to A$$

and the characteristics of the relationships are given as:

$$A = \{m, n\}$$
$$K_1 = \{r, u\}$$
$$K_2 = \{c, i\}$$

The question is whether A is a member of G, denoted by m, or not a member of G, denoted by n. As far as K_1 is concerned, he might be telling us what he thinks we want to hear, so his judgment is classed as reliable, denoted by r, or unreliable, denoted by u. K_2 is simply correct or incorrect, denoted by c or i, respectively. Through a method known as belief propagation (Katzan 2010a), the knowledge is transferred from the problem space to the solution space, resulting in the following representation:

Source	Representation
K_1	$\{[(m), p]. [(m, n), 1\text{-}p]\}$
K_2	$\{[(n), q]. [(m, n), 1\text{-}q]\}$

The results of belief propagation assign the mass (p) of the information received from K_1 to (m) and the remainder of the belief is assigned to (m, n). A similar argument applies to K_2 such that the mass (q) of that belief is assigned to (n) and the remainder to (m, n). Using Dempster's rules of combination (Dempster 1967), the resulting forms can be combined yielding the following assessment in the solution space:

$$\left[(m), \frac{p(1-q)}{1-pq}\right], \left[(n), \frac{(1-p)q}{1-pq}\right] \cdot \left[(m,n), \frac{(1-p)(1-q)}{1-pq}\right]$$

using symbolic math from calculations in *Mathematica*™. Applying the expression to several values of p and q yields the following results:

$K_1(p)$	$K_2(q)$	$K_1 \oplus K_2$
.6	.7	$\{[(m), 0.310], [(n), 0.483], [(m,n), 0.207]\}$
.7	.5	$\{[(m), 0.538], [(n), 0.231], [(m,n), 0.231]\}$

This is what we wanted to show. QED.

An alternate methodology, known as *abductive inference*, is used to determine the probable cause of group membership. (Josephson 1996) As with many forms of diagnosis, we have an event or condition and wish to determine the probable cause of the occurrence. A person may have a condition, such as liver disease, or a physical system may fail, such as a fighter aircraft. The list of probable causes in each instance is called the *differential*. Abductive inference is often referred to as, "turning modus ponens induction on its head." Abduction takes the following pattern:

> E is an event or a collection of data
> C explains E
> No other hypothesis can explain E and well as C
> \-
> Therefore, C is probably true

For example, J attends a training camp that is associated with membership in a militant group. There could be several possible causes for this phenomenon, two of which are that J is a militant or wants to be one. J could also be a journalist wanting to find out about things, but that is definitely less probable. The use of subjective probabilities, assigned through abductive inference, can be an analytic technique in its own right, or it can be used as input to a "combination of evidence" methodology.

Abductive inference and consensus theory would appear to be promising research topics for the modern world.

SUMMARY

Personal identity and privacy are important topics in the modern world of communications and the Internet. Most citizens are not aware of the major issues or do not realize the serious nature of identity theft and privacy invasion. The academic community is needed to foster attention to this subject, and this paper attempts to spotlight the major concerns. Accordingly, this paper is an admixture of topics that include identity, identity theory, privacy, and privacy theory, along with a summary of the major aspects of each domain. There is due consideration given to identity requirements through a set of identity principles and some proposals for identity analytics. In the latter instance, evidential methods are presented as promising research topics.

REFERENCES

1   ACLU of Northern California. 2010. *Cloud Computing: Storm Warning for Privacy?* www.dotrights.org, (downloaded 3/11/2010).

2   Black, M. 1952. Identity of Indiscernibles. *Mind* 61:153. (Secondary reference.)

3   Cavoukian, A. 2009. *Privacy in the Clouds.* Toronto: Information and Privacy Commission of Ontario (www.ipc.on.ca).

4   Cavoukian, A. 2010. 7 Laws of Identity: The Case for Privacy-Embedded Laws of Identity I the Digital Age." Toronto: Information and Privacy Commission of Ontario (www.ipc.on.ca).

5   Katzan, H. 2010. *Privacy, Identity, and Cloud Computing*, New York: iUniverse, Inc.

6   OECD 2010. OECD Guidelines on the Protection of Privacy and Transborder Flows of Personal Data. www.oecd.org. (downloaded 3/23/2010).

7   Salido, J. and P. Voon. 2010. A Guide to Data Governance for Privacy, Confidentiality, and Compliance: Part 1. The Case for Data Governance. Microsoft Corporation.

8   Windley, P. 2005. *Digital Identity*, Sebastopol: O'Reilly Media, Inc.

***** End of Chapter 11 *****

12

ESSENTIALS OF RANSOMWARE FOR BUSINESS AND MANAGEMENT

INTRODUCTION

Any incident that affects the continued operation of a person's or an organization's computer facilities can be annoying, frustrating, and even terrifying. In the case of health-care facilities, it can be life threatening. Even though your computer – including tablets and smartphones – may not contain personal identifiable information (PII), any event that prevents access to *your* information can be a serious matter.

Here is how it happens. A user clicks on a hot link or a web site that places an element of malware, i.e., a malicious program, on the computer to be affected. That program then executes the encryption of or prevents access to the stored data files on that computer. The malware program then effectively locks the computer and displays a message on the screen informing the user that access is denied unless a ransom is paid.

If and when the user pays the requested sum of money, procedures are then given to unlock the data files. The cyber criminal may be reputable or not. If the object pays the ransom amount and the criminal is reputable, then the user is back in business. If not, then the situation requires the services of a data recovery specialist. The total cost and the operational downtime can be significant.

The subject of ransomware has become a major cybersecurity issue, because the cyber criminals have networks of server programs, i.e., botnets to facilitate the operation of ransomware, that can affect thousands of computers. There are potentially large sums of money involved.

PROTECTION FROM RANSOMWARE

Protection against ransomware is relatively straightforward. The FBI and Department of Homeland Security have given the problem some attention, and here is a short list of safeguards:Have updated antivirus software on your computer.

- Accept automated software updates to your operating system and web browser.
- Use strong passwords and change them regularly.
- Do not operate your computer in the "administrator" mode.
- Turn on the pop-up blocker on your system.
- Only download software from trusted sites.
- Do not open attachments to unsolicited emails.
- Never click on an URL, but copy and paste it into your browser.
- Use the same procedures for tablets and mobile phones as you do with your browser.
- Conduct a regular back up to an offline backup device.

TYPES OF RANSOMWARE

There are two basic forms of ransomware, even though minor variations exist: crypto ransomware and locker ransomware. The objective of cryto ransomware is to encrypt personal data and files making them unavailable to the user. The malware of locker ransomware purports to lock the computer so it is unavailable for use. There are two aspects to the study of ransomware: how the method works from a technological standpoint and the psychological impact of its use.

Locker ransomware, also known as "computer locker," prevents access to the computer interface rendering the underlying computer and data files unchanged. In the execution of a computer locker, the user is allegedly threatened by law enforcement to have committed an online indiscretion or other criminal activity, and the computer is locked from subsequent use unless a fee is paid to the cyber criminal. The ransomware program is in control of the computer and permits limited facilities for using the keyboard but enough to specify a payment code. This form of ransomware is particularly effective in cases where the end user has limited facilities for accessing the underlying system through as additional computer. With locker ransomware, the malware is easily removed through the use of tools and techniques available from security vendors. (Savage, 2015)

Crypto ransomware, also known as "data locker," detects and encrypts valuable data stored on the computer. Supposedly, the user obtains the decryption key when the ransom is paid. In the best case, the crypto ransomware detects and encrypts only critical data, such as reports and financial information. Otherwise, crypto ransomware resides beneath the surface until an appropriate time or at a point when the critical data is needed. The malware does not affect the underlying system software, such as the operating system, so that the computer can be used for normal operations.

TYPICAL SCENARIOS

The number of potential victims of ransomware attacks is extremely large and includes private individuals, students, military personnel, government employees, and business workers. There may be untold additional groups that are potential victims. So there is a very large amount of revenue just waiting to be picked up by unscrupulous persons in local and remote locations. Most private individuals have neither the time nor inclination to be concerned with persons halfway around the world attempting to load illegal software on their computer. In short, ordinary people are ostensibly too busy to be worried about cybersecurity. It is the same with students and military personnel, many of whom simply do not care about what is happening with regard to their computer. Government employees and business workers, typically operating in a complex environment, are otherwise too occupied with productive activities to be concerned with security; it is not reasonable for organizations to have to finance a totally safe workplace. Many ransomware criminals are outside of the domain of federal and local law enforcement. It is very difficult, if not impossible, to apprehend cyber criminals in foreign countries. Perhaps, the notion of the much aligned "kill switch" should be given additional consideration.

It would seem that locker ransomware would be most appropriate wherein an individual user clicks on a hot link from within a web site where he or she should not be in the first place. The ransomware installation facility places software on the target computer making the system unavailable for productive use. No files are stolen or modified, but the computer is essentially not usable by its owner or user. The ransom fee is typically $200 to $300. The amount is low enough so the victim would often just pay the amount without calling in law enforcement. Convenient facilities, such as bitcoin, are customarily used for payment. Commercial specialists, such as The Geek Squad[6], could be called in to free the system, but there is normally a fee involved.

Crypto ransomware is normally used by criminals to encrypt critical files in the operational domain of organizations that are able

---

6

to pay relatively large amounts of money, such as $10,000. The name "data locker" is appropriate since the selected files are effectively locked up until the user pays the ransom amount to the criminal. Through social engineering techniques, the ransomware software is place on the target computer through the presentation layer or the server database. Crypto ransomware is exceedingly complicated and typically uses a symmetric cryptology algorithm to encipher and decipher the critical file and uses an asymmetric public key algorithm to manage the key. Usually the AES method is used for enciphering the critical data, and either RSA or elliptic curve methods for managing the public and private keys used to manage the symmetric key. The critical files reside on the home computer during the process and the symmetric cipher key is stored with the data in an asymmetric form. In this instance, the victim usually pays the ransom fee, because the data is critical for continued operation of the enterprise or the data is associated with an exceedingly large business endeavor.

SUMMARY

Although the notion of ransom generating malware is not particularly new, its widespread use is recent. It is difficult to know how widespread it is because victims are reluctant to inform the authorities. The two main methods are locker ransomware and crypto ransomware. Locker ransomware locks up the whole system so the computer is unavailable for use. Locker ransomware is appropriate for small jobs including drive-by penetration. Crypto ransomware encrypts critical files and is difficult to crack, since advanced mathematics is involved, and time is often a critical factor.

There are two general approaches to the ransomware situation:

Ransomware attack response
Ransomware prevention

The Ransomware Hostage Rescue Manual (Alessandrini, 2015) gives operational checklists for each approach. The reality of the situation is inherent in the quote by Dustin Dykes (op cit., p.1): "The adage is true that the security systems have to win every time, the attacker only has to win once." Here is a summary of the ransomware attack response checklist:

> Disconnect everything
> Determine the scope of the infection
> Determine ransomware strain
> Determine response
>
> > -Restore your files from backup
> > -Try to decrypt
> > -Do nothing (lose files)
> > -Negotiate and/or pay the ransom
> > -Protect yourself in the future

The ransomware prevention checklist similar:

> Establish first line of defense: users
> Establish second line of defense: software
> Establish third line of defense: backups

Detailed information is clearly available from the stated reference.

REFERENCES

Alessandrini, A. (2015)." Ransomware Hostage Rescue Manual," KnowBe4 Company, File: AST-0147692-Ransomware-Hostage-Rescue-Manual, www.KnowBe4.com, 2015.

Alvarez, M. (2015). IBM MSS: Ransomware, www.ibm.com.

FBI, (2015). "Ransomware on the Rise," File: www.fbi.gov/news/stories/2015/ january/ransomware-on-the-rise/ransomware-on-the-rise.

CERT, (2014). "Crypto Ransomware," File: TA 14-295A), www.us-dert-gov/ncas/alerts/TA14-295A.

Savage, K., Coogan, P., and Lau, H. (2015). "The evolution of ransomware." Symantic, File: www.symantic.com/connect/symantic-blogs/sr.

Wyke, J and Ajjan, S. (2015). "The Current State of Ransomware," Sophos Company, File: sophos-current-state-of-ransomware, www.sophos.com/en-us/support/knowledbase/25044.aspx, 2015.

***** End of Chapter 12 *****

13

WATCHLIST CONCEPTS FOR BUSINESS AND MANAGEMENT – GETTING STARTED

INTRODUCTION

Watchlist management is customarily associated with terrorism and firearms control, but the inherent methodology is applicable to a wide variety of business and management situations. Operational procedures for federal and local facilities are commonly designed to facilitate the identification and apprehension of persons of interest. Modern government at all levels is exceedingly complex, and the protocol for Watchlist screening mirrors that complexity. This paper covers the structure and operation of the Watchlist screening process with an emphasis on terrorism and management control. The primary objective is to identify persons of interest, leaving incident handling and social issues to subsequent papers. There are benefits to employers from watchlist screening because background checks historically fail to expose the complicated psychological picture of an employee, and subsequent updates from watchlist systems can provide an additional level of control.

Most managers are familiar with the process of background checks for determining the eligibility of an individual for the acquisition of firearms from a licensed gun dealer. The National Instant Criminal Background Check System (NICS) is commonly used for this purpose. The 2009 Fort Hood shooting and the 2013 Boston Marathon bombing generated renewed interest in terrorist watchlist screening. The alleged perpetrators were possibly entered in the National Counterterrorism Center's (NCTC's) Terrorist Identities Datamart Environment (TIDE), and consequently watchlisted in the FBI-led Terrorist Screening Center's Terrorist Screening Database. (Krause, 2013) In the latter case, the Russian Federal Security Service (FSB, which stands for Federal'naya Sluzba Bbezopasnost) notified the FBI and the CIA that one of the terrorists had possibly become an Islamic extremist and subsequently relevant information had been entered into the Department of Homeland Security's TECS (Treasury Enforcement Communications System) and the National Counterterrorism's TIDE system. However, because of the complexity of terrorist databases and the technicalities of information quality, none of the intelligence agencies was alerted.

In the United States, there are several databases related to terrorist activities and more than a few federal agencies and departments in the intelligence community that include: the Office of the Director of National Intelligence (ODNI); Central Intelligence Agency (CIA); the National Security Agency (NSA); the Defense Intelligence Agency (DIA); the National Geospatial-Intelligence Agency (NGA); the National Reconnaissance Office (NRO); the other DOD offices that specialize in national intelligence through reconnaissance programs; the intelligence components of the Army, Navy, Air Force, and Marine Corps; the FBI; the Drug Enforcement Agency (DEA); the Department of Energy; the Coast Guard; the Bureau of Intelligence and Research (INR) at the Department of State (DOS); the Office of Intelligence and Analysis at the Department of the Treasury; and elements of the Department of Homeland Security (DHS) that are concerned with the analyses of foreign information. It would seem clear at this point that the maintenance and use of terrorist watchlists is a major undertaking. (Krause, op cit, p.9)

ORGANIZATION AND OPERATION
OF THE WATCHLIST SYSTEM

In order to have a collection of files and databases that store the information that constitutes the watchlist system, it is necessary to have sophisticated groups of individuals that build, maintain, and use the data. A terrorist database can be managed by an established department from within the intelligence community. For example, the government contains an FBI-led Terrorist Screening Center (TSC) that runs its Terrorist Screening Database (TSDB). This makes good sense because the FBI does the terrorist screening for both international and domestic terrorists. In other cases, such as the Terrorist Identities Datamart Environment (TIDE), the maintenance is achieved by a special organization that in this instance is the National Counterterrorism Center (NCTC). The TIDE and TSDB are typical but not the only conceivable watchlist databases.

The various groups within the intelligence community forward watchlist nominations on to the NCTC for inclusion in the TIDE database and possibly to the TSDB database for screening. Alternately, entries are entered directly into TSDB. In actual practice, less than 2% of TIDE entries are domestic. The remaining entries are from international sources. The criteria for an entry into the TIDE database are based on a candidate's conduct is a variety of areas, such as the following:

- Performs international terrorist activity
- Plans international terrorist activity
- Gathers information concerning potential targets for terrorist activity
- Collects funds to support terrorist activity
- Offers membership in terrorist organizations
- Supports terrorist activity – such as housing or transportation
- Is a member of a terrorist group

Supporting agencies generally adhere to their own criteria for nomination to a watchlist. This has been a topic of intense discussion.

It is not entirely clear how entries are made into a watchlist database, and some sources are more reliable than others. An individual usually does not know if he or she is in a terrorist database until their name appears on a No-Fly list. It is almost impossible to have it removed, once it is discovered, and the source of the nomination cannot be determined in most cases. (American Civil Liberties Union, 2014) For example, Ted Kennedy, former U.S. Senator from Massachusetts, was frequently placed on a No-Fly list, as was a 8-year old Cub Scout. (Terror, nd) In spite of the inherent difficulties of terrorist watchlists, the U.S. government has had extremely good results with terrorism research, as evidenced by the quote by G. Weimann:

The threat posed by Cyberterrorism has grabbed headlines and the attention of politicians, security experts, and the public. But just how real is the threat? Could terrorists cripple critical military, financial, and service computer systems? ... Many of these fears, the report contends, are exaggerated: not a single case of terrorism has been recorded, hackers are regularly mistaken for terrorists, and cyberdefenses are more robust than is commonly supposed. (Weimann, 2004)

WATCHLIST PROCESS

The basic objective of this paper is to describe the watchlist process, since it applies to employee management. As covered in the next section, the idea is that real-time updates on employees could be useful in some areas of U.S. business. Whether it applies to outsourcing is another question. The subject of this section is to present a generic description of a watchlist process. Clearly, there could be other ways of instantiating the process.

There are numerous definitions of terrorism and terrorists. The important aspects of a suitable definition would be that it is related to the following attributes or activities: coerce a civilian population, influence the effectiveness of a government policy, threaten national security, or to influence the execution of one of the stated activities. Further, an individual that is so engaged is identified by or through an intelligence agency. Associated with that individual is relevant personal identifiable information (PII), which is an enormous problem in its own right. The terrorist identifiers are the identity elements that enable a watch list to be effective. The originating agency is known as the originator of the known or suspected terrorist. There is wide range of behaviors that can be classed as terrorist in nature at varying degrees of severity.

The originator thereby nominates an individual for inclusion is a watchlist database and probably only a nomination is needed to get on a preliminary watch list. In a typical scenario, the NCTC, mentioned above, might be a receiving group. Next an analytic process – for lack of a better word – takes place and information is collected and consolidated. When necessary, screening takes place, followed by appropriate action, as required.

Unfortunately, there are lots of people who are jealous, or something else, of their neighbors. There is a story floating around of some guy who removed the back seat of his car. A nosy neighbor figured he was going to use the car to transport a bomb and notified a government agency. As it turns out, the car owner was just putting in new seats. Anyone who has taken a taxi to the airport in a major city has had to listen to the ranting and raving of a taxi driver, so it is easy to imagine how much work is involved with Watchlisting.

WATCHLISTING FOR BUSINESS AND MANAGEMENT

There have been several cases where an employee has checked out OK during pre-employment screening, but later turned out to be a terrorist. There have been several civilian instances of this situation, but the major one is the Fort Hood shooting, where a Major in the

Army, who was an Army psychiatrist, killed several soldiers. At some point during his enlistment, he was in contact with a terrorist organization that influenced his behavior.

The FBI has proposed or made a service whereby personnel in certain areas are placed on appropriate watch lists with the facility to obtain necessary feedback. This is an interesting topic for the future in modern management.

SUMMARY

Watchlist management is customarily associated with terrorism and firearms control, but the inherent methodology is applicable to a wide variety of business and management situations. Operational procedures for federal and local facilities are commonly designed to facilitate the identification and apprehension of persons of interest. Modern government at all levels is exceedingly complex and the protocol for Watchlist screening mirrors that complexity. There are benefits to employers from watchlist screening because background checks historically fail to expose the complicated psychological picture of an employee, and subsequent updates from watchlist systems can provide an additional level of control.

Most managers are familiar with the process of background checks for determining the eligibility of an individual for the acquisition of firearms from a licensed gun dealer. The National Instant Criminal Background Check System (NICS) is commonly used for this purpose. In the United States, there are several databases related to terrorist activities and more than a few federal agencies and departments in the intelligence community that include: the Office of the Director of National Intelligence (ODNI); Central Intelligence Agency (CIA); the National Security Agency (NSA); the Defense Intelligence Agency (DIA); the National Geospatial-Intelligence Agency (NGA); the National Reconnaissance Office (NRO); the other DOD offices that specialize in national intelligence through reconnaissance programs; the intelligence components of the Army, Navy, Air Force, and Marine Corps; the FBI; the Drug Enforcement Agency (DEA); the Department of Energy; the Coast Guard; the Bureau of Intelligence and Research (INR) at the Department of State (DOS); the Office of Intelligence and Analysis at the Department of the Treasury; and elements of the Department of Homeland Security (DHS) that are concerned with the analyses of foreign information.

In order to have a collection of files and databases that store the information that constitutes the watchlist system, it is necessary to have sophisticated groups of individuals that build, maintain, and use the data. A terrorist database can be managed by an established department from within the intelligence community. For example, the government contains an FBI-led Terrorist Screening Center (TSC) that runs its Terrorist Screening Database (TSDB). This makes good sense because the FBI does the terrorist screening for both international and domestic terrorists. In other cases, such as the Terrorist Identities Datamart Environment (TIDE), the maintenance is achieved by a special organization that in this instance is the National Counterterrorism Center (NCTC). The TIDE and TSDB are typical but not the only conceivable watchlist databases. The criteria for an entry into the TIDE database are based on a candidate's conduct is a variety of areas, such as the following:

- Performs international terrorist activity
- Plans international terrorist activity
- Gathers information concerning potential targets for terrorist activity
- Collects funds to support terrorist activity
- Offers membership in terrorist organizations
- Supports terrorist activity – such as housing or transportation
- Is a member of a terrorist group

Supporting agencies generally adhere to their own criteria for nomination to a watchlist.

There are numerous definitions of terrorism and terrorists. The important aspects of a suitable definition would be that it is related to the following attributes or activities: coerce a civilian population, influence the effectiveness of a government policy, threaten national security, or to influence the execution of one of the stated activities. Further, an individual that is so engaged is identified by or through an intelligence agency. Associated with that individual is relevant personal identifiable information (PII), which is an enormous problem in its own right. The terrorist identifiers are the identity elements that enable a watch list to be effective. The originating agency is known as the originator of the known or suspected terrorist. There is wide range of behaviors that can be classed as terrorist in nature at varying degrees of severity.

There have been several cases where an employee has checked out OK during pre-employment screening, but later turned out to be a terrorist. The FBI has proposed or made a service whereby personnel in certain areas are placed on appropriate watch lists with the facility to obtain necessary feedback. This is an interesting topic for the future in modern management.

REFERENCES AND ADDITIONAL READING

American Civil Liberties Union (2014). *U.S. Government Watchlisting: Unfair Process and Devastating Consequences,* March, 2014.

Currier, C. and Hussain, M. (2017). "48 Questions the FBI Uses to Determine if Someone is s Likely Terrorist," *The Intercept,* February 13, 2017.

Kofman, A. (2017). "The FBI is Building a National Watchlist That Gives Companies Real-Time Updates on Employees," *The Intercept,* February 4, 2017.

Krause, W.J. (2013), *Terrorist Watch List Screening and Background Checks for Forearms,* Congressional Research Service, 7-5700, www.crs.gov, R42336, May 1, 2013.

Larence, E. (2010). *FBI Has Enhanced Its Use of Information from Firearm and Explosives Background Checks to Support Counterterrorism Efforts,*

Testimony Before the Senate Committee on Homeland Security and Government Affairs, U.S. Senate, May 5, 2010.

Terror (nd). *The Terror Watch List Database's Troubles Continue,* Case Study from Information Technology Infrastructure.

Weimann, G. (2004). *Cyberterrorism: How Real is the Threat?* United States Institute of Peace, December, 2004.

***** End of Chapter 13 *****

14

CYBERSPACE POLICY REVIEW AND THE NATIONAL STRATEGY FOR TRUSTED IDENTITY IN CYBERSPACE

INTRODUCTION

Cyberspace policy and a national strategy for trusted identity are in the news, because the current digital infrastructure is inadequate to satisfy the operational needs of a modern society based on computers and the Internet. (White House 2010a and 2010b) An identity ecosystem is proposed to mitigate identity theft, fraud, and digital crime through an overall awareness of the root causes of information and communications security problems. (OECD 2008) The existing Internet is based on an open society, and a myriad of operational and security problems have evolved. It is generally felt that "leadership from the top" is needed to remedy the existing situation. Accordingly, the United States Office of the President has orchestrated a public/private 60-day clean-slate review of the existing U.S. policies and structures for cybersecurity. (White House 2010a) This paper gives a review of that initiative from a service science perspective. We will be taking a look at two documents, available from the White House at www.whitehouse.gov: *Cyberspace Policy Review* and the *National Strategy for Trusted Identity in Cyberspace.*

BACKGROUND

Several definitions are relevant to the ensuing review: identity, mission, strategy, governance, policy, service, and service system. *Identity* is means of denoting a subject in a particular namespace and is the cornerstone of security and privacy. A subject may have several identities and be associated with more than one namespace. A subject's identity may be self-determined or determined by others. The most trustworthy identities are determined by trusted authorities and established through an identity credential, such as a birth certificate, driver's license, passport, or military ID card. When one identity management system accepts the identity certification of another, a phenomenon known as "trust" is established, often facilitated by a third party.

Four organizational concepts are important, because they reflect the substance of presentation: mission, strategy, governance, and policy. (Katzan 2008) A *strategy* is "a long-term plan of action designed to achieve a particular goal," and *governance* is "the set of processes, customs, policies, laws, and institutions affecting the way an endeavor is directed, administered, or controlled. (Wiki 2008) The basic tenet of strategy is that a principal entity desires to accomplish an objective called a *mission*, required in order that an entity knows its direction, and the strategy determines how to get there. Thus, the mission is the subject's goal, and the strategy is the roadmap for achieving that goal. A strategy is a plan of action. A *policy* – the most problematic of the definitions – is commonly regarded as a set of guiding principles or procedures considered to be advantageous for influencing decisions or establishing courses of action.

Since we will be taking a service perspective, a brief mention of that approach is entertained. A *service* is generally regarded as work performed by one person or group that benefits another. Another definition is that it is a type of business that provides assistance and expertise rather than a tangible product. Still another definition is that it is after-purchase support offered by a product manufacturer or retailer. We are going to refer to it as a provider/client interaction in which both parties participate and both parties obtain some benefit from the relationship. The provider and the client exchange information and adopt differing roles in the process. A *service system* is a collection of resources, economic entities, and other services capable of engaging in and supporting one or more service events. Services, i.e., service processes, may interact or they may be included in a service value chain. This is a recursive definition of a service system that would support the following modalities of service operation: *tell me, show me, help me, and do it for me.* Service systems are inherently multidisciplinary, since a service provider may not have the knowledge, skill, time, resources, and inclination to perform all of the steps in a service process and require the services of an external service provider. (Katzan 2009) The service perspective is particularly appropriate to the study of interacting components in a trusted identity system.

CYBERSPACE POLICY PRELIMINARIES

Within this paper, *cyberspace* is defined as the interdependent network of information technology components that underpin most of our digital communications. (White House 2010b, p. 1) Many persons are affected by cyberspace, since it is a platform for business, education, government, and daily affairs. There is an overwhelming concern for the security of cyberspace, since its use has exceeded the original architecture. Cyberspace is additionally a convenient means for government, business, and education to exercise their responsibility to their constituents and serves as backbone for social networking. Many persons feel that software errors and negligent human behavior are responsible for Internet security problems, and are as much a security problem as the technical infrastructure. (OECD 2008)

Regardless of the root causes of concerns over security in cyberspace, it would appear that the following tenets apply, since a secure cyberspace is necessary for continued support for the U.S. economy, civil infrastructure, public safety, and national security: (White House 2010a)

- The Nation is at a crossroads
- The status quo is no longer acceptable
- A national dialogue on cybersecurity is needed
- The U.S. cannot succeed with cybersecurity in isolation
- The U.S. cannot outsource its responsibility
- A public and private dialogue is required for the establishing of a secure cyber infrastructure

It follows that cybersecurity should address mission-critical principles for computer network defense, law enforcement investigations, military and intelligence activities, and the intersection of information assurance, counterintelligence, counterterrorism, telecommunications policies, and general critical infrastructure protection. (White House 2010a, p.2)

CYBERSECURITY POLICY PRINCIPLES

In order to make cybersecurity a national priority affecting the U.S. goals of economic growth, civil liberties, privacy protection, national security, and social advancement, a set of guiding principles would necessarily apply. Here is the set of principles as espoused by the subject documentation.

Principle #1: Leading from the Top
The intension of this principle is that leadership should emanate from the White House, since no other entity has responsibility to

coordinate Federal government cybersecurity-related activities. A cybersecurity policy official is proposed with operational authority to assure effective implementation of the strategy.

Principle #2: Building Capacity for a Digital Nation

The Internet and computers have transformed most aspects of daily life, and in order for security to persist, risk awareness should be addressed through a "public awareness" program, an enhanced educations system, and a capable workforce to address the relevant subjects.

Principle #3: Sharing Responsibility for Cybersecurity

This principle insures that developments in cybersecurity will result from a partnership between the private sector and the government, as well as with the international community.

Principle #4: Creating Effective Information Sharing and Incident Response

A comprehensive framework for coordinated response from relevant parties to cybersecurity events is necessary for continued success and enhancement of a cyber ecosystem. Information sharing is required for this endeavor with the overall accountability being anchored in the office of the cybersecurity policy official.

Principle #5: Encouraging Innovation

Technical innovation in telecommunications infrastructure products and service is anticipated and encouraged. A single vision is needed to guide decision-making by the private sector, academia, and government. An R&D framework to link research to development, that is lead by the cybersecurity official, is proposed.

The Cyberspace Policy Review document concludes with near-term and mid-term action plans for the implementation of cybersecurity.

Analysis. The document entitled "Cyberspace Policy Review" is an exceedingly well-written and comprehensive review of Internet security provisions sponsored by the Federal Government with public/private cooperation. However, the content of the policy review reads more as a mission statement than a set of policy principles. The report succeeds, because it resists the temptation to venture into strategy and cybersecurity technology. The policy review presents a service system where the Federal Government is the service provider, and the stakeholders are the service clients. In fact, the proposed identity management system demonstrates two concepts in service science: collectivism and duality. (Katzan 2010) Collectively, the ontological elements of the identity management system provide a service to a subscriber, and the subscriber demonstrates service duality to the identity system, as a client without which the identity system could not exist.

NATIONAL STRATEGY FOR TRUSTED IDENTITY PRELIMINARIES

A key aspect of mitigating online crime and identity theft is to increase the level of trust between parties in cyberspace transactions. In this context, usage of the term "trust" is intended to imply that the subject and relying party are actually who they say they are. The strategy seeks to delineate methods to raise the level of trust associated with the digital identities of individuals, organizations, services, and digital components through a trusted cyber ecosystem so as to enhance the following: (White House 2010b)

- Security
- Efficiency
- Ease of use
- Confidence
- Increased privacy
- Greater choice
- Innovation

The overall objectives of the endeavor are to increase the protection of personal privacy through the following goals: (White House *op cit.*, p. 2)

Goal 1: Develop a comprehensive Identity Ecosystem Framework

Goal 2: Build and implement an interoperable identity infrastructure aligned with the Identity Ecosystem Framework

Goal 3: Enhance confidence and willingness to participate in the Identity Ecosystem

Goal 4: Ensure the long-term success of the Identity Ecosystem

Nine comprehensive actions are anticipated to align the strategy with operational reality: (White House *op cit.*, p. 2-3)

Action 1: Designate a Federal Agency to lead the public/private sector efforts associated with achieving the goals of the strategy

Action 2: Develop a shared, comprehensive public/private sector implementation plan

Action 3: Accelerate the expansion of Federal services, pilots, and policies that align with the identity ecosystem

Action 4: Work among the public/private sectors to implement enhanced privacy protections

Action 5: Coordinate the development and refinement of risk models and interoperability standards

Action 6: Address the liability concerns of service providers and individuals

Action 7: Perform outreach and awareness across all stakeholders

Action 8: Continue collaborating in international efforts

Action 9: Identity other means to drive adoption of the identity ecosystem across the Nation

It is anticipated that the Executive Office of the President (EOP) will be the lead agency in the above actions.

The *identity ecosystem*, comprised of transaction participants and an operational trust infrastructure, is the paradigm for the national strategy. The guiding principle for trusted identity is that there will be standardized and reliable identical credentials, methods of insuring those credentials, and relying parties that accept the trusted identities. It is up to the designers of the identity ecosystem to determine how the presented ideas will interoperate.

IDENTITY ECOSYSTEM FRAMEWORK (IEF)

The IEF is conceptualized as being comprised of three layers:

- The *execution layer* that conducts transactions according to rules of the identity ecosystem
- The *management layer* that applies and enforces the rules
- The *governance layer* establishes the rules and operations

The *executive layer* is the place where participants and service components come together to instantiate a trusted transaction. The subject will possess an *identity credential* and the relying party will possess a *trustmark*. Both participants can request verification from a *certified provider*, which can supply identity attribute data, as required. Subjects and relying parties register with the identity provider beforehand. A sponsor may be required for proper registration.

Clearly, the subject and relying party are outside of the basic cyber infrastructure, whereas the identity provider and supporting elements are subsumed in the identity ecosystem framework. The ecosystem provides a service to the relying party, and the relying party provides a service to the subject.

The *management layer* is the component that handles credentials, attributes, and registration. A subject and a relying party must register with at least one identity provider. Identity validation is performed by the identity provider according to rules established at the governance layer for use in the management layer. The notion of an attribute provider is conceptualized but appears to be an operational item requiring further study.

The *governance layer* will provide facilities for assessing and certifying identity ecosystem service providers through a Governance Authority, conceptualized to control the rules for identity and trusted certification to identity providers and service providers (i.e., relying parties). Before any participant, with the exception of individuals, can join the identity ecosystem framework, it must be certified by an accreditation authority to insure that the service provider is trustworthy.

As a conceptual entity, the identity ecosystem will have the following characteristics: (White House op cit., p. 17)

- Individuals and organizations choose the providers they use and the way they conduct transactions securely.
- Participants can trust one another and have confidence that their transactions are secure.
- Individuals can conduct transactions online with multiple organizations without sacrificing privacy.
- Identity solutions are simple for individuals to use and efficient for providers.
- Identity solutions are scalable and evolve over time.

and provide the following benefits for individuals:

- Security
- Efficiency
- Ease-of-use
- Confidence
- Privacy
- Choice

Analysis. The proposed National Strategy for Trusted Identity in Cyberspace appears to be a well-conceived vision for future operations in a global society based on the Internet. Many persons feel that the Internet security problems are simply the result of buggy code and careless users. However, the identity problem still remains. Without a trusted authority, how do you know that the participant on the other end of the line is who he says he is?

SUMMARY

The reports addressed by this paper are long and complex document, consisting of 65 and 36 pages, respectively. A comprehensive summary would be long and tedious. One approach could be that the contents be summarized by the 8 Fair Information Practice Principles (FIPPs): (White House op cit., p. 36):

- Transparency
- Individual Participation
- Purpose Specification
- Data Minimization
- Use Limitation
- Data Quality and Integrity
- Security
- Accountability and Auditing

The principles are rooted in the United States Department of Health, Education, and Welfare's report entitled *Records, Computers, and the Rights of Citizens.* "The universal application of FIPPs provides the basis for confidence and trust in online transactions."

REFERENCES

1   Katzan, H. 2008. *Foundations of Service Science: A Pragmatic Approach*, New York: iUniverse, Inc.

2   Katzan, H. 2009. Principles of Service Systems: An Ontological Approach. *Journal of Service Science*, 2(2): 35-52.

3   Katzan, H. 2010a. *Privacy, Identity, and Cloud Computing*, New York: iUniverse, Inc.

4   Katzan, H. 2010b. Service Collectivism, Collaboration, and Duality Theory, *IABR Conference*, Orlando, Florida.

5   Katzan, H. 2010c. Service Analysis and Design, *IABR Conference*, Orlando, Florida.

6   Katzan, H. 2010d. Toward a Unified Ontology of Trusted Identity in Cyberspace, (this proceedings).

7   OECD 2008. Scoping Paper on Online Identity Theft: Ministerial Background Report, June 17-18, 2008, (DSTI/CP(2007)3/FINAL, Organization for Economic Co-Operation and Development.

8   White House 2010a. Cyberspace Policy Review: Assuring, a Trusted and Resilient Information and Communications Infrastructure, Office of the President, 2010, (www.whitehouse,gov).

9   White House 2010b. National Strategy for Trusted Identities in Cyberspace: Creating Options for Enhanced Online Security and Privacy, Office of the President, June 25, 2010, (www.whitehouse,gov).

10 Wiki 2008. Articles on Strategy and Governance. (www.wikipedia.con), 2008.

***** End of Chapter 14 ******

15

INTRODUCTION TO TERRORISM FOR MANAGERS

INTRODUCTION

Terrorism is a tactic for eliciting fear among its targets for a defined purpose; it is used in times of peace and conflict by nation states, organized groups, and individuals. Most people in the course of everyday affairs experience a minor form of terror from clergy, teachers, doctors, and criminals. This kind of terror, however threatening it may be, is not the subject of this paper. We are going to investigate the use of violence for political, religious, or ideological reasons against noncombatant targets with the ultimate objective of causing societal change, even though the exact nature of that change varies widely and at times would seem to be ill-directed. Historically, terror was used extensively for totalitarian domination and revolution against it. In more modern times, terrorism addressed selected targets. We are going to refer to domination, revolution, and selectivity as the "old terrorism." The *new terrorism* is aimed at a broad spectrum of society so that it causes as many casualties as possible and a widespread societal disruption. [5]

The precise forms that terrorism can take include any or all of the following:

- Threats of terrorist activity
- Assassination
- Kidnapping
- Hijacking
- Bomb scares and bombing
- Cyber disruption and warfare
- Use of chemical, nuclear, and radiological weapons

Moreover, terrorist acts may result from a terrorist organization or a "lone wolf" cell structure. The organization may have a hierarchical or horizontal structure and span multiple countries and be comprised of leaders, planners, trainers, specialists, and large groups of individuals that actually execute an asymmetrical form of warfare, wherein a weaker group attacks a stronger group outside of the conventional form of violence. The RAND terrorist database reflects that 96% of the persons killed by terrorist attacks killing persons in the US, Russia, and Eastern Europe in the period 2000-2010 were committed by Muslim terrorists. The terrorist objectives have evolved from political demands to a destruction of modern society. [6,8]

CAUSES OF TERRORISM

Terrorism has a long and extremely violent history, and there are differing views of the subject matter. It is important to note that one person's terrorist is another's freedom fighter. Even residents of countries in which the violence occurs commit some terrorist acts, although most acts of terrorism originate from within foreign borders. Even though most terrorism is rooted in the Muslim community, radical Christian groups have supported the bombing of abortion clinics. There are many root causes that exist in the literature. Here are a few:

- *Religion* – Fanaticism inherent in an ideological focus
- *Oppression* – Opposition to a governmental state-of-affairs

- *Historical grievances* –Targeting of governmental views as being responsible for historical injustices
- *Violations of international law* – Infringement of a right valued by the terrorist
- *Relative deprivation* – Limited relative economic opportunities
- *Financial gain* – Kidnapping or hostage taking for ransom
- *Racism* – Dehumanizing adversaries
- *Guilt by association* –Terrorism against groups or individuals sympathetic to an unpopular cause of a terrorist group
- *Narcissism* – Defensive grandiosity caused by personal inadequacy
- *Communication and publicity* – Killing adversaries or innocent civilians to promote a particular cause

Even though the causes of terrorism are varied and diverse, many scholars refer to terrorists as individuals in search for an ascribed identity – i.e., an identity created for oneself, as opposed to an identity assumed through innate human characteristics or attribution by others. Most modern societies focus on unacceptable levels of death or destruction caused by terrorism as a means of identifying the individuals involved.

Both men and women have been engaged in terrorism, and women have occasionally been leaders. However, most leaders have been men, and women have been followers. Less physical roles, such as making bombs explode, are particularly appropriate to women since they are less closely scrutinized than men. Most male terrorists are between the ages of 19 and 23 and women over 24. Many female terrorists are widows of men killed by the opposition (sometimes referred to as "black widows").

FORMS OF TERRORISM

A useful definition of terrorism, to frame the various forms it could take, is that it is the calculated use of unlawful violence or threat of unlawful violence to inculcate fear; intended to coerce or to intimidate governments or societies in the pursuit of goals that are generally political, religious, or ideological. [7 p. 2] The vectors of action by terrorists are political, psychological, violent, and deliberate action. *Political terrorism* reflects a deeply held grievance over some form of injustice. *Psychological terrorism* is intended to produce a negative psychological effect on a target population. *Violent terrorism* intends to produce a physical effect that can contribute to other forms of activity. *Deliberate terrorism* is purposeful selection of a target audience, which may appear to be random, but is designed with a terrorist objective. [*op cit.* p.1-4] Here are the various forms of terrorism:

- Threat or hoax
- Arson
- Sabotage
- Bombing
- Chemical/biological
- Kidnapping
- Hostage taking
- Hijack-seizure
- Raid or ambush
- Assassination
- Weapons of mass destruction (WMD)
- Maritime threats
- Suicide tactics

The forms of terrorism may be introduced to disrupt or dismantle a variety of activities and facilities, such as practices/procedures/routines, residences and workplaces, transportation facilities, and the very facilities designed to protect against terrorism.

TERRORISM MANIFESTATIONS

Terrorist threats can be grouped into four distinct categories: explosions, biological threats, chemical threats, and nuclear blasts. The effective manager should provide countermeasures and response scenarios in each of these categories. [1]

Explosions

One of the most common forms of terrorist weapons is explosive devices, since information on their construction is readily available. Moreover, explosive devices are easily detonated from remote locations or by suicide bombers. Surveillance is an effective countermeasure, as well as the identification of packages containing bombs. Here are several ways of identifying suspicious packages:

- Unexpected from an unfamiliar source
- Have no return address
- Marked with restrictive denotations
- Have protruding wires
- Variance between return address and postmark
- Unusual weight for the size
- Unusual labeling
- Have excessive packaging material
- Have misspellings of common words
- Addressed to someone no longer in your organization
- Have incorrect titles
- Not addressed to a specific person
- Have hand-written addresses

Telephoned bomb threats are also common. The usual procedures apply, such as keeping the caller online and notifying the proper authorities.

Biological Threats

Biological agents are organisms that can kill or incapacitate people, livestock, and crops. The most common threats are bacteria, viruses, and toxins. Agents in this category are easily dispersed by spraying them into the air, through animals, and through food and beverages. Here are the most common examples to guard against:

- Aerosols
- Animals
- Food and water contamination
- Person-to-person

Limiting physical contact, filtering systems, and personal hygiene are effective countermeasures to be implemented, since governmental facilities have a definite lag time.

Chemical Threats

Chemical agents are poisonous vapors, aerosols, liquids, and solids with dangerous properties. Chemical agents may be released via aircraft, boats, and vehicles. Chemical agents may have delayed effect and may dissipate rapidly. Physical and organizational countermeasures are effective against chemical threats.

Nuclear Blast

A nuclear attack is characterized by intense light and heat. However, dirty bombs are particularly convenient to terrorists and contain low-level radiation components as well as various forms of metal debris. Radiation poisoning can have a delayed response and medical countermeasures are commonly available. In the event of a nuclear attack or incident, distance, shielding, and time are particularly good defenses.

PRIMARY RECOMMENDATIONS

Recommendations for the protection of public health are readily available from government reports and are generally grouped into biodefense, food and water safety, citizen self-help, and a national readiness strategy. The government can help with preparedness through a public health system and definitive communications in the event of a terrorist attack, or with an effective alert system.

Business also should have a role in preparing employees and insuring business continuity. A terrorist attack could easily disrupt a supply chain with serious economic condequences.

GOVERNMENT RESPONSE

Leadership in the event of a terrorist attack must come primarily from government – at the federal, state, and local levels. However, there are things that individuals and businesses can do to protect their respective domains. Self-protection should involve the purchase of civil defense items, such as filter masks, safe rooms, and emergency kits. Knowledge of an appropriate response to an attack is of prime importance, and this knowledge can be obtained through publicity and familiarization with the threats of an attack. [2,3]

As stated in the US Strategy for Counterterrorism, core principles, building security partnerships, applying counterterrorism tools and capabilities appropriately, and building a culture of resilience guide the US position. [4] Governed by the rule of law, the core principles are summarized as:

- Respect for human rights
- Encouraging responsive governance
- Respect for privacy rights, civil liberties, and civil rights
- Balancing security and transparency
- Upholding the rule of law

Security partnerships are:

- Accepting varying degrees of partnerships
- Leveraging multinational institutions

Applying counterterrorism tools and capabilities appropriately include:

- Pursuing a "whole of government" effort
- Balancing near and long-term counterterrorism considerations

Building a culture of resilience necessarily involves:

- Building essential components of resilience

The four areas of focus provide the foundation for an extensive set of "overachieving" goals for the nation that include protecting the American people and homeland, disrupting terrorist organizations, preventing the acquisition of weapons of mass destruction, the elimination of safehavens, building enduring partnerships, degrading links between terrorist organizations and affiliates, diminishing the drivers of violence, and the elimination of enabling means for terrorist organizations.

SUMMARY

This paper defines terrorism and gives its causes. The forms of terrorism are described, and its destructive form is explored. The subject of a proper response and government support are covered. The subject matter is preliminary but necessary for a proper business response to terrorism.

REFERENCES

1   American Red Cross, *Homeland Security Advisory System Recommendations for Individuals, Families, Neighborhoods, Schools, and Businesses*: www.redcross.com.

2   Augustine, N. (ed), *The Science and Technology of Combating Terrorism*, The President's Council of Advisors on Science and Technology, July, 2003.

3   *National Strategy for Combating Terrorism*, Washington: The White House, September 2006.

4   National Strategy for Counterterrorism, Washington: The White House, June 2011.

5   Primoratz, I., *Terrorism*, Stanford Encyclopedia of Philosophy, 2011.

6   Sekulow, J., *Rise of ISIS: A Threat We Can't Ignore*, New York: Howard Books, 2014.

7   US Army TRADOC, *A Guide to Terrorism in the Twenty-First Century*, TRADOC G2 Handbook No. 1, Fort Leavenworth, Kansas, 2007.

***** End of Chapter 15 *****

***** End of Book *****

ABOUT THE AUTHOR

Harry Katzan, Jr. is a professor who has written several books and peer-reviewed technical papers on computer science and service science. He wrote one of the first books on computer security - perhaps the first on this interesting subject. He has been a consultant on computer security and cryptography and has taught cybersecurity in the graduate level at a large university. He and his wife have lived in Switzerland where he was a executive consultant and a visiting professor. He holds bachelors, masters, and doctorate degrees.

BOOKS BY HARRY KATZAN, JR.

COMPUTERS AND INFORMATION SYSTEMS

Advanced Programming
APL Programming and Computer Techniques
APL Users Guide
Computer Organization and the System/370
A PL/I Approach to Programming Languages
Introduction to Programming Languages
Operating Systems
Information Technology
Computer Data Security
Introduction to Computer Science
Computer Systems Organization and Programming
Computer Data Management and Database Technology
Systems Design and Documentation
Microprogramming Primer
The IBM 5100 Portable Computer
Fortran 77
The Standard Data Encryption Algorithm
Introduction to Distributed Data Processing
Distributed Information Systems
Invitation to Pascal
Invitation to Forth
Microcomputer Graphics and Programming Techniques
Invitation to Ada
Invitation to Ada and Ada Reference Manual
Invitation to Mapper
Operating Systems (2nd Edition)
Local Area Networks
Invitation to MVS (with D. Tharayil)
Privacy, Identity, and Cloud Computing

BUSINESS AND MANAGEMENT

Multinational Computer Systems
Office Automation
Management Support Systems
A Manager's Guide to Productivity, Quality
Circles, and Industrial Robots
Quality Circle Management
Service and Advanced Technology

RESEARCH

Managing Uncertainty

SERVICE SCIENCE

A Manager's Guide to Service Science
Foundations of Service Science
Service Science
Introduction to Service
Service Concepts for Management
A Collection of Service Essays
Hospitality and Service

NOVELS

The Mysterious Case of the Royal Baby
The Curious Case of the Royal Marriage
The Auspicious Case of the General and the Royal Family
A Case of Espionage
Shelter in Place
The Virus
The Pandemic
Life is Good

The Vaccine
A Tale of Discovery
The Terrorist Plot
An Untimely Situation

LITTLE BOOKS

The Little Book of Artificial Intelligence
The Little Book of System Management
The Little Book of Cybersecurity

*****

***** End of the Book *****